Langenscheidt's European Phrasebook

Kerry Payne

LANGENSCHEIDT

NEW YORK · BERLIN · MUNICH · VIENNA · ZURICH

Phonetic Transcriptions: The Glanze Intersound System
Translations:
French: Sabine Lippi; Italian: Silvana Brusati;
German: Barbara Holle; Spanish: Celia Robledo;
Portuguese: Helena Cunha e Silva; Dutch: Maud Beersmans

Cover photos: Corbis images

This phrasebook contains all of the most important expressions and words you'll need for your trip. They have been divided up according to languages and organized into 6 chapters. A color-coded edge index helps you find things even more quickly.

Each chapter consists of example sentences and lists of words. This will help you put together exactly the right sentence you need for any situation. Metric conversion charts and the most commonly used pictograms found in European airports and rail-road stations will give you further support.

Of course you can just show the person you're talking to the translation of the sentence you wish to say. But the easily distinguished, blue phonetic alphabet will enable you to speak your chosen phrase without any knowledge of the foreign language whatsoever. In order to give you an indication of the proper intonation, we have inserted punctuation marks into the phonetic spellings.

There are two equivalents in the European languages of the English you (and your), depending on whether you are talking to a close friend or a child or to someone you do not know or are merely acquainted with. We generally give the more formal form in the example sentences. In some languages, however, particularly in Italian, the familiar form is more common.

CONTENTS

SPANISH

PORTUGUESE

DUTCH

7

All words and phrases are accompanied by simplified pronunciation. The sound symbols you find in **Langenscheidt's European Phrasebook** are the symbols you are familiar with from your high-school or college dictionaries of the *English* language.

For French, these basic symbols are supplemented mainly by ā, ē and N. These three sounds have no English equivalents and have to be learned by listening.

Symbol	Approximate Sound	Examples
	VOWELS	
ä	The *a* of *father*.	*madame* mädäm
		garage gäräzh
		tasse täs
ā	The *a* of *fate* (but without the "upglide").	*été* ātā
ā	A sound that has to be learned by listening: round the lips for the *o* of *nose*; then, without moving the lips, try to pronounce the *a* of *fate*.	*deux* dā
		œuf āf
		fleur flār
e	The *e* of *met*.	*adresse* ädres
ē	The *e* of *he*.	*midi* mēdē
		dire dēr
ē	A sound that has to be learned by listening: round the lips for the *o* of *nose*; then, without moving the lips, try to pronounce the *e* of *he*.	*fumer* fēmā
		le fumeur lə fēmār

Symbol	Approximate Sound	Examples
ō	The *o* of *nose*, but without the "upglide".	*rideau* rēdō *rôle* rōl
ô	The *o* of *often*. In French, sometimes shorter, as in *moment*; sometimes longer, as in *sport*.	*moment* mômäN *sport* spôr
ōō	The *u* of *rule* (but without the "upglide").	*trou* trōō *rouge* rōōzh
ə	The neutral sound (unstressed): the *a* of *ago* or the *u* of *focus*.	*je* zhə *demi* dəmē
N	This symbol does not stand for a sound but shows that the preceding vowel is nasal – is pronounced through nose and mouth at the same time. Nasal sounds have to be learned by listening. Try not to use the *ng* of *sing* in their place.	*temps* täN *nom* nôN *matin* mäteN *parfum* pärfeN
CONSONANTS		
g	The *g* of *go*.	*gare* gär
l	The *l* of *love* (not of *fall*).	*volar* vôlä
ng	The *ng* of *sing*. (Occurs in some foreign words in French.)	*parking* pärkēng
r	The French "fricative" *r*. It is similar to the *j* of Spanish *Juan* and softer than the *ch* of Scottish *loch* or German *Bach*.	*rue* rē *rire* rēr
s	The *s* of *sun* (not of *praise*.)	*salle* säl *garçon* gärsôN

Symbol	Approximate Sound	Examples
sh	The *sh* of *shine*.	*chapeau* shäpō
v	The *v* of *vat*.	*avant* äväN
y	The *y* of *year*.	*payer* pāyā *avion* ävyôN
z	The *z* of *zeal* or the *s* of *praise*.	*blouse* blōōz
zh	The *s* of *measure* or the *si* of *vision*.	*jour* zhōōr *genou* zhənōō

The symbols b, d, f, k, m, n, p, and t are basically pronounced as in *boy, do, far, key, me, no, pin,* and *toy,* respectively.

The syllables of a French word are usually stressed evenly, with slightly more emphasis on the last syllable of a word or sentence. Therefore, stress is not indicated in this sound system – except in the following four situations in which the last syllable is not only stress-free but is barely pronounced as a syllable.

This absence of stress is shown through a preceding accent mark:

'ē: ē'ē	as in **fille** fē'ē
e'ē	as in **bouteille** bōōte'ē or **appareil** äpäre'ē
ä'ē	as in **paille** pä'ē
ä'ē	as in **feuille** fä'ē
ōō'ē	as in **grenouille** grənōō'ē.
'lə: b'lə	as in **table** täb'lə
k'lə	as in **siècle** syek'lə
g'lə	as in **triangle** trē-äNg'lə'
'rə	as in **libre** lēb'rə or **quatre** kät'rə or **descendre** däsäNd'rə
n'yə	as in **ligne** lēn'yə or **campagne** käNpän'yə

Combinations like the following are pronounced as a single "gliding" sound:

11

ô·ä	as in **roi** rô·ä or **voyage** vô·äyäzh
ô·eN	as in **loin** lô·eN
yeN	as in **bien** byeN
ē·ē	as in **nuit** nē·ē or **conduire** kôNdē·ēr
ōō·ē	as in **oui** ōō·ē or **weekend** ōō·ēkend
ōō·e	as in **souhaiter** sōō·etā

The final sound of a word is often linked with the initial sound of the next: **il y a** ēlyä, and a silent consonant may then become pronounced: **ils** ēl + **on** ôN = ēlzôN. This transition, called "liaison", is used quite frequently in French, but only the most important and common cases are rendered in this phrasebook. (As you progress in French, you will learn to use "liaison" with great frequency.)

A raised dot separates two neighboring vowel symbols: **réalité** rā·älētā. This dot is merely a convenience to the eye; it does not indicate a break in pronunciation.

Try to produce French sounds by speaking at the front of the mouth, with vigorous movement of the lips, unlike English, which is spoken in the back of the mouth, and with "lazy" lips.

EVERYDAY EXPRESSIONS

Yes.	**Oui.** ōō·ē.
No.	**Non.** nôN.
Please.	**S'il vous plaît.** sēl vōō plā.
Thank you.	**Merci.** mersē'.
You're welcome.	**De rien/Je vous en prie.** də rē·eN'/zhə vōōzäN prē.
Excuse me.	**Excusez-moi.** ekskēzā'-mô·ä.
I beg your pardon.	**Je vous demande pardon.** zhə vōō dəmäNd' pärdôN'.
Sorry.	**Pardon.** pärdôN'.
How much is this/that?	**Combien ça coûte?** kōNbyeN sä kōōt?
What time is it?	**Quelle heure est-il?** kelār etēl'?
At what time does the ... open/close?	**A quelle heure ouvre/ferme le/la ...?** ä kelār ōōvrə/färm lə/lä ...?
Where can I find the/a restroom?	**Où sont les toilettes?** ōō sôN lā tô·älet?
Is the water safe to drink?	**(Est-ce que) l'eau est potable?** (eskə) lō ā pōtäb'lə?
Is this free? (city map, museum, etc.)	**C'est gratuit?** sā grätē·ē?

NOTEWORTHY SIGNS

Avancez lentement/Attention äväNsā' läNtmäN/ätäNsyôN'	Caution
Fermé pour travaux färmā' pōōr trävō'	Closed for Restoration

FRENCH

GREETINGS

Prière de ne pas toucher/Défense de toucher prē·âr də nə pä tōōshä'/dāfäNs də tōōshä'	Do Not Touch
Sortie de Secours sôrtē' də səkōōr'	Emergency Exit
Entrée interdite äNtrā' eNterdēt	Do Not Enter
Entrée libre äNtrā' lēbrə	Free Admission
Défense d'entrée/Accès interdit dāfäNs däNtrā'/äksā eNterdē'	Keep Out
Entrée interdite/(in one way-street) Sens interdit äNtrā' eNterdēt'/säNs eNterdē'	No Entry
Prière de ne pas fumer/Défense de fumer prē·âr də nə pä fēmä'/dāfäNs də fēmä'	No Smoking
Ouvert de …à … ōōvâr' də … ä …	Open from … to …
Eau non potable ō nôN pōtäb'lə	Undrinkable Water
Hommes ôm	Men
Dames däm	Women

GREETINGS

Good morning.	**Bonjour.** bôNzhōōr.
Good afternoon.	**Bon après-midi.** bônäprä-mēdē.
Good night.	**Bonne nuit.** bôn nē̄-ē̄.
Hello/Hi.	**Salut.** sälē̄.
What's your name?	**Comment vous appelez-vous?** kōmäN' vōōzäplā-vōō?
My name is …	**Je m'appelle …** zhə mäpel' …
How are you?	**Comment allez-vous?** kōmäNtälā-vōō?
Fine, thanks. And you?	**Bien, merci. Et vous?** byeN, mersē'. ā vōō?

CONVERSING

FRENCH

Where are you from?	**Vous êtes d'où?** vōōzät dōō?
I'm from …	**Je suis de …** zhə svē də …
It was nice meeting you.	**Je suis ravi(e) d'avoir fait votre connaissance.** zhə svē rävē dävô·är fā vôtrə kōnesäNs.
Good-bye.	**Au revoir.** ō revô·är.
Have a good trip.	**Bon voyage.** bôN vô·äyäzh.
Miss	**Mademoiselle** mädmô·äzel'
Mrs./Madam	**Madame** mädäm'
Mr./Sir	**Monsieur** məsyā

CONVERSING & GETTING TO KNOW PEOPLE

Do you speak English/French/Italian/German/Spanish?	**Vous parlez anglais/français/italien/allemand/espagnol?** vōō pärlā äNglā/fräNsä/ētälyeN/älmäN/espänyōl?
I don't understand.	**Je ne comprends pas.** zhə nə kôNpräN pä.
Could you speak more slowly please?	**Vous pouvez parler plus lentement, s'il vous plaît?** vōō pōōvā pärlā plē läNtmäN, sēl vōō plä?
Could you repeat that please?	**Vous pouvez répéter, s'il vous plaît?** vōō pōōvā rāpātā, sēl vōō plä?
I don't speak French/Italian/German/Spanish.	**Je ne parle pas français/italien/allemand/espagnol.** zhə nə pärl pä fräNsä/ētälyeN/älmäN/espänyōl.
Is there someone here who speaks English?	**(Est-ce que) quelqu'un parle anglais ici?** (eskə) kelkeN pärl äNglā ēsē?
Do you understand?	**Vous comprenez?** vōō kôNprənā?

CONVERSING

Just a moment. I'll see if I can find it in my phrasebook.	**Attendez. Je vais regarder si je trouve ça dans mon petit livre de conversation.** ätäNdā. zhə vä regärdā sē zhə trōōv sä däN môN pətē lēvrə də kōNversäsyôN.
Please point to your question/answer in the book.	**Montrez-moi votre question/réponse dans le livre, s'il vous plaît.** môNtrā-mô·ä vôtrə kestyôN/rāpôNs däN lə lēvrə, sēl vōō plä.
My name is … What's yours?	**Je m'appelle … Et vous?** zhə mäpel … ā vōō?
It's nice to meet you.	**Ravi(e) de vous rencontrer.** rävē də vōō räNkôNtrā.
This is my friend/sister/brother/wife/husband/daughter/son …	**C'est mon ami(e)/ma sœur/mon frère/ma femme/mon mari/ma fille/mon fils …** sä mônämē/mä sär/môN frär/mä fäm/môN märē/mä fē'ē/môN fēs …
Where are you from?	**Vous êtes d'où?** vōōzät dōō?
What city?	**De quelle ville?** də kel vēl?
I'm from the United States/Canada/Australia/England.	**Je suis des États-Unis/du Canada/d'Australie/d'Angleterre.** zhə svē dāzätäzēnē/dē känädä/dōsträlē/däNglətär.
Are you here on vacation?	**Vous êtes en vacances ici?** vōōzät äN väkäNs ēsē?
Do you like it here?	**Ça vous plaît ici?** sä vōō plä ēsē?
How long have you been here?	**Depuis quand vous êtes ici?** dəpē·ē käN vōōzät ēsē?
I just got here.	**Je viens juste d'arriver.** zhə vyeN zhēst därēvā.
I've been here for … days.	**Je suis là depuis … jours.** zhə svē lä dəpē·ē … zhōōr.

16

FRENCH

I love it.	**Ça me plaît beaucoup.** sä mə plä bōkōō.
It's okay.	**Ça va.** sä vä.
I don't like it.	**Ça ne me plaît pas.** sä nə mə plä pä.
It's too noisy/crowded.	**Il y a trop de bruit/monde.** elyä trō də brē-ē/môNd.
It's too dirty/boring.	**C'est trop sale/ennuyeux.** sä trō säl/änēyä.
Where are you staying?	**Vous logez/Tu loges où?** vōō lōzhä/tē lōzh ōō?
I'm staying at the youth hostel/camp-ground.	**Je loge à l'auberge de jeunesse./ Je campe.** zhə lōzh ä lōbärzh də zhänes./zhə käNp.
Where were you before you came here?	**Vous étiez/tu étais où avant d'arriver ici?** vōōzätyā/tē ätä ōō äväN därēvā ēsē?
Did you stay at a youth hostel/campground there?	**Tu as logé à l'auberge de jeunesse? Tu as campé?** tē ä lōzhā ä lōbärzh də zhänes? tē ä käNpä?
Did you like that city/country/youth hos-tel/campground?	**C'était bien cette ville/ce pays/cette auberge de jeunesse/ce terrain de camping?** sätä byeN set vēl/sä pä-ē/set ōbärzh də zhänes/sä tereN də käNpēng?
Why not?	**Pourquoi pas?** pōōrkô·ä pä?
Where are you going from here?	**Et après, tu vas où?** ä äprä, tē vä ōō?
Did you ever stay at the youth hostel in …?	**Tu a déjà logé dans cette auberge de jeunesse à …?** tē ä däzhä lōzhā däN set ōbärzh də zhänes ä …?
I'm going there next.	**C'est ma prochaine étape.** sä mä prōshen ätäp.

ARRIVAL & DEPARTURE

It was nice meeting you.	**C'était sympa de te rencontrer.** sätä seNpä də tə räNkôNträ.
Here is my address. Write to me sometime.	**Voilà mon adresse. Écris-moi à l'occasion.** vô·älä mônädres. ākrē-mô·ä ä lōkäsyôN.
May I have your address? I'll write to you.	**Je peux avoir ton adresse? Je t'écrirai.** zhə pÃ ävô·är tônädres? zhə tākrērä.

USEFUL WORDS & EXPRESSIONS

Is it …?	**C'est …?** sä …?
Is it … or …?	**C'est … ou …?** sä … o͞o …?
It is …	**C'est …** sä …
cheap/expensive	**pas cher/cher** pä shār/shār
early/late	**tôt/tard** tō/tär
near/far	**près/loin** prä/lô·eN
open/closed	**ouvert/fermé** o͞ovär/färmā
right/left	**à droite/à gauche** ä drô·ät/ä gôsh
vacant/occupied	**libre/occupé** lēbrə/ōkēpā
entrance/exit	**entrée/sortie** äNtrā/sôrtē
with/without	**avec/sans** ävek/säN

ARRIVAL & DEPARTURE

Your passport please.	**Votre passeport, s'il vous plaît.** vôtrə päspôr, sēl vo͞o plä.
I'm here on vacation/business.	**Je suis ici en vacances/pour le travail.** zhə so͞o·ē ēsē äN väkäNs/po͞or lə trävä'ē.
I have nothing to declare.	**Je n'ai rien à déclarer.** zhə nā rē·eN ä dāklärā.
I'll be staying …	**Je vais loger …** zhə vā lōzhā

18

a week	**une semaine** ēn sǝmen'
two/three weeks	**deux/trois semaines** dā/trô·ä sǝmen'
a month	**un mois** eN mô·ä
two/three months	**deux/trois mois** dā/trô·ä mô·ä

That's my backpack. | **C'est mon sac à dos.** sā môN säk ä dō.

Where can I catch a bus/the subway into town? | **Pour aller en ville, je peux prendre un bus/le métro où?** pōōr älā äN vēl, zhǝ pā präNdreN bēs/lǝ mātrō ōō?

Which number do I take? | **Quel numéro de bus/de métro je dois prendre?** kel nēmārō dǝ bēs/dǝ mātrō' zhǝ dô·ä präNdrǝ?

Which stop do I get off for the center of town? | **Je dois descendre à quelle station pour le centre-ville?** zhǝ dô·ä desäNdrä kel stäsyôN' pōōr lǝ säNtrǝ-vēl?

Can you let me know when we get to that stop? | **Vous pouvez me dire quand on arrive à cette station?** vōō pōōvä mǝ dēr käNdôN ärēv ä set stäsyôN'?

Where is gate number …? | **Où est la porte numéro …?** ōō ā lä pôrt nēmārō …?

CHANGING MONEY

Excuse me, can you tell me where the nearest bank is? | **Excusez-moi, vous pouvez me dire où se trouve la banque la plus proche?** ekskēzā-mô·ä, vōō pōōvä mǝ dēr ōō sǝ trōōv lä bäNk lä plē prôsh?

… money exchange is? | **… le bureau de change le plus proche?** … lǝ bērō dǝ shäNzh lǝ plē prôsh?

… cash machine is? | **… le distributeur de billets le plus proche?** … lǝ dēstrēbētär dǝ bēyä lǝ plē prôsh?

19

YOUTH HOSTELS

I would like to exchange this currency.	**Je voudrais changer cet argent.** zhə vōōdrä shäNzhä setärzhäN.
I would like to exchange these traveler's checks.	**Je voudrais changer ces chèques de voyage.** zhə vōōdrä shäNzhā sā shek də vô·äyäzh'.
What is your exchange rate for U.S. dollars/traveler's checks?	**Quel est votre taux de change pour les dollars américains/chèques de voyage?** kel ā vôtrə tō də shäNzh pōōr lā dōlär' ämärēkeN/shek də vô·äyäzh'?
What is your commission rate?	**Quel est votre taux de commission?** kel ā vôtrə tô də kōmēsyôN'?
Is there a service charge?	**Il y a des frais d'agence?** ēlyä dā frā däzhäNs'?
I would like a cash advance on my credit card.	**Je voudrais retirer de l'argent avec ma carte de crédit.** zhə vōōdrä retērä də lärzhäN ävek mä kärt də krädē.
I would like small/large bills.	**Je voudrais de petites/grandes coupures.** zhə vōōdrä də pətēt'/gräNd kōōpēr'.
I think you made a mistake.	**Je crois que vous avez fait une erreur.** zhə krô·ä kə vōōzävä fā ēn erär'.

YOUTH HOSTELS

Excuse me, can you direct me to the youth hostel?	**Excusez-moi, vous pouvez me dire où se trouve l'auberge de jeunesse?** ekskēzā'-mô·ä, vōō pōōvä' mə dēr ōō sə trōōv lōberzh' də zhänes'?
Do you have any beds available?	**Vous avez encore des lits disponibles?** vōōzävä' äNkôr dā lē dēspōnēb'lə?
For one/two.	**Pour une/deux personnes.** pōōr ēn/dā persôn.

20

… women	**… femmes** … fäm
… men	**… hommes** … ôm

We'd like to be in the same room.

On voudrait être dans la même chambre.
ôN vōōdrā etrə däN lä mām shäNbrə.

How much is it per night?

C'est combien la nuit? sā kôNbyeN' lä nē·ē?

Is there a limit on how many nights I/we can stay?

Je peux/On peut passer combien de nuits au maximum? zhə pā/ôN pā päsā kôNbyeN' də nē·ē ō mäksēmôm'?

I'll/We'll be staying …

Je vais/On va passer …
zhə vā/ôN vä päsā …

tonight only
two/three nights
four/five nights
a week

cette nuit seulement set nē·ē sälmäN
deux/trois nuits dā/trô·ä nē·ē
quatre/cinq nuits kätrə/seNk nē·ē
une semaine ēn səmen'

Does it include breakfast?

Le petit déjeuner est inclus?
lə pətē' dāzhānā' āteNklē'?

Do you serve lunch and dinner?

Vous servez le déjeuner et le dîner?
vōō servā' lə dāzhānā' ā lə dēnā'?

What are the hours for breakfast/lunch/dinner?

A quelle heure on prend le petit-déjeuner/déjeuner/dîner? ä kelār ôN präN lə pətē' dāzhānā'/dāzhānā'/dēnā'?

What are the lockout hours?

Quels sont les horaires de fermeture de l'auberge de jeunnesse? kel sôN läzôrār də fermətēr də lōberzh' də zhānes'?

Can I leave my bags here during lockout?

(Est-ce que) je peux laisser mes sacs ici pendant la fermeture? eskə zhə pā lesā mā säk ēsē' päNdäN lä fermətēr'?

21

HOTEL OR OTHER ACCOMMODATIONS

Do I take my key with me or leave it with you when I go out?
Je prends ma clé avec moi ou je vous la laisse quand je sors? zhə präN mä klä ävek' mô·ä ōō zhə vōō lä les käN zhə sôr?

Do you have lockers?
Vous avez des coffres? vōōzävä' dā kôfrə?

What time is the curfew?
A quelle heure vous fermez les portes le soir? ä kelär vōō fermä lä pôrt lə sô·är?

What time is checkout?
A quelle heure on doit payer la note et quitter la chambre? ä kelär ôN dô·ä pāyā lä nōt ā kētā lä shäNbrə?

Are there cooking/laundry facilities?
On peut faire la cuisine/la lessive? ôN pə fär lä kē·ēzēn/lä lesēv?

Is there a reduction for children?
Il y a une réduction pour les enfants? ēlyä ēn rädēksôN pōōr läzäNfäN?

HOTEL OR OTHER ACCOMMODATIONS

chambres à louer/complet shäNbrä lōō·ā/kôNplä
vacancy/no vacancy

chambres à louer shäNbrä lōō·ā
Rooms for Rent

fermé pour congés fermä pōōr kôNzhā
Closed for Vacation

I'm looking for ...
Je cherche ... zhə shersh ...

    an inexpensive hotel.
un hôtel pas cher. enôtel pä shär.

    a pension.
une pension. ēn päNsyôN.

    a room.
une chambre. ēn shäNbrə.

I have a reservation.
J'ai fait une réservation. zhā fā ēn räzerväsyôN.

Do you have a room for tonight?
Vous avez une chambre pour cette nuit? vōōzävä ēn shäNbrə pōōr set nē·ē?

I'd like your cheapest room.	**Je voudrais la chambre la moins chère.** zhə vōōdrā lä shäNbrə lä mô·eN shär.
I'd like a single/double room …	**Je voudrais une chambre pour une personne/deux personnes.** zhə vōōdrā ēn shäNbrə pōōr ēn persôn/dā persôn.
with a private bath.	**avec salle de bain (particulière)** ävek' säl də beN (pärtēkēlyär')
with a shared bath.	**avec salle de bain commune** ävek säl də beN kōmēn.
for … days/a week.	**pour … jours/une semaine** pōōr … zhōōr/ēn səmen'.
How much is the room?	**Combien fait la chambre?** kôNbyeN fā lä shäNbrə?
May I see the room?	**Je peux voir la chambre?** zhə pā vô·är lä shäNbrə?
Does it include break-fast?	**Le petit-déjeuner est inclus dans le prix?** le pətē' dāzhānā' eteNklē däN lə prē?
I'll take it.	**Je la prends.** zhə lä präN.
Do you have anything cheaper?	**Vous n'avez rien de moins cher?** vōō nävā rē·eN' də mô·eN shär?
What time is check-out?	**A quelle heure on doit payer la note et quitter la chambre?** ä kelär ôN dô·ä pāyā lä nōt ā kētā lä shäNbrə?

CAMPING ACCOMMODATIONS

Can you direct me to the nearest camp-ground?	**Vous pouvez m'indiquer le camping le plus proche?** vōō pōōvā meNdēkā lə käNpēng' lə plē prôsh?

CAMPING ACCOMMODATIONS

How much is it per night/per person/ per tent?	**C'est combien la nuit/par personne/par tente?** sā kôNbyeN lä nē-ē/pär persôn'/pär täNt?
Are showers included?	**Les douches sont incluses dans le prix?** lā dōōsh sôN eNklēz däN lə prē?
Where can I buy a shower token?	**Pour la douche, je peux acheter un jeton où?** pōōr lä dōōsh, zhə pā äshtā eN zhətôN ōō?
How much are they?	**Ils coûtent combien?** ēl kōōt kôNbyeN?
How many do I need?	**J'en ai besoin de combien?** zhäNā bəzô-eN də kôNbyeN?
Are there cooking/ laundry facilities?	**On peut faire la cuisine/la lessive?** ôN pā fār lä kē-ēzēn'/lä lesēv?
Can we rent a bed/mat- tress/tent?	**On peut louer un lit/un matelas/une tente?** ôN pā lōō-ā eN lē/eN mätlä/ēn täNt?
May we light a fire?	**On a le droit de faire du feu?** ônä lə drô-ä də fār dē fā?
Where can I find ...	**Où (est-ce que) je peux trouver** ... ōō (eskə) zhə pā trōōvā ...
the drinking water?	**de l'eau potable?** də lō pōtäb'lə?
a camping equip- ment store?	**un magasin de matériel de camping?** eN mägäzeN də mätāryel də käNpēng?
a grocery store?	**une épicerie?** ēn āpēsrē?
a bank?	**une banque?** ēn bäNk?
laundry facilities?	**le lave-linge?** lə läv-leNzh?
a telephone?	**un téléphone?** eN tālāfôn?
a restaurant?	**un restaurant?** eN restöräN?
electric hook-ups?	**des relais électriques?** dā rəlā ālektrēk?
Is there a swimming pool?	**Il y a une piscine?** ēlyä ēn pēsēn?

How much does it cost?	**Elle coûte combien?** el kōōt kôNbyəN?
May we camp here/ over there?	**On peut camper ici/là-bas?** ôN pā käNpä ēsē/lä-bä?

SIGNS

Camping interdit käNpēng eNtərdē	No Camping
Entrée interdite/Propriété privée äNtrā eNtərdēt/prōprē-ātā prēvā	No Trespassing
Propriété privée prōprē-ātā prēvā	Private Property

CAMPING EQUIPMENT

I'd like to buy a/an/ some …	**Je voudrais acheter …** zhə vōōdrā äshtā …
I'd like to rent a/an/ some …	**Je voudrais louer …** zhə vōōdrā lōō·ā …

air mattress/air mattresses.	**un matelas pneumatique/des matelas pneumatiques.** eN mätlä pnᾱmätēk/dā mätlä pnᾱmätēk
butane gas.	**un butagaz.** eN bētägäz
charcoal.	**du charbon de bois.** dē shärbôN də bô·ä
compass.	**une boussole.** ēn bōōsôl
eating utensils.	**des ustensiles pour manger.** dāzēstäN-sēl pōōr mäNzhā
flashlight.	**une lampe électrique.** ēn läNp älektrēk
folding chairs/ table.	**des chaises pliantes/une table pliante.** dā shāz plē·äNt/ēn täb'lə plē·äNt
ground sheet.	**un tapis de sol.** eN täpē də sōl
ice pack.	**une glacière.** ēn gläsyär
insect spray.	**un insecticide en spray.** eneNsektēsēd äN sprā

kerosene.	**du pétrole.** dē pātrōl
lantern.	**une lanterne.** ēn läNtärn
matches.	**des allumettes.** dāzälēmet
rope.	**une corde.** ēn kôrd
sleeping bag.	**un sac de couchage.** eN säk də kōōshäzh
soap.	**du savon.** dē sävôN
tent.	**une tente.** ēn täNt
towel/towels.	**une serviette/des serviettes de toilette.** ēn servyet/dā servyet də tô·älet

CHECKING OUT

I'd like to check out. May I have my bill please?	**Je voudrais partir. Je peux avoir ma note, s'il vous plaît?** zhə vōōdrā pärtēr. zhə pə ävô·är mä nōt, sēl vōō plā?
Could you give me a receipt.	**Vous pouvez me donner un reçu?** vōō pōōvā mə dōnā eN rəsē?
Could you explain this item/charge?	**Vous pouvez m'expliquez ce chiffre/supplément?** vōō pōōvā meksplēkā sā shēfrə/sēplämäN?
Thank you. I enjoyed my stay.	**Merci. C'était très bien.** mersē. sātā trā byeN.
We enjoyed our stay.	**C'était très bien.** sātā trā byeN.

TRANSPORTATION BY AIR

Is there a bus/train to the airport?	**Il y a un bus/train qui va à l'aéroport?** ēlyä eN bēs/treN kē vä ä lä·ärōpôr?
At what time does it leave?	**A quelle heure il part?** ä kelār ēl pär?
How long does it take to get there?	**Il met combien de temps pour arriver?** ēl mā kôNbyeN də täN pōōr ärēvā?

Is there an earlier/later bus/train?	**Il y a un bus/train plus tôt/plus tard?** ēlyä eN bēs/treN plē tō/plē tär?
How much does it cost?	**Combien ça coûte?** kôNbyeN sä kōōt?
I'd like a flight to …	**Je voudrais un vol pour …** zhə vōōdrā eN vōl pōōr …
a one-way/round trip ticket	**un aller simple/aller retour** enälä seNp'lə/älä rətōōr.
your cheapest fare	**le tarif le moins cher** lə tärēf lə mô·eN shär
an aisle/window seat	**une place couloir/fenêtre** ēn pläs kōōlô·är/fənetrə
Is there a bus/train to the center of town?	**Il y a un bus/train qui va au centre-ville?** ēlyä eN bēs/treN kē vä ō säNtrə-vēl?

RIDING THE BUS & SUBWAY

Could you tell me where the nearest bus/subway station is?	**Vous pouvez me dire où se trouve la station de bus/métro la plus proche?** vōō pōōvä mə dēr ōō sə trōōv lä stäsyôn də bēs/mätrō lä plē prôsh?
Could you tell me where the nearest bus/subway stop is?	**Vous pouvez me dire où se trouve l'arrêt de bus/métro le plus proche?** vōō pōōvä mə dēr ōō sə trōōv lärä bēs/mätrō lə plē prôsh?
Where can I buy a ticket?	**Où (est-ce que) je peux acheter un ticket?** ōō (eskə) zhə pä äshtā eN tēkä?
How much does it cost?	**Combien il coûte?** kôNbyeN ēl kōōt?
Can I use this ticket for the subway and the bus?	**Je peux utiliser ce ticket pour le métro et le bus?** zhə pä ētēlēzā sə tēkä pōōr lə mätrō ā lə bēs?

27

TRAIN-STATION & AIRPORT SIGNS

I'd like to buy … tickets.
Je voudrais acheter … tickets.
zhə vōōdrä äshtā … tēkā.

I'd like to buy a book of tickets/weekly pass.
Je voudrais acheter un carnet de tickets/une carte hebdomadaire. zhə vōōdrä äshtā eN kärnä də tēkā/ēn kärt ebdōmädär.

Which bus/train do I take to get to …?
Quel bus/train je dois prendre pour aller à …?
kel bēs/treN zhə dô·ä präNdrə pōōr älä ä …?

Do I have to change buses/trains to get to …?
(Est-ce que)je dois changer de bus/train pour aller à …? (eskə) zhə dô·ä shäNzhā də bēs/treN pōōr älä ä …?

When is the next/last bus/train to …?
Quand arrive le prochain/dernier bus/train pour …? käNdärēv lə prōsheN/dernyā bēs/treN pōōr …?

Can you tell me when we reach …?
Vous pouvez me dire quand nous arrivons à …? vōō pōōvā mə dēr käN nōōzärēvôN ä …?

Do I get off here for …?
Je dois descendre ici pour …?
zhə dô·ä desäNdrēsē pōōr …?

Please let me off here.
Pardon! Je dois descendre ici. Merci!
pärdôN! zhə dô·ä desäNdrēsē. mersē!

TRAIN-STATION & AIRPORT SIGNS

Arrivée ärēvā	Arrival
Bulletin de consigne bəlteN də kôNsēn'yə	Baggage Check
Livraison des bagages lēvrāzôN dā bägäzh	Baggage Pick-up
Change shäNzh	Change
Douanes dōō·än	Customs
Départ däpär	Departure

TAKING THE TRAIN

FRENCH

Entrée äNtrā	Entrance
Sortie sôrtē	Exit
Renseignements räNsenymäN	Information
Les objets trouvés lāzōbzhā trōōvā	Lost & Found
La consigne lä kôNsēn'y	Luggage Lockers
Prière de ne pas fumer/Défense de fumer prēyār də nə pä fēmā/dāfäNs də fēmā	No Smoking
Réservations rāzervāsyôN	Reservations
Billets bēyā	Tickets
Toilettes tô·älet	Toilets
Vers les quais/trains vār lā kā/treN	To the Platforms/Trains
Salle d'attente säl dätäNt	Waiting Room

TAKING THE TRAIN

Could you tell me where the train station is?	**Vous pouvez me dire où la station de train se trouve?** vōō pōōvā mə dēr ōō lä stäsyôN də treN sə trōōv?
Could I have a train schedule to …	**Je peux avoir un horaire des trains pour …?** zhə pā ävô·är enôrär dā treN pōōr …?
When is the next/last train to …?	**Quand arrive le prochain/dernier train pour …?** käNdärēv lə prōsheN/dernyā treN pōōr …?
I would like to reserve a seat/couchette in 1st/2nd class.	**Je voudrais réserver une place assise/une couchette en première/deuxième classe.** zhə vōōdrā räzervā ēn pläs äsēz/ēn kōōshet äN prəmyār/dāzyäm kläs.

29

TAKING THE TRAIN

one-way/round trip	**un aller simple/un aller retour** enälä seNp'lə/enälä rətōōr
smoking/non-smoking	**fumeur/non-fumeur** fēmȧr/nôN-fēmȧr
aisle/window seat	**une place couloir/fenêtre** ēn pläs kōōlô·är/fənetrə
At what time does the night train to ... leave?	**A quelle heure part le train de nuit pour ...?** ä kelȧr pär lə treN də nē·ē pōōr ...?
At what time does it arrive?	**A quelle heure il arrive?** ä kelȧr ēl ärēv?
Do I have to change trains? At what stop?	**(Est-ce que) je dois changer de train? A quel arrêt?** (eskə) zhə dô·ä shäNzhā də treN? ä kel ärā?
I have a rail pass. Must I pay a supplement to ride this train?	**J'ai une carte d'abonnement/Inter-Rail. Je dois payer un supplément sur ce train?** zhā ēn kärt däbônmäN/eNterāl. zhə dô·ä päyā eN sēplämäN sẽr sə treN?
Could you tell me where platform/track ... is?	**Vous pouvez me dire où se trouve le quai/la voie ...?** vōō pōōvā mə dēr ōō sə trōōv lə kā/lä vô·ä ...?
Could you tell me where car number ... is?	**Vous pouvez me dire où se trouve la voiture numéro ...?** vōō pōōvā mə dēr ōō sə trōōv lä vô·ätẽr nēmärō ...?
Could you help me find my seat/couchette, please?	**Vous pouvez m'aider à trouver ma place/couchette, s'il vous plaît?** vōō pōōvā mādä ä trōōvā mä pläs/kōōshet, sēl vōō plä?
Is this seat taken?	**Cette place est occupée?** set pläs etōkōōpā?
Excuse me, I think this is my seat.	**Excusez-moi, je crois que c'est ma place.** ekskēzā-mô·ä, zhə krô·ä kə sā mä pläs.
Could you save my seat, please?	**Vous pouvez garder ma place, s'il vous plaît?** vōō pōōvā gärdā mä pläs, sēl vōō plä?

| Where is the dining car? | **Où se trouve la voiture restaurant?** ōō sə trōōv lä vô·ätēr restōräN? |
| Where are the toilets? | **Où sont les toilettes?** ōō sôN lā tô·älet? |

**For Europass and Flexipass users. With these passes you will only have access to certain countries. If your train goes through a country that is not on your pass, you will be required to pay an extra fare.

My rail pass only covers Spain/Portugal/France/Italy/Switzerland/Germany/Austria.	**Avec mon pass Inter-Rail, je peux seulement aller en Espagne/au Portugal/en France/en Italie/en Allemagne/en Autriche.** ävek môN päs eNterāl, zhə pā sälmäN älä änespän'y/ō pôrtēgäl/äN fräNs/änētälē/änälmän'y/änōtrēsh.
How much extra do I have to pay since my train goes through …?	**Combien je dois payer de supplément si mon train traverse le/la …?** kôNbyeN zhə dô·ä päyä də sēplämäN sē môN treN trävers lə/lä …?
Is there another way to get to … without having to go through …?	**Il y a un autre trajet pour aller à … sans devoir traverser le/la …?** ēlyä enōtrə träzhā pōōr älä ä … säN dəvô·är träversä lə/lä …?

BY BOAT

| Is there a boat that goes to …? | **Il y a un bateau qui va à …?** ēlyä eN bätō kē vä ä …? |
| When does the next/last boat leave? | **Quand part le prochain/dernier bateau?** käN pär lə prōsheN/dernyä bätō? |

31

ROAD SIGNS

I have a rail pass. Do I get a discount? How much?	**J'ai un pass Inter-Rail. Je peux avoir une réduction? De combien?** zhã eN päs eNterāl. zhə pā ävô·är ēn rādēksôN? də kôNbyeN?
At what time does the boat arrive?	**A quelle heure arrive le bateau?** ä kelār ärēv lə bätō?
How early must I get on board?	**A quelle heure je dois embarquer?** ä kelār zhə dô·ä äNbärkā?
Can I buy seasickness pills nearby?	**Je peux acheter des comprimés contre le mal de mer dans le coin?** zhə pā äshtā dā kôNprēmā kôNtrə lə mäl də mär däN lə kô·eN?

GETTING AROUND BY CAR

I'd like to rent a car.	**Je voudrais louer une voiture.** zhə vōōdrā lōō·ā ēn vô·ätēr.
for … days	**pour … jours** pōōr … zhōōr
for a week	**pour une semaine** pōōr ēn səmen'
What is your daily/ weekly rate?	**Quels sont vos prix pour la journée/ la semaine?** kel sôN vō prē pōōr lä zhōōrnā/lä səmen'?
Do I need insurance?	**J'ai besoin d'une assurance?** zhã bəzô·eN dēn äsēräNs?
Is mileage included?	**Le kilométrage est inclus?** lə kēlōmäträzh eteNklē?
How much is it?	**Combien ça coûte?** kôNbyeN sä kōōt?

ROAD SIGNS

Stop stôp	Stop
Sens unique säNsēnēk	One Way

FRENCH

Sens interdit säNseNterdē Do Not Enter

Route prioritaire rōot prē·ôrētär Yield

Parking interdit pärkēng eNterdē No Parking

TAXI

I'd like to go to …	**Je voudrais aller à …** zhə vōōdrā älä ä …
What is the fare?	**Combien coûte la course?** kôNbyeN kōōt lä kōōrs?
Please stop here.	**Arrêtez-vous là, s'il vous plaît.** ärātā-vōō, sēl vōō plā.
Can you wait for me?	**Vous pouvez m'attendre?** vōō pōōvā mätäNdrə?

GETTING AROUND ON FOOT

Excuse me, could you tell me how to get to …?	**Excusez-moi, vous pouvez me dire comment aller à …?** ekskēzā-mô·ä, vōō pōōvā mə dēr kōmäN älä ä …?
Is it nearby/far?	**C'est près/loin d'ici?** sā prā/lô·eN dēsē?
Can I walk or should I take the bus/subway?	**Je peux y aller à pied ou je dois prendre le bus/métro?** zhə pä ē älä ä pyā ōō zhə dô·ä präNd(rə) lə bēs/mātrō?
Could you direct me to the nearest subway station/bus stop?	**Vous pouvez m'indiquer la station de métro la plus proche/l'arrêt de bus le plus proche?** vōō pōōvā meNdēkā lä stäsyôN də mātrō lä plē prôsh/lärä də bēs lə plē prôsh?
Straight ahead.	**Tout droit.** tōō drô·ä.
Go right/left.	**Tournez à droite/gauche.** tōōrnā ä drô·ät/gôsh.

EATING OUT

At the corner/traffic light.	**Au coin/au feu.** ō kô·eN/ō fä
I'm lost.	**Je suis perdu.** zhə svē perdē.
Could you show me where we are on this map?	**Vous pouvez me montrer où on est sur cette carte?** vōō pōōvä mə môNtrā ōō ônä sēr set kärt?

EATING OUT

EATING OUT

Could we have a table outside/inside?	**On peut avoir une table dehors/ dedans?** ôN pä ävô·är ēn täb'lə də·ôr/dədäN?
Do you have a fixed-price menu?	**Vous avez un menu à prix fixe?** vōōzävä eN menē ä prē fēks?
Is service included?	**Le service est inclus?** lə servēs eteNklē?
Is there a cover charge?	**On doit payer pour le couvert?** ôN dô·ä päyā pōōr lə kōōvär?
Separate checks, please.	**Une addition pour chacun, s'il vous plaît.** ēn ädēsyôN pōōr shäkeN, sēl vōō plā.
I'd like some apple/ orange/grapefruit juice.	**Je voudrais un jus de pomme/d'orange/ de pamplemousse.** zhə vōōdrā eN zhē də pôm/dōräNzh/də päNpləmōōs.
I'd like some coffee with cream/tea with lemon.	**Je voudrais un café-crème/thé-citron.** zhə vōōdrä eN käfā-krām/tā-sētrôN.
I'd like a soda/beer/ mineral water.	**Je voudrais un soda/une bière/une eau minérale.** zhə vōōdrä eN sōdä/ēn byär/ēn ō mēnäräl.
I'd like a glass/bottle of red/white/rose wine.	**Je voudrais un verre/une bouteille de vin rouge/blanc/rosé.** zhə vōōdrä eN vär/ēn bōōtä'ē də veN rōōzh/bläN/rōzä.

FRENCH

dry/sweet	**sec/doux** sek/dōo
Cheers!	**à votre/ta santé!** ä vôtrə/tä säNtä!
What is the special of the day?	**Quel est le plat du jour?** kelä lə plä dē zhōōr?
Do you have a tourist menu?	**Vous avez un menu touristique?** vōōzävä eN menē tōōrēstēk?
What is this? (pointing to item on menu)	**Qu'est-ce que c'est?** keskə sä?
I'll have this.	**Je prendrai ça.** zhə präNdrā sä.
I'd like some salt/pepper/cheese/sugar/milk.	**Je voudrais du sel/poivre/fromage/sucre/lait.** zhə vōōdrā dē sel/pô·ävrə/frōmäzh/sēkrə/lā.
More juice/coffee/tea/beer.	**Un autre jus/café/thé/une autre bière.** enōtrə zhē/käfä/tā/ēn ōtrə byär.
More lemon/milk/wine.	**Encore du citron/lait/vin.** äNkôr dē sētrôN/lā/veN.
I cannot eat/drink sugar/salt/alcohol.	**Je ne peux pas manger/boire de sucre/sel/d'alcool.** zhə nə pā pä mäNzhā/bô·är də sēkrə/sel/dälkôl.
I am a diabetic.	**Je suis diabétique.** zhə svē dē·äbātēk.
I am a vegetarian.	**Je ne mange pas de viande.** zhə nə mäNzh pä də vyäNd.
May I have the check, please.	**L'addition, s'il vous plaît.** lädēsyôN, sēl vōō plä.
Keep the change.	**Gardez la monnaie.** gärdā lä monā.

35

FOOD SHOPPING & PICNIC FOOD

Can you make me a sandwich?	**Vous pouvez me faire un sandwich?** vōō pōōvā mə fār eN säNdvētsh?
To take out.	**Pour emporter.** pōōr äNpôrtā.
I'd like some …	**Je voudrais du/de la …** zhə vōōdrä dē/də lä …
I'll have a little more.	**J'en voudrais un peu plus.** zhə vōōdrä eN pä plē.
That's too much.	**C'est trop.** sä trō.
Do you have …	**Vous avez …** vōōzävä …
I'd like …	**Je voudrais …** zhə vōōdrä …
a box of	**un paquet de** eN päkā də …
a can of	**une boîte de** ēn bô·ät də …
a jar of	**une bouteille de** ēn bōōtä'ē də …
a half kilo of	**une livre de** eN lēvrə də …
a kilo of	**un kilo de** eN kēlō də …
a half liter	**un demi-litre de** eN dəmē-lētrə de
a liter	**un litre de** eN lētrə də
a packet of	**un paquet de** eN päkā də …
a slice of	**un tranche de** ēn träNsh də …
a bottle opener	**un ouvre-bouteille** enōōvrə-bōōtä'ē
a can opener	**un ouvre-boîte** enōōvrə-bô·ät
a cork screw	**un tire-bouchon** eN tēr-bōōshôN.
it sliced	**C'est coupé en tranches.** sä kōōpā äN träNsh.
Do you have any plastic forks/spoons/knives and napkins?	**Vous avez des fourchettes/cuillers/couteaux en plastique et des serviettes en papier?** vōōzävä dā fōōrshet/kē·ēyār/kōōtō äN plästēk ā dā servyet äN päpyä?
May I have a bag?	**Je peux avoir un sac?** zhə pä ävô·är eN säk?

Is there a park nearby?	**Il y a un parc dans le coin?**	
	ēlyä eN pärk däN lə kô·eN?	
May we picnic there?	**On a le droit d'y pique-niquer?**	
	ônä lə drô·ä dē pēknēkā?	
May we picnic here?	**On peut pique-niquer ici?**	
	ôN pä pēknēkā ēsē?	

Fruits

apples	**des pommes (une)** dā pôm (ēn)
apricots	**des abricots (un)** dāzäbrēkō (eN)
bananas	**des bananes (une)** dā bänän (ēn)
blueberries	**des myrtilles (une)** dā mērtē·ē (ēn)
cantaloupe	**melon (un)** məlôN (eN)
cherries	**des cerises (une)** dā serēz (ēn)
dates	**des dattes (une)** dā dät (ēn)
figs	**des figues (une)** dā fēg (ēn)
grapefruit	**des pamplemousses (un)** dā päNpləmōōs (ēn)
grapes	**des raisins (un)** dā räzeN (eN)
lemons	**des citrons (un)** dā sētrôN (eN)
nectarines	**des nectarines (une)** dā nektärēn (ēn)
oranges	**des oranges (une)** dāzôräNzh (ēn)
peaches	**des pêches (une)** dā pāsh (ēn)
pears	**des poires (une)** dā pô·är (ēn)
pineapple	**ananas (un)** änänä (eN)
plums	**des prunes (une)** dā prēn (ēn)
raisins	**des raisins secs (un)** dā räzeN (eN)
raspberries	**des framboises (une)** dā fräNbô·äz (ēn)
strawberries	**des fraises (une)** dā frāz (ēn)
tangerines	**des mandarines (une)** dā mäNdärēn (ēn)
watermelon	**pastèque (une)** pästāk (ēn)

FOOD SHOPPING

Vegetables

artichokes	**des artichauts (un)** dāzärtēshō (eN)
asparagus	**des asperges (une)** dāzäsperzh (ēn)
green/kidney beans	**des haricots verts/rouges (un)** dā ärēkō vär/rōōzh (eN)
broccoli	**des brocolis (un)** dā brōkōlē (eN)
red/cabbage	**un chou rouge** eN shōō rōōzh
carrots	**des carottes (une)** dā kärōt (ēn)
cauliflower	**un chou-fleur** eN shōō-flär
celery	**du céleri** dē sälerē
corn	**du maïs** dē mä-ēs
cucumber	**un concombre** eN kôNkôNbrə
eggplant	**une aubergine** ēn ōberzhēn
fennel	**du fenouil** dē fenōō'ē
french fries	**des frites** dā frēt
garlic	**de l'ail** də lä'ē
leeks	**des poireaux (un)** dā pô·ärō (eN)
lentils	**des lentilles (une)** dā läNtē'ē
lettuce	**une laitue/salade verte** ēn letē/säläd värt
mushrooms	**des champignons (un)** dā shäNpēnyōN (eN)
black/green olives	**des olives noires/vertes (une)** dāzōlēv nô·är/värt (ēn)
onions	**des oignons (un)** dāzônyôN (eN)
peas	**des petits pois (un)** dā pətē pô·ä (eN)
hot/sweet peppers	**des piments/des poivrons (un)** dā pēmäN/dā pô·ävrôN (eN)
pickles	**des cornichons (un)** dā kôrnēshôN (eN)
potatoes	**des pommes de terre (une)** dā pôm də tär (ēn)
radishes	**des radis (un)** dā rädē (eN)
rice	**du riz** dē rē
sauerkraut	**de la choucroute** də lä shōōkrōōt
spinach	**des épinards** dāzāpēnär
tomatoes	**des tomates (une)** dā tōmät (ēn)
zucchini	**des courgettes (une)** dā kōōrzhet (ēn)

Meats/Cold Cuts

beef	**du bœuf** dē bəf
bologna	**de la mortadelle** də lä môrtädel
chicken	**du poulet** dē pōōlā
fish	**du poisson** dē pô·äsôN
ham	**du jambon** dē zhäNbôN
hamburger/ground beef	**un hamburger/de la viande hachée** eN äNbōōrgär (äNbĕrzhā)/də lä vē·äNd äshā
hot dogs/frankfurters	**des saucisses de hot-dogs/de Francfort (une)** dā sōsēs də ōt-dôg/də fräNkfôr (ēn)
lamb	**de l'agneau** də länyō
pork	**du porc** dē pôr
roast beef	**du rosbif** dē rōsbēf
salami	**du saucisson** dē sōsēsôN
sausage	**des saucisses (une)** dā sōsēs (ēn)
turkey	**de la dinde** də lä deNd
veal	**du veau** dē vō

Nuts

almonds	**des amandes (une)** dāzämäNd (ēn)
brazil nuts	**des noix du Brésil (une)** dā nô·ä dē brāzēl (ēn)
cashews	**des noix de cajou** dā nô·ä də käzhōō
chestnuts	**des châtaignes (une)** dā shäten'yə (ēn)
hazelnuts	**des noisettes (une)** dā nô·äzet (ēn)
peanuts	**des cacahuètes (une)** dā käkähōō·et (ēn)
walnuts	**des noix (une)** dā nô·ä (ēn)

Condiments

butter	**le beurre** lə bär
honey	**le miel** lə myel
horseradish	**le raifort** lə räfôr
jam/jelly	**la confiture/la gelée** lä kôNfētēr/lä zhelā

FOOD SHOPPING

ketchup	**le ketchup** lə ketshäp
margarine	**la margarine** lä märgärēn
mayonnaise	**la mayonnaise** lä mäyōnäz
mustard	**la moutarde** lä mōōtärd
vegetable/olive oil	**l'huile végétale/d'olive** lə̄-ēl väzhätäl/dōlēv
pepper	**le poivre** lə pô·ävrə
mild/hot salsa	**la sauce portoricaine peu épicée/épicée** lä sōs pōrtōrēken pä āpēsä/āpēsä
salt	**du sel** dē sel
sugar	**du sucre** dē sēkrə
tabasco/hot sauce	**du tabasco/de la sauce épicée** dē täbäskō/də lä sōs āpēsä
vinegar	**du vinaigre** dē vēnāgrə

Miscellaneous

bread	**du pain** dē peN
cake	**du gâteau** dē gätō
candy	**des bonbons (un)** dā bôNbôN (eN)
cereal	**des céréales** dā särä·äl
cheese	**du fromage** də frōmäzh
chocolate	**du chocolat** dē shōkōlä
cookies	**des petits gâteaux** dā pətē gätō
crackers	**des crakers/biscuits salés** dā kräkär/bēskē·ē sälä
eggs	**des œufs (un œuf)** dāzə (enəf)
ice cream	**une glace** ēn gläs
popcorn	**des pop-corn** dā pôp-kôrn
potato chips	**des chips** dā shēps
rolls	**des petits pains (un)** dā pətē peN (eN)
spaghetti	**des spaghettis** dā spägetē
yogurt	**un yaourt** eN ē·ä·ōōr

FRENCH

Drinks

beer	**une bière** ēn byär
coffee	**un/du café** eN/dē käfā
hot chocolate	**un/du chocolat chaud** eN/dē shōkōlä shō
apple juice	**un/du jus de pommes** eN/dē zhē də pôm
cranberry juice	**un/du jus de canneberge** eN/dē zhē də känbärzh
grapefruit juice	**un/du jus de pamplemousse** eN/dē zhē də päNpləmōōs
orange juice	**un/du jus d'orange** eN/dē zhē də dōräNzh
tomato juice	**un/du jus de tomates** eN/dē zhē də tōmät
milk	**du lait** dē lā
soft drinks	**des boissons sans alcool** dā bô·äsôN säN älkôl
tea	**un/du thé** eN/dē tā
sparkling/mineral water	**de l'eau gazeuse/minérale** də lō gäzēz/mēnäräl
red/white/rose wine	**du vin rouge/blanc/rosé** dē veN rōōzh/bläN/rōzā
dry/sweet	**sec/doux** sek/dōō

USING THE TELEPHONE

Can I use local currency to make a local/long-distance call or do I need to buy a phone card?	**Je peux utiliser de la monnaie pour une communication urbaine/à l'étranger ou je dois acheter une carte téléphone?** zhə pā ētēlēzā də lä mōnā pōōr ēn kōmēnēkäsyôN ērben/ä läträNzhā ōō zhə dô·ä äshtā ēn kärt tālāfōn?
Do I need to buy tokens?	**Je dois acheter des jetons?** zhə dô·ä äshtā dā zhetôN?

41

POST OFFICE

Where can I buy tokens/a phone card?	**Où (est-ce que) je peux acheter des jetons de téléphone/une carte téléphone?** ōō (eskə) zhə pä äshtä dā zhətôN də tālāfōn/ ēn kärt tālāfōn?
… tokens, please. How much?	**… jetons, s'il vous paît. Ça fait combien?** … zhetôN, sēl vōō plä. sä fä kôNbyeN?
I'd like to buy phone card. How much does it cost?	**Je voudrais acheter une carte téléphone. Combien elle coûte?** zhə vōōdrä äshtä ēn kärt tālāfōn. kôNbyeN el kōōt?
How do you use the phone card?	**Comment on se sert de la carte téléphone?** kōmäN ôN sə sār də lä kärt tālāfōn?
Excuse me, where is the nearest phone?	**Excusez-moi, où se trouve la cabine téléphonique la plus proche?** ekskēsä- mô'ä, ōō sə trōōv lä käbēn tālāfōnēk lä plē prôsh?
I'd like to make a col- lect call.	**Je voudrais téléphoner en PCV.** zhə vōōdrä tālāfōnä äN pā sä vä.
The number is …	**Le numéro est …** lə nēmerō ā …
Hello. This is …	**Bonjour. C'est …à l'appareil.** bôNzhōōr. sä … ä läpärä'ē
May I speak to …	**Je voudrais parler à …s'il vous plaît.** zhə vōōdrä pärlä ä … sēl vōō plä.

POST OFFICE

Can you direct me to the nearest post office?	**Vous pouvez m'indiquer le bureau de poste le plus proche, s'il vous plaît?** vōō pōōvā meNdēkā lə bērō də pôst lə plē prôsh, sēl vōō plä?
Which window is for …?	**Quel guichet est pour …?** kel gēshā ā pōōr …?
stamps	**les timbres (un)** lā teNbrə (eN)

42

FRENCH

sending/cashing a money order	**envoyer/toucher un mandat postal.** äNvô·äyä/tōōshä eN mäNdə pōstäl.
airmail writing paper	**le papier à lettres pelure.** lə päpyä ä letrə pelēr.

I'd like ... stamps for postcards/letters to America.

Je voudrais ... timbres pour cartes postales/lettres pour l'Amérique. zhə vōōdrā ... teNbrə pōōr kärt pōstäl/letrə pōōr lämärēk.

I'd like to send this airmail.

Je voudrais envoyer ce courrier par avion. zhə vōōdrā äNvô·äyā sə kōōryä pär ävyôN.

How much does it cost?

Combien ça coûte? kôNbyeN sä kōōt?

PHARMACY & DRUGSTORE

Can you direct me to the nearest pharmacy?

Vous pouvez m'indiquer la pharmacie la plus proche? vōō pōōvā meNdēkā lä färmäsē lä plē prôsh?

I'd like a/an/some ...

Je voudrais ... zhə vōōdrā ...

aspirin	**de l'aspirine** də läspērēn
Band-Aids	**des pansements (un)** dā päNsmäN (eN)
cough medicine	**un médicament contre la toux** eN mādēkämäN kôntrə lä tō
contraceptives	**des contraceptifs** dā kônträseptēv
eye drops	**des gouttes pour les yeux** dā gōōt pōōr läzyə
insect repellant	**de la crème anti-insectes** də lä krãm äNtē-eNsekt
sanitary napkins	**des serviettes hygiéniques (une)** dā servyet ēzhē·änēk (ēn)

43

PHARMACY

Could you give me something for …?	**Vous pouvez me donner quelque chose pour …?** vōō pōōvä mə dōnä kelkə shōz pōōr …
constipation	**la constipation** lä kôNstēpäsyôN
diarrhea	**la diarrhée** lä dē·ärā
a headache	**la mal de tête** lə mäl də tät
hay fever	**le rhume des foins** lə rēm dā fô·eN
indigestion	**l'indigestion** leNdēzhestyôN
itching	**la démangeaison** lä dämäNzhāzôN
nausea/travel sickness	**la nausée/le mal de la route** lä nōzā/lə mäl də lä rōōt
a rash	**l'urticaire** lērtēkär
sore throat	**le mal de gorge** lə mäl də gôrzh
sunburn	**le coup de soleil** lə kōō də sōläᵉ
May I have a/an/some …	**Je peux avoir …** zhə pāzävô·är …
deodorant	**un déodorant** eN dā·ōdōräN
razor	**un rasoir** eN räzô·är
razor blades	**des lames de rasoir (une)** dā läm də räzô·är (ēn)
shampoo/conditioner	**du shampoing/du baume démêlant** dē shäNpô·eN/dē bōm dāmäläN
soap	**du savon** dē sävôN
suntan oil/cream/lotion	**de l'huile/de la crème/du lait solaire** də lē·ēl/də lä kräm/dē lä sōlär
tissues	**des mouchoirs en papier (un)** dā mōōshô·är äN päpyä (eN)
toilet paper	**du papier hygiénique/toilette** dē päpyä ēzhē·änēk/tô·älet
toothbrush	**une brosse à dents** ēn brôs ä däN
toothpaste	**du dentifrice** dē däNtēfrēs

FRENCH

cleaning/soaking solution for contact lenses	**une solution d'aseptisation/de conservation pour les lentilles de contact** ēn sōlēsyôN däseptēzäsyôN/ də kôNserväsyôN pōōr lä läNtē'ē də kôNtäkt
How much does it cost?	**Combien ça coûte?** kôNbyeN sä kōōt?

TOBACCO SHOP

I'd like to buy …	**Je voudrais acheter …** zhə vōōdrä äshtä …
a pack/carton of cigarettes	**un paquet/une cartouche de cigarettes** eN päkā/ēn kärtōōsh də sēgäret
a cigarette lighter	**un briquet** eN brēkä
a cigar	**un cigare** eN sēgär
May I have some matches?	**Je peux avoir des allumettes?** zhə pā ävô·är däzälēmet?

PHOTOGRAPHY

I'd like to buy a roll of film.	**Je voudrais acheter une pellicule photo.** zhə vōōdrä äshtä ēn pelēkēl fōtō.
Black and white/Color.	**Noir et blanc/Couleur.** nô·är ā bläN/kōōlär.
How much are they?	**Elles coûtent combien?** el kōōt kôNbyeN?
I'd like to buy batteries for this camera.	**Je voudrais acheter des piles pour cet appareil photo.** zhə vōōdrä äshtä dä pēl pōōr setäpärä'ē fōtō.

HEALTH

The Doctor

I don't feel well.	**Je ne me sens pas bien.** zhə nə mə säN pä byeN.

45

Could you direct me to a doctor that speaks English?	**Vous pouvez m'indiquer un médecin/ docteur qui parle anglais?** vōō pōōvä meNdēkä eN mädseN/dōktär kē pärl äNglä?
I have (a) …	**J'ai …** zhā (eN/ēn) …

burn   **une brûlure** ēn brēlēr

chest pains   **des douleurs de poitrine** dā dōōlár də pô·ätrēn

cold   **un rhume** eN rhēm

cough   **une mauvaise toux** ēn mōväz tō

cramps   **des crampes** dā kräNp

cut   **une coupure** ēn kōōpēr

diarrhea   **la diarrhée** lä dē·ärā

fever   **de la fièvre** də lä fyävrə

flu   **la grippe** lä grēp

infection   **une infection** ēn eNfeksyôN

nausea   **des nausées** dā nōzā

rash   **de l'urticaire** də lērtēkär

sore throat   **mal à la gorge** mäl ä lä gôrzh

sprained ankle   **une entorse à la cheville** ēn äNtôrs ä lä shevē'ē

stomach ache   **mal au ventre** mäl ō väNtrə

It hurts here.	**Ça fait mal ici.** sä fā mäl ēsē.
I've been vomiting.	**J'ai vomi.** zhā vōmē.
I'm having difficulty breathing.	**J'ai du mal à respirer.** zhā dē mäl ä respērā.
I'm allergic to penicillin.	**Je suis allergique à la pénicilline.** zhə svē älerzhēk ä lä pänēsēlēn.
I'm diabetic.	**Je suis diabétique.** zhə svē dē·äbātēk.
I don't smoke/drink.	**Je ne fume/bois pas.** zhə nə fēm/bô·ä pä.

FRENCH

The Dentist

Could you direct me to a dentist that speaks English?

Vous pouvez m'indiquer un dentiste qui parle anglais?
vōō pōōvä meNdēkä eN däNtēst kē pärl äNglä?

I have a toothache. This tooth.

J'ai mal aux dents. Cette dent me fait mal. zhā mäl ō däN. set däN mə fä mäl.

My tooth is loose.

Ma dent bouge. mä däN bōōzh.

My tooth is broken.

Ma dent est cassée. mä däN ā käsā.

I've broken/lost a filling.

J'ai cassé/perdu un plombage.
zhā käsā/perdē eN plôNbāzh.

Paying

How much does this cost?

Combien ça coûte? kôNbyeN sä kōōt?

I have health insurance.

J'ai une assurance maladie.
zhā ēn äsēräNs mälädē.

I'm supposed to call this number.

Je devrais appeler ce numéro.
zhə dəvrā äplä sə nēmārō.

How much do I owe you?

Combien je vous dois?
kôNbyeN zhə vōō dô·ä?

SIGHTSEEING

Can you recommend a good, inexpensive restaurant?

Vous pouvez recommander un bon restaurant pas cher?
vōō pōōvä rekōmändä eN bōN restōräN pä shär?

a fun nightclub?
a good place to dance?

une boîte sympa? ēn bô·ät seNpä?
un endroit sympa où danser?
enäNdrô·ä seNpä ōō däNsä?

47

SIGHTSEEING

Can you tell me where the tourist office is?	**Vous pouvez me dire où se trouve l'office de tourisme?** vōō pōōvā mə dēr ōō sə trōōv lōfēs də tōōrēsm?
What are the main points of interest here?	**Quels sont les endroits les plus intéressants à visiter ici?** kel sôN lāzäNdrô·ä lā plē eNtāresäN ä vēzētā ēsē?
What time does it open/close?	**A quelle heure ça ouvre/ferme?** ä kelär sä ōōvrə/färm?
What time is the last entry?	**A quelle heure ferment les guichets?** ä kelär färm lā gēshä?
How much is the admission? Free.	**Combien coûte l'entrée? C'est gratuit.** kôNbyeN kōōt läNtrā? sä grätē·ē.
Is there a discount for students/children/ teachers/senior citizens?	**Il y a une réduction pour les étudiants/ enfants/professeurs/seniors?** ēlyä ēn rādēksyôN pōōr lā ātēdyäN/äNfäN/ prōfesār/senyôr?
Is the ticket good all day?	**Le ticket est valable toute la journée?** lə tēkā ā väläb'lə tōōt lä zhōōrnā?
Is there a sightseeing tour?	**Il y a une visite guidée?** ēlyä ēn vēzēt gēdā?
What time does it start?	**Elle commence à quelle heure?** el kōmäNs ä kelär?
How much does it cost?	**Combien elle coûte?** kôNbyeN el kōōt?
How long is it?	**Combien de temps dure la visite?** kôNbyeN də täN dēr lä vēzēt?
Does the guide speak English?	**Le guide parle anglais?** lə gēd pärl äNglä?

48

Am I allowed to take pictures/a video?	**(Est-ce que) je peux prendre des photos/ filmer?** (eskə) zhə pä präNdrə dā fōtō/fēlmā?
Can you direct me to the …?	**Vous pouvez m'indiquer …?** vōō pōōvā meNdēkä …?

art gallery	**la galerie de peinture** lä gälrē də peNtēr
beach	**la plage** lä pläzh
castle	**le château** lə shätō
cathedral	**la cathédrale** lä kätādräl
cemetery	**le cimetière** lə sēmətyār
church	**l'église** lāglēz
fountain	**la fontaine** lä fôNten
gardens	**les jardins** lā zhärdeN
harbor	**le port** lə pôr
lake	**le lac** lə läk
monastery	**le monastère** lə mōnästār
mountains	**la montagne** lä môNtän'yə
movies	**le cinéma** lə sēnämä
museum	**le musée** lə mēzā
old city	**la vieille ville** lä vyā'ē vēl
palace	**le palais** lə pälā
ruins	**les ruines** lā rē·ēn
shops/bazaar	**les magazins/le bazar** lā mägäzeN/lə bäzär
statue	**la statue** lä stätē
tomb	**le tombeau** lə tôNbō
trails (for hiking)	**les sentiers (de randonnée)** lā säNtyā (də räNdōnā)
university	**l'université** lēnēversētā
zoo	**le zoo** lə zō·ō

Is it far from here?	**C'est loin d'ici?** sā lô·eN dēsē?
Can we walk there?	**On peut y aller à pied?** ôN pä ē älä ä pyā?
Straight ahead.	**Tout droit.** tōōt drô·ä.

EMERGENCIES

Go right/left.	**Tournez à droite/gauche.** tōōrnā ä drô·ät/gôsh.
At the corner/traffic light.	**Au coin/carrefour.** ō kô·eN/kärfōōr.

DISCOUNT INFORMATION

Do I get a discount with my student/teacher's/senior citizens card?	**Je peux bénéficier d'une réduction avec ma carte d'étudiant/de professeur/de senior?** zhə pə̄ bānāfēsyā dēn rādēksyôN ävek mä kärt dātēdyäN/də prōfesär/də senyôr?
Do I get a discount with my Eurailpass/Europass/Flexipass?	**Je peux bénéficier d'une réduction avec ma carte d'abonnement/mon Europass/Flexipass?** zhə pə̄ bānāfēsyā dēn rādēksyôN ävek mä kärt däbōnmäN/môN ārōpäs/fleksēpäs?
How much of a discount?	**La réduction est de combien?** lä rādēksyôN ā də kôNbyeN?
How much do I owe?	**Combien je vous dois?** kôNbyeN zhə vōō dô·ä?

EMERGENCIES & ACCIDENTS

Please call the police.	**Appelez la police, s'il vous plaît.** äplā lä pōlēs, sēl vōō plā.
Please call a doctor/an ambulance, quickly!	**Appelez un médecin/une ambulance, vite!** äplā eN mādseN/ēn äNbəläNs, vēt!
Hurry!	**Vite/Dépêchez-vous!** vēt! dāpāshā-vōō!
Danger!	**Attention!** ätäNsyôn!
Someone has been hurt/robbed.	**Quelqu'un a été blessé/ volé.** kelkeN ä ātā blesā/vōlā.
I'm hurt.	**Je suis blessé.** zhə svē blesā.

50

Where is the hospital?	**Où est l'hôpital?** ōō ā lōpētäl?
There's a fire.	**Il y a un incendie/le feu.** ēlyä eneNsäNdē/lə fä.
Help!/Thief!/Pickpocket!	**A l'aide! (Au secours!)/Au voleur!** äläd! (ō səkōōr!)/ō vōlär!
Police!	**Police!** pōlēs!
Stop that man/woman!	**Arrêtez cet homme/cette femme!** ärātā setôm/set fäm!

LOSS & THEFT

Can you help me, please?	**Pouvez-vous m'aider, s'il vous plaît?** pōōvā-vōō mādā, sēl vōō plä?
Where is the police station?	**Où est le poste de police?** ōō ā lə pôst də pōlēs?
Where is the American consulate/embassy?	**Où est le consulat américain/** **l'ambassade américaine?** ōō ā lə kôNsēlä ämārēkeN/läNbäsäd ämārēken?
Can you tell me where the lost and found is?	**Pouvez-vous me dire où se trouvent les** **objets trouvés?** pōōvā-vōō mə dēr ōō sə trōōv läzôbzhā trōōvā?
Someone has stolen my …	**Quelqu'un m'a volé mon/ma/mes …** kelkeN mä vōlā môN/mä/mā …
I have lost my …	**J'ai perdu …** zhā perdē …
I left my … on the bus/train.	**J'ai oublié … dans le bus/train.** zhā ōōblē·ā … däN lə bēs/treN.

backpack	**mon sac à dos** môN säk ä dō
camera	**mon appareil photo** mônäpärä'ē fōtō
credit cards	**mes cartes de crédit** mā kärt də krädē
glasses	**mes lunettes** mā lēnet

luggage	**mes bagages** mā bägäzh
money	**mon argent** mônärzhäN
passport	**mon passeport** môN päspôr
rail pass	**ma carte d'abonnement/mon pass Inter-Rail**
	mä kärt däbônmäN/môN päs eNteräl
traveler's checks	**mes chèques de voyage**
	mā shek də vô·äyäzh
wallet	**mon porte-monnaie** môN pôrt-mōnā

DEALING WITH PROBLEM PEOPLE

Leave me alone or I'll call the police.	**Laissez-moi tranquille, sinon j'appelle la police.**
	lesā-mô·ä träNkēl, sēnôN zhäpel lä pōlēs.
Stop following me.	**Arrêtez de me suivre.** ärätā də mə svēvrə.
I'm not interested.	**Ça ne m'intéresse pas.** sä nə meNtäres pä.
I'm married.	**Je suis marié/mariée.**
	zhə svē märē·ā/märē·ā.
I'm waiting for my boyfriend/husband.	**J'attends mon ami/mari.**
	zhätäN mônämē/môN märē.
Enough!	**Ça suffit!** sä sēfē!
Go away!	**Allez-vous-en !** älā-vōōzäN!

NUMBERS

zero	**zéro** zārō
one	**un** eN
two	**deux** dā
three	**trois** trô·ä
four	**quatre** kätrə
five	**cinq** seNk
six	**six** sēs

seven	**sept** set
eight	**huit** *ē*·ēt
nine	**neuf** n*ä*f
ten	**dix** dēs
eleven	**onze** ôNz
twelve	**douze** dōōz
thirteen	**treize** trez
fourteen	**quarorze** kätôrz
fifteen	**quinze** keNz
sixteen	**seize** sez
seventeen	**dix-sept** dēset
eighteen	**dix-huit** dēz*ē*·ēt
nineteen	**dix-neuf** dēzn*ä*f
twenty	**vingt** veN
twenty-one	**vingt-et-un** veNtā·eN
twenty-two	**vingt-deux** veNt·d*ä*
twenty-three	**vingt-trois** veNt·trô·ä
twenty-four	**vingt-quatre** veNt·kät′rə
thirty	**trente** träNt
forty	**quarante** käräNt
fifty	**cinquante** seNkäNt
sixty	**soixante** sô·äsäNt
seventy	**soixante-dix** sô·äsäNt·dēs
eighty	**quatre-vingts** kätrəveN
ninety	**quatre-vingt-dix** kätrəveNdēs
one hundred	**cent** säN
one thousand	**mille** mēl
one million	**un million** eN mēlyôN

DAYS

What day is today?	**Quel jour sommes-nous?** kel zhōōr sôm-nōō?
It's Monday.	**C'est lundi.** sā leNdē.
… Tuesday.	**… mardi.** … märdē.

... Wednesday.	**... mercredi.** ... merkrədē.
... Thursday.	**... jeudi.** ... zhädē.
... Friday.	**... vendredi.** ... väNdrədē.
... Saturday.	**... samedi.** ... sämdē.
... Sunday.	**... dimanche.** ... dēmäNsh.

TIME

Time is told by the 24-hour clock. You can also reference the numbers section.

Excuse me. Can you tell me the time?	**Excusez-moi/Excuse-moi. Vous pouvez/ Tu peux me dire l'heure?** ekskēzä-mô·ä/ ekskēz-mô·ä. vōō pōōvā/tē pä mə dēr lär?

I'll meet you in ...	**On se voit dans ...** ôN sə vô·ä däN ...
ten minutes	**dix minutes** dē mēnēt
a quarter of an hour	**un quart d'heure.** eN kär där.
a half hour	**une demi-heure.** ēn dəmē-är.
three quarters of an hour	**trois quarts d'heure.** trô·ä kär där.

It is ...	**Il est ...** ēl ä ...
five past one.	**une heure cinq.** ēnär seNk.
ten past two.	**deux heures dix.** dāzär dēs.
a quarter past three.	**trois heures et quart.** trô·äzär ā kär.
twenty past four.	**quatre heures vingt.** käträr veN.
twenty-five past five.	**cinq heures vingt-cinq.** seNkär veN-seNk.
half past six.	**six heures et demie.** sēsär ā dəmē.
twenty-five to seven.	**sept heures moins vingt-cinq.** setär mô·eN veN-seNk.
twenty to eight.	**huit heures moins vingt.** hē·ētär mô·eN veN.

54

a quarter to nine.	**neuf heures moins le quart.**
	nāfār mô·eN lə kär.
ten to ten.	**dix heures moins dix.** dēsār mô·eN dēs.
five to eleven.	**onze heures moins cinq.**
	ôNzār mô·eN seNk.
noon.	**midi.** mēdē.
midnight.	**minuit.** mēn*é*·ē.

yesterday	**hier** ē·ār
last night	**hier soir** ē·ār sô·är
today	**aujourd'hui** ōzhōōrdvē
tonight	**ce soir/cette nuit** sā sô·är/set n*é*·ē
tomorrow	**demain** dəmeN
morning	**le matin** lə mäteN
afternoon	**l'après-midi** läprä-mēdē
evening	**le soir** lə sô·är
night	**la nuit** lä n*é*·ē
day before yesterday	**avant-hier** äväNtē·ār
in two/three days	**dans deux/trois jours** däN d*ā*/trô·ä zhōōr

MONTHS

January	**janvier** zhäNvyā
February	**février** fāvrē·ā
March	**mars** märs
April	**avril** ävrēl
May	**mai** mā
June	**juin** zh*é*·eN
July	**juillet** zh*é*·ēyā
August	**août** ōō (ōōt)
September	**septembre** septäNbrə
October	**octobre** ōktōbrə
November	**novembre** nōväNbrə
December	**décembre** dāsäNbrə

| Merry Christmas! | **Joyeux Noël!** zhô·äy*ā* nō·el! |
| Happy Easter! | **Joyeuses Pâques!** zhô·äy*ā*z päk! |

COLORS

Happy New Year!   **Bonne année!** bônänā!
Happy Birthday!   **Joyeux anniversaire!** zhô·äy*a* änēversär!

COLORS

beige	**beige** bāzh
black	**noir** nô·är
blue	**bleu** bl*a*
brown	**brun/marron** breN/märôN
gold	**or** ôr
green	**vert** vār
gray	**gris** grē
yellow	**jaune** zhōn
orange	**orange** öräNzh
pink	**rose** rōz
purple	**violet** vyōl*a*
red	**rouge** rōōzh
silver	**argent** ärzhäN
white	**blanc** bläN

HOW DO YOU PRONOUNCE IT?

All words and phrases are accompanied by simplified pronunciation. The sound symbols are the ones you are familiar with from your high-school or college dictionaries of the *English* language, but applied here to foreign languages – a unique feature of **Langenscheidt's European Phrasebook**.

Symbol	Approximate Sound	Examples
	VOWELS	
ä	The *a* of *father*.	*facile* fä'tshēle
e	Either the *e* of *met* (as in Italian *festa*) or the *a* of *fate* (as in Italian *sera*). The difference is not shown here; it has to be learned by listening.	*festa* fe'stä *sera* se'rä
ē	The *e* of *he*.	*piccolo* pē'kōlō
ī	The *i* of *time*.	*dai* dī *traino* trī'no
ō	Either the *o* of *nose* (as in Italian *sole*) or the *o* of *often* (as in Italian *donna*). The difference is not shown here; it has to be learned by listening.	*sole* sō'le *donna* dō'nä
oi	The *oi* of *voice*.	*poi* poi
o͞o	The *u* of *rule* (but without the "upglide").	*luna* lo͞o'nä
ou	The *ou* of *house*.	*laudare* loudä're

ITALIAN

CONSONANTS

b	The *b* of *boy*.	*bello* be'lō
d	The *d* of *do*.	*dare* dä're
f	The *f* of *far*.	*farina* färē'nä
g	The *g* of *go*.	*gusto* gōō'stō
j	The *j* of *John*.	*giorno* jōr'nō *oggetto* ōje'tō
k	The *k* of *key*, the *c* of *can*.	*casa* kä'sä *scherzo* sker'tsō
l	The *l* of *love* (not of *fall*).	*mela* me'lä
m	The *m* of *me*.	*mano* mä'nō
n	The *n* of *no*.	*nome* nō'me
ng	The *ng* of *sing*. (Occurs in some foreign words in Italian.)	*bowling* bō'lēng
p	The *p* of *pin*.	*pane* pä'ne
r	The *r* of *run* (but with a slight "trill").	*roba* rō'bä *carta* kär'tä
s	The *s* of *sun* (See also z, below.)	*sala* sä'lä *casa* kä'sä
sh	The *sh* of *shine*.	*lasciare* läshä're
t	The *t* of *toy*.	*tempo* tem'pō
tsh	The *ch* of *much*.	*cento* tshen'tō
v	The *v* of *vat*.	*vita* vē'tä
y	The *y* of *year*.	*gennaio* jenä'yō *stiamo* styä'mō
z	The *z* of *zeal*.	*paese* pä·e'ze *sbaglio* zbä'lyō

Note these frequent combinations:

'ly	as in *meglio* me'lyō
'ny	as in *agnello* änye'lō or *legno* le'nyō
ts	as in *rizzare* rētsä're or *zampa* tsäm'pä
dz	as in *mezzo* me'dzō or *zebra* dze'brä
tsy	as in *negozio* negō'tsyō
ōō·e	as in *guerra* gōō·e'rä
ōō·ē	*as in qui* kōō·ē' *or guidare* gōō·ēdä're

A raised dot separates two neighboring vowel symbols. This dot is merely a convenience to the eye; it does not indicate a break in pronunciation.

EVERYDAY EXPRESSIONS

Yes.	**Sì.** sē.
No.	**No.** nō.
Please.	**Per favore.** per fävō′re.
Thank you.	**Grazie.** grä′tsye.
You're welcome.	**Prego!** pre′gō!
Excuse me.	**Scusa!** skōō′zä!
I beg your pardon.	**Come scusa?** kō′me skōō′zä?
Sorry.	**Scusa.** skōō′zä.
How much is this/that?	**Quant'è?** kōō′änte′?
What time is it?	**Che ora è?** kē ō′rä e?
At what time does the … open/close?	**A che ora apre …/chiude …?** ä ke ō′rä ä′pre …/kyōō′de …?
Where can I find the/a restroom?	**Dov'è la/una toilette, per favore?** dōve′ lä/ōō′na tōle′te, per fävō′re?
Is the water safe to drink?	**L'acqua è potabile?** lä′kōō·ä e pōtä′bēle?
Is this free? (city map, museum, etc.)	**È gratis?** e grä′tēs?

ITALIAN

NOTEWORTHY SIGNS

Attenzione ätentsyō′ne	Caution
Chiuso per restauri Kyōō′zō per restou′rē	Closed for Restoration
Non toccare non tōkä′re	Do Not Touch
Uscita d'emergenza ōōshē′tä demerjen′tsä	Emergency Exit
Divieto d'accesso dēvye′tō dätshe′sō	Do Not Enter

61

GREETINGS

Entrata libera enträ'tä lē'berä	Free Admission
Non altrepassare nōn ältrepäsä're	Keep Out
Entrata vietata enträ'tä vyetä'tä	No Entry
Vietato fumare vyetä'tō fōōmä're	No Smoking
Aperto dalle … alle … äper'tō dä'le … ä'le …	Open from … to …
Acqua non potabile ä'kōō-ä nōn pōtä'bēle	Undrinkable Water
Signore/Donne sēnyō're/dō'ne	Women
Signori/Uomini sēnyō'rē/ōō-ō'mēnē	Men

GREETINGS

Good morning.	**Buongiorno.** bōō-ōnjōr'nō
Good afternoon.	**Buonasera.** bōō-ō'nä se'rä.
Good night.	**Buonanotte.** bōō-ōnänō'te.
Hello/Hi.	**Ciao/salve.** tshou/säl've.
What's your name?	**Come ti chiami?** kō'me tē kyä'mē?
My name is …	**Mi chiamo …** mē kyä'mō …
How are you?	**Come stai?** kō'me stī?
Fine thanks. And you?	**Sto bene, e tu?** stō be'ne, e tōō?
Where are you from?	**Di dove sei?** dē dō've se'ē?
I'm from …	**Sono di …** sō'nō dē …
It was nice meeting you.	**Mi ha fatto piacere conoscerti.** mē ä fä'tō pyätshe're kōnōsher'tē.
Good-bye.	**Ciao.** tshou.
Have a good trip.	**Buon viaggio.** bōō-ōn' vyä'jō.
Miss	**signorina** sēnyōrē'nä

| Mrs./Madam | **signora** sēnyōˈrä |
| Mr./Sir | **signor/signore** sēnyōr'/sēnyōˈre |

CONVERSING & GETTING TO KNOW PEOPLE

Do you speak English/French/Italian/German/Spanish?	**Parli inglese/francese/italiano/tedesco/spagnolo?** pärˈlē ēn·gleˈse/fräntsheˈse/ētälyäˈnō/tedesˈko/spänyōˈlō?
I don't understand.	**Non capisco.** nōn käpēsˈkō.
Could you speak more slowly please?	**Puoi parlare più lentamente, per favore?** pōō·oiˈ pärläˈre pyōō lentämenˈte, per fävoˈre?
Could you repeat that please?	**Puoi ripetere, per favore?** pōō·oiˈ rēpeˈtere, per fävoˈre?
I don't speak French/Italian/German/Spanish.	**Non parlo francese/italiano/tedesco/spagnolo.** nōn pärˈlō fräntsheˈse/ētälyäˈnō/tedesˈkō/spänyōˈlō.
Is there someone here who speaks English?	**C'è qualcuno qui che sa l'inglese?** tshe kōō·älkōōˈnō kōō·ēˈke sä lēn·gleˈse?
Do you understand?	**Hai capito?** ī käpēˈtō?
Just a moment. I'll see if I can find it in my phrasebook.	**Un attimo, guardo se lo trovo nel mio frasario.** ōōn äˈtēmō, gōō·ärˈdō se lō trōˈvō nel mēˈō fräzärˈyō.
Please point to your question/answer in the book.	**Indicami la tua domanda/risposta nel libro, per favore.** ēndēˈkämē lä tōōˈä dōmänˈdä/rēspōˈstä nel lēˈbrō, per fävoˈre.
My name is … What's yours?	**Io mi chiamo … E tu?** ēˈō mē kyäˈmō … e tōōˈ?
It's nice to meet you.	**Piacere!** pyätsheˈre!
This is my friend (male).	**Questo è il mio amico.** kōō·eˈstō e ēl mēˈō ämēˈkō.

63

CONVERSING

This is my brother/my husband/son …

Questo è mio fratello/mio marito/mio figlio … kōō·e'stō e mēō fräte'lō/mēō märē'tō/mēō fē'lyō …

This is my friend (female).

Questa è la mia amica. kōō·e'stä e lä mē'ä ämē'kä.

This is my sister/wife/daughter …

Questa è mia sorella/mia moglie/mia figlia … kōō·e'stä e mē'ä sore'lä/mē'ä mō'lye/mē'ä fē'lyä …

Where are you from?

Di dove sei? dē dō've se'ē?

What city?

Di che città? dē ke tshētä'?

I'm from …

Sono … sō'no …

    the United States.

    americano/americana. ämerēkä'nō/ämerēkä'na'.

    Canada.

    canadese. känäde'se.

    Australia.

    australiano/australiana. ousträlyä'nō/ousträlyä'nä.

    England.

    inglese. ēn·gle'se.

Are you here on vacation?

Sei qui in vacanza? se'ē kōō·ē' ēn väkän'tsä?

Do you like it here?

Ti piace qui? tē pyä'tshe kōō·ē'?

How long have you been here?

Da quanto tempo sei qui? dä kōō·än'tō tem'pō se'ē kōō·ē'?

I just got here.

Sono appena arrivato/arrivata. sō'nō äpe'nä ärēvä'tō/ärēvä'tä.

I've been here for … days.

Sono qui da … giorni. sō'nō kōō·ē' dä … jōr'nē.

I love it.

Mi piace un sacco. mē pyä'tshe ōōn sa'kō.

It's okay.

Non è male. nōn e mä'le.

I don't like it.

Non mi piace. nōn mē pyä'tshe.

64

It's too noisy.

C'è troppo rumore. tshe trō'pō rōōmō're.

It's too crowded/dirty/boring.

È troppo affollato/sporco/noioso. e trō'pō äfōlä'tō/spōr'kō/nōyō'sō.

Where are you staying?

Dove stai? dō've stī?

I'm staying at the … youth hostel/campground.

Sono all'ostello/al campeggio. sō'nō älōste'lō/äl kämpe'jo.

Where were you before you came here?

Dove sei stato/stata prima? dō've se'ē stä'tō/stä'tä prē'mä?

Did you stay at a youth hostel/campground there?

Sei stato/stata in un ostello/in un campeggio? se'ē stä'tō/stä'tä ēn ōōn ōste'lō/ēn ōōn kämpe'jo?

Did you like that city?

Ti è piaciuta quella città? tē e pyätshōō'tä kōō·e'lä tshētä'?

Did you like that country/youth hostel/campground?

Ti è piaciuto quel paese/quell'ostello/quel campeggio? tē e pyätshōō'tō kōō·el' pä·e'ze/kōō·elōste'lō/kōō·el' kämpe'jo?

Why not?

Perchè no? perke' nō?

Where are you going from here?

Dove vai adesso? dō've vī äde'sō?

Did you ever stay at the youth hostel in …?

Sei mai stato/stata all'ostello di …? se'ē mī stä'to/stä'tä älōste'lō dē …?

I'm going there next.

Ci vado adesso. tshē vä'dō äde'sō.

It was nice meeting you.

Mi ha fatto piacere conoscerti. mē ä fä'tō pyätshe're kōnōsher'tē.

Here is my address. Write to me sometime.

Ecco il mio indirizzo. Scrivimi! e'kō ēl mē'ō ēndērē'tsō. skrē'vēmē!

May I have your address? I'll write to you.

Mi dai il tuo indirizzo? Ti scrivo! mē dī ēl tōō'ō ēndērē'tsō? tē skrē'vō!

ITALIAN

USEFUL WORDS & EXPRESSIONS

Is it …?	**È …?** e …?
Is it … or …?	**È … o …?** e … ō … ?
It is …	**È …** e …

cheap/expensive	**economico/caro** ekōnō'mēkō/kä'rō
early/late	**presto/tardi** pre'stō/tär'dē
near/far	**vicino/lontano** vētshē'nō/lōntä'nō
open/closed	**aperto/chiuso** äper'tō/kyōō'zō
right/left	**destra/sinistra** de'strä/sēnē'strä
vacant/occupied	**libero/occupato** lē'berō/ōkōōpä'tō

entrance/exit	**entrata/uscita** enträ'tä/ōōshē'tä
with/without	**con/senza** kōn/sen'tsä

ARRIVAL & DEPARTURE

Your passport please.	**Il Suo passaporto, per favore.** ēl sōō'ō päsäpōr'tō, per fävō're.
I'm here on vacation/ business.	**Sono qui in vacanza/sono qui per lavoro.** sō'nō kōō·ē' in väkän'tsä/sō'nō kōō·ē' per lävō'rō.
I have nothing to declare.	**Non ho nulla da dichiarare.** nōn ō nōō'lä dä dēkyärä're.
I'll be staying …	**Resto qui per …** re'stō kōō·ē' per …

a week.	**una settimana.** ōō'nä setēmä'nä.
two/three weeks.	**due/tre settimane.** dōō'e/tre setēmä'ne.
a month.	**un mese.** ōōn me'se.
two/three months.	**due/tre mesi.** dōō'e/tre me'se.

·That's my backpack.	**Questo è il mio zaino.** kōō·e'stō e el mē'ō dzī'nō.

Where can I catch a bus/the subway into town?	**Dove si prende l'autobus/la metro per andare in centro?** dō've sē pren'de lou'tōbōōs/ lä me'trō per ändä're in tshen'trō?
Which number do I take?	**Che numero (di autobus)/che linea (della metro) devo prendere?** ke nōō'merō (dē ou'tōbōōs)/ke lē'ne·ä (de'lä me'trō) de'vō pren'dere?
Which stop do I get off for the center of town?	**A che fermata devo scendere per il centro?** ä ke fermä'tä de'vo shen'dere per ēl tshen'trō?
Can you let me know when we get to that stop?	**Mi può avvertire quando devo scendere?** mē pōō·ō' ävertē're kōō·än'dō de'vo shen'dere?
Where is gate number …?	**Dov'è l'uscita (numero) …?** dōve' lōōshē'tä (nōō'merō) …?

ITALIAN

CHANGING MONEY

Excuse me, can you tell me …	**Scusi, c'è …** skōō'zē, tshe …
where the nearest bank is?	**una banca qui vicino?** ōō'nä bän'kä kōō·ē' vētshē'nō?
where the nearest money exchange is?	**un ufficio cambio qui vicino?** ōōn ōōfē'tshō käm'byō kōō·ē' vētshē'nō?
where the nearest cash machine is?	**un bancomat qui vicino?** ōōn bänkōmät' kōō·ē vētshē'nō?
I would like to exchange this currency.	**Vorrei cambiare questa valuta.** vōre'ē kämbyä're kōō·e'stä välōō'tä.
I would like to exchange these traveler's checks.	**Vorrei cambiare questi traveller's cheques.** vōre'ē kämbyä're kōō·e'stē tre'velers sheks?

67

YOUTH HOSTELS

What is your exchange rate for U.S. dollars/traveler's checks?	**Che cambio fate per i dollari americani/per dei traveller's cheques?** ke käm'byō fä'te per ē dō'lärē ämerēkä'nē/per de'ē tre'velers sheks?
What is your commission rate?	**Che commissione fate?** ke kōmēsyō'ne fä'te?
Is there a service charge?	**Fate pagare il servizio?** fä'te pägä're ēl servē'tsyō?
I would like a cash advance on my credit card.	**Vorrei un anticipo sulla mia carta di credito.** vōre'ē ōon äntē'tshēpō sōo'lä mē'ä kär'tä dē kre'dētō.
I would like small/large bills.	**Vorrei delle banconote di taglio piccolo/grosso, per favore.** vōre'ē de'le bänkōnō'te dē tä'lyō pē'kōlō/grō'sō, per fävō're.
I think you made a mistake.	**Ci dev'essere un errore.** tshē deve'sere ōon erō're.

YOUTH HOSTELS

Excuse me, can you direct me to the youth hostel?	**Scusi, mi sa dire dov'è l'ostello?** skōo'zē, mē sä dē're dōve' lōste'lō?
Do you have any beds available?	**Avete ancora dei posti letto?** äve'te änkō'rä de'ē pō'stē le'tō?
For one/two.	**Per una persona/per due persone.** per ōo'nä perso'nä/per dōo'e persō'ne.
... women	**... donne** ... dō'ne
... men	**... uomini** ... ōo·ō'mēnē
We'd like to be in the same room.	**Vorremmo dormire nella stessa camera.** vōre'mō dōrmē're ne'lä ste'sä kä'merä.

68

How much is it per night?	**Quant'è a notte?** kōō·änte' ä nō'te?
Is there a limit on how many nights I/we can stay?	**Per quante notti si può restare qui? C'è un limite massimo?** per kōō·än'te nō'tē sē pōō·ō' restä're kōō·ē'? tshe ōōn lē'mēte mä'sēmō?
I'll/We'll be staying …	**Resto/Restiamo …** re'stō/restyä'mō …
tonight only.	**solo stanotte.** sō'lo stänō'te.
two/three nights.	**due/tre notti.** dōō'e/tre nō'tē.
four/five nights.	**quattro/cinque notti.** kōō·ä'trō/tshēn'kōō·e nō'tē.
a week.	**una settimana.** ōō'nä setēmä'nä.
Does it include breakfast?	**La colazione è inclusa?** lä kōlätsō'ne e ēnklōō'zä?
Do you serve lunch and dinner?	**Si può anche pranzare e cenare qui?** sē pōō·ō' än'ke prändzä're e tshenä're kōō·ē'?
What are the hours for breakfast/lunch/dinner?	**A che ora è la colazione/il pranzo/la cena?** ä ke ō'rä e lä kōlätsyō'ne/ēl prän'dzō/lä tshe'nä?
What are the lockout hours?	**Da che ora a che ora chiudete?** dä ke ō'rä ä ke ō'rä kyōōde'te?
Can I leave my bags here during lockout?	**Posso lasciare qui il mio bagaglio durante le ore di chiusura?** pō'sō läshä're kōō·ē' ēl mē'ō bägä'lyō dōōrän'te le ō're dē kyōōzōō'rä?
Do I take my key with me or leave it with you when I go out?	**Devo portare la chiave con me o lasciarla qui quando esco?** de'vō pōrtä're lä kyä've kōn me ō läshär'lä kōō·ē' kōō·än'dō es'kō?
Do you have lockers?	**Ci sono degli armadietti?** tshē sō'nō de'lyē ärmädye'tē?
What time is the curfew?	**Qual è l'ora di chiusura serale?** kōō·ä'l e lō'rä dē kyōōzōō'rä serä'le?

HOTEL OR OTHER ACCOMMODATIONS

What time is check-out?	**A che ora devo liberare la camera?** ä ke ō'rä de'vō lēberä're lä kä'merä?
Are there cooking/laundry facilities?	**È possibile cucinare/lavare qualcosa?** e pōse'bēle kōotshēnä're/lävä're kōo-älkō'sä?
Is there a reduction for children?	**C'è una riduzione per i bambini?** tshe ōō'nä rēdōotsyō'ne per ē bämbē'nē?

HOTEL OR OTHER ACCOMMODATIONS

libero/completo lē'berō/kōmple'tō	vacancy/no vacancy
camere libere kä'mere lē'bere	Rooms for Rent
chiuso per ferie kyōō'zō per fer'ye	Closed for Vacation

I'm looking for …	**Cerco …** tsher'kō …
an inexpensive hotel.	**un hotel economico.** ōōn ōtel' ekōnō'mēkō.
a pension.	**una pensione.** ōō'nä pensyō'ne.
a room.	**una stanza.** ōō'nä stän'tsä.
I have a reservation.	**Ho prenotato.** ō prenōtä'tō.
Do you have a room for tonight?	**Ha una stanza per questa notte?** ä ōō'nä stän'tsä per kōo·e·stä nō'te?
I'd like your cheapest room.	**Vorrei avere la stanza più economica.** vōre'ē äve're lä stän'tsä pyōō ekōnō'mēkä.
I'd like a single/double room …	**Vorrei una stanza singola/doppia.** vōre'ē ōō'nä stän'tsä sin'gōlä/dō'pyä.
with a private bath.	**con bagno privato.** kōn bä'nyō prēvä'tō.
with a shared bath.	**con bagno in comune.** kōn bä'nyō ēn kōmōō'ne.
for … days/a week.	**per … giorni/per una settimana.** per … jōr'nē/per ōō'na setēmä'nä.

How much is the room?	**Quanto costa la stanza?** koo·än'tō kō'stä lä stän'tsä?
May I see the room?	**Posso vedere la stanza?** pō'sō vede're lä stän'tsä?
Does it include breakfast?	**La colazione è compresa?** lä kōlätsyō'ne e kōmpre'zä?
I'll take it.	**La prendo.** lä pren'do.
Do you have anything cheaper?	**Ha qualcosa di più economico?** ä koo·älkō'sä dē pyoo ekōnō'mēkō?
What time is checkout?	**A che ora devo liberare la camera?** ä ke ō'rä de'vō lēberä're lä kä'merä?

ITALIAN

CAMPING ACCOMMODATIONS

Can you direct me to the nearest campground?	**Mi può dire dov'è il campeggio più vicino?** mē poo·ō' dē're dōve' ēl kämpejō pyoo vētshē'nō?
How much is it per night/per person/ per tent?	**Quant'è a notte/a persona/a tenda?** koo·änte' ä nō'te/ä persō'nä/ä ten'dä?
Are showers included?	**Le docce sono incluse?** le dō'tshe sō'nō ēnkloo·ō'ze?
Where can I buy a shower token?	**Dove si comprano i gettoni per la doccia?** dō've sē kōm'präno ē jetō'nē per lä dō'tshä?
How much are they?	**Quanto vengono?** koo·än'tō ven'gōnō?
How many do I need?	**Quanti ce ne vogliono?** koo·än'tē tshe ne vōl'yōnō?
Are there cooking/ laundry facilities?	**È possibile cucinare/lavare qualcosa?** e pōsē'bēle kootshēnä're/lävä're koo·älkō'sä?

71

SIGNS

Can we rent a bed/mattress/tent?	**Possiamo noleggiare un lettino/un materassino/una tenda?** pōsyä'mō nōlejä're ōōn letē'nō/ōōn mäteräse'nō/ōō'nä ten'dä?
May we light a fire?	**Possiamo accendere un fuoco?** pōsyä'mō ätshen'dere ōōn fōō·ō'kō?
Where can I find …	**Dove posso trovare …** dō've pō'sō trōvä're …
the drinking water?	**l'acqua potabile?** lä'kōō·ä pōtä'bēle?
a camping equipment store?	**un negozio di articoli da campeggio?** ōōn negō'tsyō dē ärtē'kōlē dä kämpe'jō?
a grocery store?	**un negozio di alimentari?** ōōn negō'tsyō dē älēmentä'rē?
a bank?	**una banca?** ōō'nä bän'kä?
the laundry facilities?	**la lavanderia?** lä lävändere'ä?
a telephone?	**un telefono?** ōōn tele'fōnō?
a restaurant?	**un ristorante?** ōōn rēstōrän'te?
electric hook-ups?	**le prese elettriche?** le pre'ze ele'trēke?
Is there a swimming pool?	**C'è una piscina?** tshe ōō'nä pēshē'nä?
How much does it cost?	**Quanto costa?** kōō·än'tō kō'stä?
May we camp here?/over there?	**possiamo campeggiare qui?/laggiù?** pōsyä'mō kämpejä're kōō·ē'?/läjōō'?

SIGNS

Vietato campeggiare vyetä'tō kämpejä're	No Camping
Non oltrepassare nōn ōltrepäsä're	No Trespassing
Proprietà privata prōprē·etä' prēvä'tä	Private Property

CAMPING EQUIPMENT

I'd like to buy a/an/ some …	**Vorrei noleggiare …** vōre'ē nōlejä're …
I'd like to rent a/an/ some …	**Vorrei comprare …** vōre'ē kōmprä're …

air mattress/air mattresses.	**un materassino/dei materassini.** un mäteräsē'nō/de'ē mäteräsē'nē.
butane gas.	**una bomboletta del gas.** ōō'nä bōmbōle'tä del gäs.
charcoal.	**del carbone.** del kärbō'ne.
compass.	**una bussola.** ōō'nä bōō'sōlä.
eating utensils.	**delle posate.** de'le pōzä'te.
flashlight.	**una torcia elettrica.** ōō'nä tōr'tshä ele'trēkä.
folding chairs/ table.	**delle sedie pieghevoli/un tavolino pieghevole.** de'le se'dye pyege'vōlē/ōōn tävōlē'nō pyege'vōle.
ground sheet.	**un telone impermeabile.** ōōn telō'ne ēmperme·ä'bēle.
ice pack.	**del ghiaccio.** del gyä'tshō.
insect spray.	**uno spray contro gli insetti.** ōō'nō spre kōn'trō lyē ēnse'tē.
kerosene.	**del cherosene.** del kerōze'ne.
lantern.	**una lanterna.** ōō'nä länter'nä.
matches.	**dei fiammiferi.** de'ē fyämē'ferē.
rope.	**della corda.** de'lä kōr'dä.
sleeping bag.	**un sacco a pelo.** ōōn sä'kō ä pe'lō.
soap.	**del sapone.** del säpō'ne.
tent.	**una tenda.** ōō'nä ten'dä.
towel/towels.	**un asciugamano/degli asciugamani.** ōōn äshōōgämä'nō/de'lyē äshōōgämä'nē.

ITALIAN

73

TRANSPORTATION BY AIR

CHECKING OUT

I'd like to check out.	**Sono in partenza.** sō'nō ēn pärten'tsä.
May I have my bill please?	**Mi può fare il conto per favore?** mē pōō·ō' fä're ēl kōn'tō, per fävōre?
Could you give me a receipt.	**Mi può fare una ricevuta?** mē pōō·ō' fä're ōō'nä rētshevōō'tä?
Could you explain this item/charge?	**Mi può spiegare questo punto/addebito?** mē pōō·ō' spyegä're kōō·e'stō pōōn'tō/äde'bētō?
Thank you.	**Grazie.** grä'tsye.
I enjoyed my stay.	**Sono stato/stata bene qui.** sō'nō stä'tō/stä'tä be'ne kōō·ē'.
We enjoyed our stay.	**Siamo stati/state bene qui.** syä'mō stä'tē/stä'te be'ne kōō·ē'.

TRANSPORTATION BY AIR

Is there a bus/train to the airport?	**C'è un autobus/un treno per l'aeroporto?** tshe ōōn ou'tōbōōs/ōōn tre'nō per lä·erōpōr'to?
At what time does it leave?	**A che ora parte?** ä ke ō'rä pär'te?
How long does it take to get there?	**Quanto tempo ci mette?** kōō·än'tō tem'pō tshē me'te?
Is there an earlier/later bus/train?	**C'è un autobus/un treno prima/più tardi?** tshe ōōn au'tōbōōs/ōōn tre'nō prē'mä/pyōō tär'dē?
How much does it cost?	**Quanto costa?** kōō·än'tō kō'stä?
I'd like a flight to …	**Vorrei un volo per …** vōre'ē ōōn vō'lō per …

74

a one-way/round trip ticket	**un biglietto di sola andata/andata e ritorno** ōōn bēlye'tō dē sō'lä ändä'tä/ändä'tä e rētōr'nō.
your cheapest fare	**la tariffa più economica** lä tärē'fä pyōō ekōnō'mēkä
an aisle/window seat	**un posto accanto al corridoio/un posto accanto al finestrino** ōōn pō'stō äkän'tō äl kōrēdō'yō/äl fēnestrē'nō
Is there a bus/train to the center of town?	**C'è un autobus/treno per il centro?** tshe ōōn au'tōbōōs/tre'nō per ēl tshen'trō?

RIDING THE BUS & SUBWAY

Could you tell me where the nearest bus/subway station is?	**Mi può dire dov'è la stazione degli autobus/della metro più vicina?** mē pōō·ō' dē're dōve' lä stätsyō'ne de'lyē au'tōbōōs/de'lä me'trō pyōō vētshē'nä?
Could you tell me where the nearest bus/subway stop is?	**Mi può dire dov'è la fermata dell' autobus/della metro più vicina?** mē pōō·ō' dē're dōve' lä fermä'tä del au'tōbōōs/de'lä me'tro pyōō vētshē'nä?
Where can I buy a ticket?	**Dove si comprano i biglietti?** dō've sē kōm'pränō ē bēlye'tē?
How much does it cost?	**Quanto costano?** kōō·än'tō kō'stänō?
Can I use this ticket for the subway and the bus?	**Posso usare questo biglietto per la metro e per l'autobus?** pō'sō ōōzä're kōō·e'stō bēlye'tō per lä me'trō e per lau'tōbōōs?
I'd like to buy ... tickets.	**Vorrei ... biglietti per favore.** vōre'ē ... bēlye'tē, per fävō're.

ITALIAN

75

TRAIN-STATION & AIRPORT SIGNS

I'd like to buy a book of tickets/weekly pass.
Vorrei comprare un carnet di biglietti/un abbonamento settimanale.
vōre'ē kōmprä're ōōn kärne' dē bēlye'tē/ōōn äbōnämen'tō setēmänä'le.

Which bus/train do I take to get to …?
Che autobus/treno devo prendere per …?
ke au'tōbōōs/tre'nō de'vō pren'dere per …?

Do I have to change buses/trains to get to …?
Devo cambiare autobus/treno per arrivare a …? de'vō kämbyä're au'tōbōōs/tre'nō per ärēvä're ä …?

When is the next/last bus/train to …?
A che ora parte il prossimo/l'ultimo autobus/treno per …? ä ke ō'rä pär'te ēl prō'sēmō/lōōl'tēmō au'tōbōōs/tre'nō per …?

Can you tell me when we reach …?
Mi può avvisare quando arriviamo a …? mē pōō·ō' ävēzä're kōō·än'dō ärēvyä'mō ä …?

Do I get off here for …?
È questa la fermata per …? e kōō·e'stä lä fermä'tä per …?

Please let me off here.
Mi faccia scendere qui, per favore. mē fä'tshä shen'dere kōō·ē', per fävō're.

TRAIN-STATION & AIRPORT SIGNS

Arrivo/Arrivi ärē'vō/ärē'vē	Arrival
Deposito bagagli depō'zētō bägä'lyē	Baggage Check
Ritiro bagagli rētē'rō bägä'lyē	Baggage Pick-up
Cambio käm'byō	Change
Dogana dōgä'nä	Customs
Partenza/Partenze pärten'tsä/pärten'tse	Departure
Entrata enträ'tä	Entrance
Uscita ōōshē'tä	Exit

76

Informazioni ēnfōrmätsyō'nē	Information
Oggetti smarriti ōje'tē zmärē'tē	Lost & Found
Deposito bagagli depō'zētō bägä'lyē	Luggage Lockers
Non fumatori nōn fōōmätō'rē	No Smoking
Prenotazioni prenōtäzyō'nē	Reservations
Biglietti bēlye'tē	Tickets
Toilette tōle'te	Toilets
Ai binari/Ai treni ī bēnä'rē/ī tre'nē	To the Platforms/ Trains
Sala d'attesa sä'lä däte'sä	Waiting Room

ITALIAN

TAKING THE TRAIN

Could you tell me where the train station is?	**Scusi, mi può dire dov'è la stazione?** skōō'zē, mē pōō·ò' dē're dōve' lä stätsyō'ne?
Could I have a train schedule to …?	**Potrei avere un orario dei treni per …?** pōtre'ē äve're ōōn ōrär'yō de'ē tre'nē per …?
When is the next/last train to …?	**A che ora parte il prossimo/l'ultimo treno per …?** ä ke ō'rä pär'te ēl prō'sēmō/ lōōl'tēmo tre'no per …?
I would like to reserve a seat/couchette in 1st/2nd class.	**Vorrei prenotare un posto/una cuccetta di prima/di seconda classe.** vōre'ē prenōtä're ōōn pō'stō/ōō'nä kōōtshe'tä dē prē'mä/dē sekōn'dä klä'se.
one-way/round trip	**solo andata/andata e ritorno** sō'lō ändä'tä/ändä'tä e rētōr'nō
smoking/non-smoking	**fumatori/non fumatori** fōōmätō'rē/nōn fōōmätō'rē

TAKING THE TRAIN

aisle/window seat	**posto corridoio/posto finestrino** pō'stō kōrēdō'yō/pō'stō fēnestrē'nō
At what time does the night train to … leave?	**A che ora parte il treno notturno per …?** ä ke ō'rä pär'te ēl tre'nō nōtōōr'nō per …?
At what time does it arrive?	**A che ora arriva?** ä ke ō'rä ärē'vä?
Do I have to change trains? At what stop?	**Devo cambiare treno? A che fermata?** de'vō kämbyä're tre'nō? ä ke fermä'tä?
I have a rail pass. Must I pay a supplement to ride this train?	**Ho un abbonamento «rail pass». Devo pagare un supplemento per questo treno?** ō ōōn äbōnämen'tō «rel päs». de'vō pägä're ōōn sōōplemen'tō per kōō·e'stō tre'nō?
Could you tell me where platform/track … is?	**Mi può dire dov'è il binario …?** mē pōō·ō' dē're dōve' ēl bēnä'rēō …?
Could you tell me where car number … is?	**Mi può dire dov'è il vagone numero …?** mē pōō·ō' dē're dōve' ēl vägō'ne nōō'merō …?
Could you help me find my seat/couchette, please?	**Scusi, mi può dire dov'è il mio posto/ la mia cuccetta, per favore?** skōō'zē, mē pōō·ō' dē're dōve' ēl mē'ō pō'stō/lä mē'ä kōōtshe'tä, per fävō're?
Is this seat taken?	**È occupato questo posto?** e ōkōōpä'tō kōō·e'stō pō'stō?
Excuse me, I think this is my seat.	**Scusi, ma questo è il mio posto.** skōō'zē, mä kōō·e'stō e ēl mē'ō pō'stō.
Could you save my seat, please?	**Mi può tenere il posto, per favore?** mē pōō·ō' tene're ēl pō'stō, per fävō're?
Where is the dining car?	**Dov'è il vagone ristorante?** dōve' ēl vägō'ne rēstōrän'te?

| Where are the toilets? | **Dov'è la toilette, per favore?** |
| | dōve' lä tōle'te, per fävö're? |

**For Europass and Flexipass users. With these passes you will only have access to certain countries. If your train goes through a country that is not on your pass, you will be required to pay an extra fare.

| My rail pass only covers Spain/Portugal/France/Italy/Switzerland/Germany/Austria. | **Il mio biglietto copre solo Spagna/Portogallo/Francia/Italia/Svizzera/Germania/Austria.** ēl mē'ō bēlye'tō kō'pre sō'lō spä'nyä/pōrtōgä'lō/frän'tshä/ētä'lē·ä/svē'tserä/jermä'nē·ä/ou'strē·ä. |

| How much extra do I have to pay since my train goes through …? | **Quando devo pagare extra, visto che il treno passa per …?** kōō·än'dō de'vō pägä're ek'strä, vē'stō ke ēl tre'nō pä'sä per …? |

| Is there another way to get to … without having to go through …? | **Esiste un altro percorso, per evitare di passare da …?** esē'ste ōōn äl'trō perkōr'sō, per evētä're dē päsä're dä …? |

BY BOAT

| Is there a boat that goes to …? | **C'è un traghetto per …?** tshe ōōn träge'tō per …? |

| When does the next/last boat leave? | **A che ora parte il prossimo/l'ultimo traghetto?** ä ke ō'rä pär'te ēl prō'sēmō/lōōl'tēmō träge'tō? |

| I have a rail pass. Do I get a discount? How much? | **Ho un biglietto «rail pass». Ho diritto a uno sconto? Quanto?** ō ōōn bēlye'tō «rel päs». ō dērē'tō ä ōō'nō skōn'tō? kōō·än'tō? |

| At what time does the boat arrive? | **A che ora arriva il traghetto?** ä ke ō'rä ärē'vä ēl träge'tō? |

ROAD SIGNS

| How early must I get on board? | **Tra quanto bisogna salire a bordo?** trä kōō·än'tō bēzō'nyä säle'̄re ä bōr'dō? |
| Can I buy seasickness pills nearby? | **Dove si possono comprare qui delle pastiglie contro il mal di mare?** dō've sē pō'sōnō kōmprä're kōō·ē' de'le pästē'lye kōn'trō ēl mäl dē mä're? |

GETTING AROUND BY CAR

I'd like to rent a car ...	**Vorrei noleggiare una macchina ...** vōre'ē nōlejä're ōō'nä mä'kēnä ...
for ... days.	**per ... giorni.** per ... jōr'nē.
for a week.	**per una settimana.** per ōō'nä setēmä'nä.
What is your daily/ weekly rate?	**Qual è la tariffa giornaliera/settimana-le?** kōō·äl' e lä tärē'fä jōrnälye'rä/setēmänä'le?
Do I need insurance?	**Devo fare un'assicurazione?** de'vō fä're ōōnäsēkōōrätsyō'ne?
Is mileage included?	**Quanti chilometri sono inclusi?** kōō·än'tē kēlō'metrē sō'nō ēnklōō'zē?
How much is it?	**Quant'è?** kōō·änte'?

ROAD SIGNS

Stop stŏp	Stop
Senso unico sen'sō ōō'nēkō	One Way
Vietato l'accesso vyetä'tō lätshe'sō	Do Not Enter
Dare la precedenza dä're lä pretsheden'tsä	Yield
Divieto di sosta dēvye'tō dē sō'stä	No Parking

TAXI

I'd like to go to …	**Vorrei andare a …** võre'ē ändä're ä …
What is the fare?	**Quanto costa una corsa?** kōō·än'tō kō'stä ōō'nä kōr'sä?
Please stop here.	**Si fermi qui, per favore.** sē fer'mē kōō·ē', per fävō're.
Can you wait for me?	**Mi può aspettare, per favore?** mē pōō·ō' äspetä're, per fävō're?

GETTING AROUND ON FOOT

ITALIAN

Excuse me, could you tell me how to get to …?	**Scusi, come si arriva a …?** skōō'zē, kō'me sē ärē'vä ä …?
Is it nearby/far?	**È vicino/lontano?** e vētshē'nō/lōntä'nō?
Can I walk or should I take the bus/subway?	**Si può andare a piedi o è meglio prendere un autobus/la metro?** sē pōō·ō' ändä're ä pye'dē ō e me'lyō pren'dere ōōn au'tōbōōs/lä me'trō?
Could you direct me to the nearest bus/subway station/stop?	**Scusi, dov'è la fermata dell'autobus/la stazione della metro più vicina?** skōō'zē, dōve' lä fermä'tä delou'tōbōōs/lä stätsyō'ne de'lä me'trō pyōō vētshē'nä?
Straight ahead.	**Sempre dritto.** sem'pre drē'tō.
Go right/left.	**Vada a destra/a sinistra.** vä'dä ä de'strä/ä sēnē'strä.
At the corner/traffic light.	**All'angolo/al semaforo.** älän'gōlō/äl semä'fōrō.
I'm lost.	**Mi sono perso/persa.** mē sō'nō per'sō/per

EATING OUT

Could you show me where we are on this map?	**Mi fa vedere dove siamo su questa cartina, per favore?** mē fä vede're dō've syä'mō sōō kōō·e'stä kärtē'nä, per fävō're?

EATING OUT

Could we have a table outside/inside?	**Possiamo sederci fuori/dentro?** pōsyä'mō seder'tshē fōō·ō're/den'trō?
Do you have a fixed-price menu?	**Avete un menù a prezzo fisso?** ävе'te ōōn menōō' ä pre'tsō fē'sō?
Is service included?	**Il servizio è incluso?** ēl servē'tsyō e ēnklōō'zō?
Is there a cover charge?	**Bisogna pagare il coperto?** bēzō'nyä pägä're ēl kōper'tō?
Separate checks, please.	**Conti separati, per cortesia.** kōn'tē sepärä'tē, per kōrtezē'ä.
I'd like some apple/orange/grapefruit juice.	**Vorrei un succo di mela/d'arancia/di pompelmo.** vōre'ē ōōn sōō'kō dē me'lä/därän'tshä/dē pompel'mō.
I'd like some coffee/tea with cream/lemon.	**Vorrei del caffè/del tè al latte/al limone.** vōre'ē del käfe'/del te äl lä'te/äl lēmō'ne.
I'd like a soda/beer/mineral water.	**Vorrei una spuma/una birra/un'acqua minerale.** vōre'ē ōō'nä spōō'mä/ōō'nä bē'rä/ōōnä'kōō·ä mēnerä'le.
I'd like a glass/bottle of red/white/rose wine.	**Vorrei un bicchiere/una bottiglia di vino rosso/bianco/rosè.** vōre'ē ōōn bēkye're/ōō'nä bōtē'lyä dē vē'nō rō'sō/byän'kō/rōze'.
dry/sweet	**secco/dolce** se'kō/dōl'tshe
Cheers!	**Salute/Cin cin!** sälōō'te!/tshēn tshēn!

What is the special of the day?	**Qual è la specialità** [del giorno?] kōō·äl e lä spetshälētä' d[...]
Do you have a tourist menu?	**Avete un menù turisti**[co?] äve'te ōōn menōō' tōōrē'st[...]
What is this? (pointing to item on menu)	**Che cos'è questo?** ke k[...] esto?
I'll have this.	**Va bene, lo prendo.** vä be'ne, lō pren'dō.
I'd like some salt/pepper/cheese/sugar/milk.	**Vorrei del sale/pepe/formaggio/ zucchero/latte.** vōre'ē del sä'le/pe'pe/fōrmä'jo/tsōō'kerō/lä'te.
More juice/coffee/tea/cream/lemon/milk/beer/wine.	**Un altro po' di succo/caffè/tè/panna/ limone/latte/birra/vino, per favore.** ōōn äl'trō pō dē sōō'kō/käfe'/tē/pä'nä/lēmō'ne/ lä'te/bē'rä/vē'nō, per fävō're.
More cream/beer.	**Dell'altra panna/birra, per favore.** deläl'trä pä'nä/bē'rä, per fävō're.
I cannot eat/drink sugar/salt/alcohol.	**Non posso assumere zuccheri/sale/ alcool.** nōn pō'sō äsōō'mere tsōō'kerē/sä'le/al'kō·ōl.
I am a diabetic.	**Sono diabetico/diabetica.** sō'nō dē·äbe'tēkō/dē·äbe'tēkä.
I am a vegetarian.	**Sono vegetariano/vegetariana.** sō'nō vejetäryä'nō/vejetäryä'nä.
May I have the check, please.	**Posso avere il conto, per favore?** pō'sō ave're ēl kōn'tō, per fävō're?
Keep the change.	**Tenga pure il resto.** ten'gä pōō're ēl re'stō.

…an you make me a sandwich.	**Mi può fare un panino, per favore?** mē pōō·ō' fä're ōōn pänē'nō, per fävō're?
To take out.	**Da portare via.** dä portä're vē·ä.
I'd like some …	**Vorrei …** vōre'ē …
I'll have a little more.	**Un po' di più, per favore.** ōōn pō dē pyōō, per fävō're.
That's too much.	**Così è troppo.** kōsē' e trōpō.
Do you have …	**Ha …** ä …
I'd like …	**Vorrei …, per favore.** vōre'ē …, per fävō're.
a box of	**una scatola di** ōō'nä skä'tōlä dē
a can of	**una lattina di** ōō'nä latē'nä dē
a jar of	**un barattolo di** ōōn bärä'tōlō dē
a half kilo of	**mezzo chilo di** me'dzō kē'lō dē
a kilo of	**un chilo di** ōōn kē'lō dē
a half liter	**mezzo litro di** me'dzō lē'trō dē
a liter	**un litro di** ōōn lē'trō dē
a packet of	**un pacchetto di** ōōn päke'tō dē
a slice of	**una fetta di** ōō'nä fe'tä dē
a bottle opener	**un apribottiglie** ōōn äprēbōtē'lye
a can opener	**un apriscatole** ōōn äprēskä'tōle
a cork screw	**un cavatappi** ōōn kävätä'pē
I'd like it sliced.	**Lo vorrei a fette, per favore.** lō vōre'ē ä fe'te, per fävō're.
Do you have any plastic forks/spoons/knives and napkins?	**Avete forchette/cucchiai/coltelli di plastica e dei tovaglioli?** äve'te fōrke'te/kōōkyä'ē/kōlte'lē dē plä'stēkä e de'ē tōvälyōle'nē?
May I have a bag?	**Mi può dare un sacchetto, per favore?** mē pōō·ō' dä're ōōn säke'tō, per fävō're?

Is there a park nearby?	**C'è un parco qui vicino?** tshe ōōn pär'kō kōō·ē' vētshē'nō?
May we picnic there?	**È possibile fare un picnic là?** e pōsē'bēle fä're ōōn pēk'nēk lä?
May we picnic here?	**Si può fare un picnic qui?** sē pōō·ō' fä're ōōn pēk'nēk kōō·ē'?

Fruits

apples	**mele** me'le	
apricots	**albicocche** älbēkō'ke	
bananas	**banane** bänä'ne	
blueberries	**mirtilli** mērtē'lē	
cantaloupe	**melone** melō'ne	
cherries	**ciliegie** tshēlye'je	
dates	**datteri** dä'terē	
figs	**fichi** fē'kē	
grapefruit	**pompelmi** pōmpel'mē	
grapes	**uva** ōō'vä	
lemons	**limoni** lēmō'nē	
nectarines	**pesche noci** pes'ke nō'tshē	
oranges	**arance** arän'tshe	
peaches	**pesche** pes'ke	
pears	**pere** pe're	
pineapple	**ananas** ä'nänäs	
plums	**prugne** prōō'nye	
raisins	**uvetta** ōōve'tä	
raspberries	**lamponi** lämpō'nē	
strawberries	**fragole** frä'gōle	
tangerines	**mandarini** mändärē'nē	
watermelon	**anguria** ängōō'rē·ä	

ITALIAN

Vegetables

artichokes	**carciofi** kärtshō'fē

85

FOOD SHOPPING

asparagus	**asparagi** äspä'räjē
green/kidney beans	**fagiolini/fagioli** fäjōlē'nē/fäjō'lē
broccoli	**broccoli** brō'kōlē
cabbage	**cavolo** kä'välō
carrots	**carote** kärō'te
cauliflower	**cavolfiore** kävōlfyō're
celery	**sedano** se'dänō
corn	**granoturco** gränōtōōr'kō
cucumber	**cetriolo** tshetrē-ō'lō
eggplant	**melanzana** meländzä'nä
fennel	**finocchio** fēnō'kyō
french fries	**patatine fritte** pätätē'ne frē'te
garlic	**aglio** ä'lyō
leeks	**porro** pō'rō
lentils	**lenticchie** lentē'kye
lettuce	**lattuga** lätōō'gä
mushrooms	**funghi** fōōn'gē
black/green olives	**olive nere/verdi** ōlē've ne're/ver'dē
onions	**cipolle** tshēpō'le
peas	**piselli** pēze'lē
hot/sweet peppers	**peperoncini/peperoni** peperōntshē'nē/peperō'nē
pickles	**cetrioli sottaceti** tshetrē-ō'le sōtätshe'te
potatoes	**patate** päta'te
radishes	**ravanelli** rävane'lē
rice	**riso** rē'sō
sauerkraut	**crauti** krou'tē
spinach	**spinaci** spēnä'tshē
tomatoes	**pomodori** pōmōdō'rē
zucchini	**zucchini** tsōōkē'nē

Meats/Cold Cuts

beef	**manzo** män'dzō
bologna	**mortadella** mōrtäde'lä
chicken	**pollo** pō'lō

fish	**pesce** pe'she
ham	**prosciutto** prōshōō'tō
hamburger/ground beef	**hamburger/carne di manzo macinata** ämbōōr'ger/kär'ne dē män'dzō mätshēnä'tä
hot dogs/frankfurters	**hot dogs/würstel** ōt dōgz/vēr'stel
lamb	**agnello** änye'lō
pork	**maiale** mäyä'le
roast beef	**roast beef** rōst bēf
salami	**salame** sälä'me
sausage	**salciccia** sältshē'tshä
turkey	**tacchino** täkē'nō
veal	**vitello** vēte'lo

ITALIAN

Nuts

almonds	**mandorle** män'dōrle
brazil nuts	**noci del Parà** nō'tshē del Pärä'
cashews	**anacardi** änäkär'dē
chestnuts	**castagne** kästä'nye
hazelnuts	**nocciole** nōtshō'le
peanuts	**noccioline/arachidi** nōtshōlē'ne/ärä'kēdē
walnuts	**noci** nō'tshē

Condiments

butter	**burro** bōō'rō
honey	**miele** mye'le
horseradish	**rafano** rä'fänō
jam/jelly	**marmellata/gelatina di frutta** märmelä'tä/jeläte'nä dē frōō'tä
ketchup	**ketchup** ke'tshōp
margarine	**margarina** märgärē'nä
mayonnaise	**maionese** mī·ōne'se
mustard	**senape** se'näpe
vegetable/olive oil	**olio vegetale/d'oliva** ō'lyō vejetä'le/dōlē'vä
pepper	**pepe** pe'pe

87

FOOD SHOPPING

mild/hot salsa	**una salsa dolce/piccante**
	ōō'nä säl'sä dōl'tshe/pēkän'te
salt	**sale** sä'le
sugar	**zucchero** tsōō'kerō
tabasco/hot sauce	**tabasco/salsa piccante**
	täbäs'kō/säl'sä pēkän'te
vinegar	**aceto** ätshe'tō

Miscellaneous

bread	**pane** pä'ne
cake	**torta** tōr'tä
candy	**caramelle** käräme'le
cereal	**cereali** tshere·ä'lē
cheese	**formaggio** fōrmä'jō
chocolate	**cioccolata** tshōkōlä'tä
cookies	**biscotti** bēskō'tē
crackers	**cracker** kre'ker
eggs	**uova** ōō·ō'vä
ice cream	**gelato** jelä'tō
popcorn	**popcorn** pōp'kōrn
potato chips	**patatine** pätätē'ne
rolls	**panini** pänē'nē
spaghetti	**spaghetti** späge'tē
yogurt	**yogurt** yō'gōōrt

Drinks

beer	**birra** bē'rä
coffee	**caffè** käfe'
hot chocolate	**cioccolata calda** tshōkōlä'tä käl'dä
apple juice	**succo di mela** sōō'kō dē me'lä
cranberry juice	**succo di mirtillo rosso**
	sōō'kō dē mērtē'lō rō'sō
grapefruit juice	**succo di pompelmo** sōō'kō dē pōmpel'mō
orange juice	**succo d'arancia** sōō'kō därän'tshä

88

tomato juice	**succo di pomodoro** sōō'kō dē pōmōdō'rō
milk	**latte** lä'te
soft drinks	**bibite analcoliche** bē'bēte änälkō'lēke
tea	**té** te
sparkling mineral water	**acqua minerale gassata** ä'kōō·ä mēnerä'le gäsä'tä
red/white/rose wine	**vino rosso/bianco/rosé** vē'nō rō'sō/byän'kō/rōze'
dry/sweet	**secco/dolce** se'kō/dōl'tshe

ITALIAN

USING THE TELEPHONE

Can I use local currency to make a local/long-distance call or do I need to buy a phone card?	**Posso usare delle monete per telefonare all'estero o devo comprare una scheda telefonica?** pō'sō ōōzä're de'le mōne'te per telefōnä're alle'sterō ō de'vō kōmprä're ōō'na ske'dä felefō'nēka?
Do I need to buy tokens?	**Devo comprare dei gettoni?** de'vō kōmprä're de'ē jetō'nē?
Where can I buy tokens/a phone card?	**Dove posso comprare dei gettoni/una scheda telefonica?** dō've pō'so kōmprä're de'ē jetō'nē/ōō'nä ske'dä telefō'nēkä?
… tokens, please. How much?	**… gettoni, per favore. Quanto fa?** … jetō'nē, per fävō're. kōō·än'tō fä?
I'd like to buy a phone card. How much does it cost?	**Vorrei una scheda telefonica. Quanto costa?** vōre'ē ōō'nä ske'dä telefō'nēkä. kōō·än'tō kō'stä?
How do you use the phone card?	**Come si usa la scheda telefonica?** kō'me se ōō'zä lä ske'dä telefō'nēkä?
Excuse me, where is the nearest phone?	**Scusa, dov'è il telefono più vicino?** skōō'zä, dōve' ēl tele'fonō pyōō vētshē'nō?

POST OFFICE

I'd like to make a collect call.	**Vorrei fare una telefonata a carico del destinatario.** vōre'ē fä're ōō'nä telefōnä'tä ä kä'rēkō del destēnätär'yō.
The number is …	**Il numero è …** ēl nōō'merō e …
Hello. This is …	**Pronto? Sono …** prōn'to? sō'nō …
May I speak to …	**Vorrei parlare con …** vōre'ē pärlä're kōn …

POST OFFICE

Can you direct me to the nearest post office?	**Mi può indicare l'ufficio postale più vicino?** mē pōō·ō' ēndēkä're lōōfē'tshō pōstä'le pyōō vētshē'nō?
Which window is for …	**Qual è lo sportello per …** kōō·äl'e lō spōrte'lō per …
stamps?	**i francobolli?** ē fränkōbō'lē?
sending/cashing a money order?	**spedire/incassare un vaglia?** spedē're/ēnkäsä're ōōn vä'lyä?
airmail writing paper?	**carta da lettere per via aerea?** kär'tä dä le'tere per vē'ä ä·e're·ä?
I'd like … stamps for postcards/letters to America.	**Vorrei … francobolli da cartolina/lettera per l'America.** vōre'ē … fränkōbō'lē dä kärtōlē'nä/le'terä per läme'rēkä.
I'd like to send this airmail.	**Per via aerea, per favore.** per vē'ä ä·e're·ä, per fävō're.
How much does it cost?	**Quant'è?** kōō·änte'?

90

PHARMACY & DRUGSTORE

Can you direct me to the nearest pharmacy?	**Dov'è la farmacia più vicina, per favore?** dōve' lä färmätshē'ä pyōō vētshē'nä, per fävō're?
I'd like a/an/some …	**Vorrei …** vōre'ē …
aspirin.	**delle aspirine.** de'le äspērē'ne.
Band-Aids.	**dei cerotti.** de'ē tsherō'tē.
cough medicine.	**qualcosa per la tosse.** kōō·älkō'sä per lä tō'se.
contraceptives.	**dei contraccettivi.** de'ē kōnträtshetē'vē.
eye drops.	**un collirio.** ōōn kōlēr'yō.
insect repellant.	**un insettifugo.** ōōn insetē'fōōgō.
sanitary napkins.	**degli assorbenti.** de'lyē äsōrben'tē.
Could you give me something for …?	**Mi può dare qualcosa per …?** mē pōō·ō' dä're kōō·älkō'sä per …?
constipation	**la stitichezza** lä stētēke'tsä
diarrhea	**la diarrea** lä dē·äre·ä
a headache	**il mal di testa** ēl mäl dē te'stä
hay fever	**l'allergia da fieno** lälerjē'ä dä fye'nō
indigestion	**l'indigestione** lēndējestyō'ne
itching	**il prurito** ēl prōōrē'tō
nausea	**la nausea** lä nou'ze·ä
travel sickness	**il mal d'auto/d'aereo** ēl mäl dou'tō/dä·er'e·ō
a rash	**un'eruzione cutanea** ōōnerōōtsyō'ne kōōtä'ne·ä
sore throat	**il mal di gola** ēl mäl dē gō'lä
sunburn	**una scottatura solare** ōō'nä skōtätōō'rä sōlä're
May I have a/an/some …?	**Potrei avere … , per favore?** pōtre'ē äve're …, per fävō're?
deodorant	**un deodorante** ōōn de·ōdōrän'te
razor	**un rasoio** ōōn räzō'yō

ITALIAN

91

razor blades	**delle lamette** de'le läme'te
shampoo/conditioner	**uno shampoo/un balsamo** ōō'no shäm'pōō/ōōn bäl'sämō
soap	**un sapone** ōōn säpō'ne
suntan oil/cream/lotion	**un olio/una crema/una lozione solare** ōōn ō'lyō/ōō'nä kre'mä/ōō'na lōtsyō'ne sōlä're
tissues	**dei fazzolettini di carta** de'ē fätsōlete'nē dē kär'tä
toilet paper	**della carta igienica** de'lä kär'tä ējē·e'nēkä
toothbrush	**uno spazzolino** ōō'nō spätsōle'nō
toothpaste	**un dentifricio** ōōn dentēfrē'tshō
cleaning/soaking solution for contact lenses	**una soluzione detergente/conservante per lenti a contatto** ōō'nä sōlōōtsyō'ne deterjen'te/konservän'te per len'tē ä kōntä'tō

How much does it cost?	**Quant'è/quanto costa?** kōō·änte'/kōō·än'tō kō'stä?

TOBACCO SHOP

I'd like to buy …	**Vorrei comprare …** vōre'ē kōmprä're …
a pack/carton of cigarettes.	**un pacchetto/una stecca di sigarette.** ōōn päke'tō/ōō'nä ste'kä dē sēgäre'te.
a cigarette lighter.	**un accendino.** ōōn ätshende'nō.
a cigar.	**un sigaro.** ōōn sē'gärō.
May I have some matches?	**Ha dei fiammiferi/cerini, per favore?** ä de'ē fyämē'ferē/tsherē'nē, per fävō're?

PHOTOGRAPHY

I'd like to buy a roll of film.	**Vorrei un rullino.** vōre'ē ōōn rōōle'nō.

92

Black and white/Color.	**In bianco e nero/A colori.** in byän'kō e ne'rō/ä kōlō'rē.
How much are they?	**Quant'è?/Quanto costano?** kōō·änte'?/kōō·än'tō kō'stänō?
I'd like to buy batteries for this camera.	**Vorrei delle batterie per questa macchina fotografica.** vōre'ē de'le bäterē'e per kōō·e'stä mä'kēnä fōtōgrä'fēkä.

HEALTH

The Doctor

I don't feel well.	**Non mi sento bene.** nōn mē sen'tō be'ne.
Could you direct me to a doctor that speaks English.	**Mi può consigliare un medico che parla l'inglese?** mē pōō·ō' kōnsēlyä're ōōn me'dēkō ke pär'lä lēn·gle'se?
I have (a) ...	**Ho ...** ō ...
burn.	**una scottatura.** ōō'nä skōtätōō'rä.
chest pains.	**dei dolori al petto/male al torace.** de'ē dōlō'rē äl petō/mä'le äl tōrä'tshe.
cold.	**un raffreddore.** ōōn räfredō're.
cough.	**la tosse.** lä tō'se.
cramps.	**dei crampi.** de'ē kräm'pē.
cut.	**un taglio.** ōōn tä'lyō.
diarrhea.	**la diarrea.** lä dē·äre'ä.
fever.	**la febbre.** lä fe'bre.
flu.	**l'influenza.** lēnflōō·en'tsä.
infection.	**un'infezione.** ōōnēnfetsyō'ne.
nausea.	**nausea.** nou'ze·ä.
rash.	**un'eruzione cutanea.** ōōnerōōtsyō'ne kōōtä'ne·ä.
sore throat.	**mal di gola.** mäl dē gō'lä.
sprained ankle.	**una caviglia slogata.** ōō'nä kävē'lyä zlōgä'tä.

ITALIAN

93

stomach ache.	**mal di stomaco.** mäl dē stō'mäkō
It hurts here.	**Mi fa male qui.** mē fä mä'le kōō·ē'.
I've been vomiting.	**Ho vomitato.** ō vōmētä'tō.
I'm having difficulty breathing.	**Faccio fatica a respirare.** fä'tshō fätē'kä ä respērä're.
I'm allergic to penicillin.	**Sono allergico/allergica alla penicillina.** sō'no äler'jēkō/äler'jēkä ä'lä penētshēlē'nä.
I'm diabetic.	**Sono diabetico/diabetica.** sō'nō dē·äbe'tēkō/dē·äbe'tēkä.
I don't smoke/drink.	**Non fumo/Non bevo.** nōn fōō'mō/nōn be'vō.

The Dentist

Could you direct me to a dentist that speaks English?	**Mi può consigliare un dentista che parla l'inglese?** mē pōō·ō' kōnsēlyä're ōōn dentē'stä ke pär'lä lēn·gle'se?
I have a toothache. This tooth.	**Mi fa male un dente. Questo dente.** mē fä mä'le ōōn den'te. kōō·e'stō den'te.
My tooth is loose.	**Mi si è staccato un dente.** mē sē e stäkä'tō ōōn den'te.
My tooth is broken.	**Mi si è rotto un dente.** mē sē e rō'tō ōōn den'te.
I've broken/lost a filling.	**Mi si è rotta/ho perso un'otturazione.** mē sē e rō'tä/ō per'sō ōōnōtōōrätsyō'ne.

Paying

How much does this cost?	**Quanto costa?/Quant'è?** kōō·än'to kō'stä?/kōō·änte'?

I have health insurance.	**Ho un'assicurazione malattie.** ō ōōnäsēkōōrätsyō'ne mälätē'e.
I'm supposed to call this number.	**Devo chiamare questo numero.** de'vō kyämä're kōō·e·stō nōō'merō.
How much do I owe you?	**Quanto Le devo?** kōō·än'tō le de'vō?

SIGHTSEEING

Can you recommend …?	**Mi puoi consigliare …** mē pōō·oi' kōnsēlyä're …
a good, inexpensive restaurant?	**un buon ristorante non troppo caro?** ōōn bōō·ōn' rēstörän'te nōn trō'pō kä'rō?
a fun nightclub?	**un nightclub divertente?** ōōn nīt'klōōb dēverten'te?
a good place to dance?	**una buona discoteca?** ōō'nä bōō·ō'nä dēskōte'kä?
Can you tell me where the tourist office is?	**Dov'è l'ufficio informazioni turistiche?** dōve' lōōfē'tshō ēnförmätsyō'ne tōōrē'stēke?
What are the main points of interest here?	**Cosa c'è da vedere qui?** kō'sä tshe dä vede're kōō·ē'?
What time does it open/close?	**A che ora apre/chiude?** ä ke ō'rä ä'pre/kyōō'de?
What time is the last entry?	**Fino a che ora si può entrare?** fē'nō ä ke ō'rä sē pōō·ō' enträ're?
How much is the admission?	**Quanto costa l'ingresso?** kōō·än'tō kō'stä lēngre'sō?
Free.	**(Ingresso) libero.** (ēngre'sō) lē'berō.

ITALIAN

95

SIGHTSEEING

Is there a discount for students/children/ teachers/senior citizens?	**C'è uno sconto per studenti/bambini/ insegnanti/pensionati?** tshe ōō'nō skōn'tō per stōōden'tē/bämbē'nē/ ēnsenyän'tē/pensyōnä'tē?
Is the ticket good all day?	**Il biglietto è valido tutto il giorno?** ēl bēlye'tō e vä'lēdō tōō'tō ēl jōr'nō?
Is there a sightseeing tour?	**C'è una visita guidata?** tshe ōō'nä vē'zētä gēdä'tä?
What time does it start?	**A che ora inizia?** ä ke ō'rä ēnē'tsyä?
How much does it cost?	**Quanto costa?** kōō·än'tō kō'stä?
How long is it?	**Quanto dura?** kōō·än'tō dōō'rä?
Does the guide speak English?	**La guida parla l'inglese?** lä gē'dä pär'lä lēn·gle'se?
Am I allowed to take pictures/a video?	**È possibile fotografare/filmare?** e pōsē'bēle fōtōgräfä're/fēlmä're?
Can you direct me to the …?	**Come arrivo …?** kō'me ärē'vō …?

art gallery	**alla galleria d'arte** ä'lä gälerē'ä där'te
beach	**alla spiaggia** ä'lä spyä'jä
castle	**al castello** äl käste'lō
cathedral	**alla cattedrale** ä'lä kätedrä'le
cemetery	**al cimitero** äl tshēmēte'rō
church	**alla chiesa** ä'lä kye'zä
fountain	**alla fontana** ä'lä fōntä'nä
gardens	**ai giardini pubblici/al parco** ī järdē'nē pōō'blētshē/äl pär'kō
harbor	**al porto** äl pōr'tō
lake	**al lago** äl lä'gō
monastery	**al monastero** äl mōnäste'rō

96

mountains	**in montagna** ēn mōntä'nyä
movies	**al cinema** äl tshē'nemä
museum	**al museo** äl mōōze'ō
old city	**alla città vecchia** ä'lä tshetä' ve'kyä
palace	**al palazzo** äl pälä'tsō
ruins	**alle rovine** ä'le rōvē'ne
shops/bazaar	**ai negozi/al bazar** ī negō'tsē/äl bätsär'
statue	**al monumento** äl mōnōōmen'tō
tomb	**alla tomba** ä'lä tom'bä
trails (for hiking)	**sentieri (per escursioni)** sentye'rē (per eskōōrsyō'nē)
university	**all'università** älōōnēversētä'
zoo	**allo zoo** ä'lō dzō'ō

ITALIAN

Is it far from here?	**È lontano da qui?** e lōntä'nō dä kōō·ē'?
Can we walk there?	**Ci si arriva a piedi?** tshē sē ärē'vä ä pye'dē?
Straight ahead.	**Sempre dritto.** sem·pre drē'tō.
Go right/left.	**Vai a destra/sinistra.** vī ä de'strä/sēnē'strä.
At the corner/traffic light.	**All'angolo/Al semaforo.** älän'gōlō/äl semä'fōrō.

DISCOUNT INFORMATION

Do I get a discount with my student/teacher's/senior citizens card?	**C'è uno sconto per studenti/insegnanti/pensionati?** tshe ōō'nō skōn'tō per stōōden'tē/ēnsenyän'tē/pensyōnä'tē?
Do I get a discount with my Eurailpass/Europass/Flexipass?	**Ho uno sconto con il mio Eurailpass/Europass/Flexipass?** ō ōō'nō skōn'tō kōn ēl mē'ō yōō'relpäs'/yōō'rōpäs/fle'ksēpäs?
How much of a discount?	**Quanto sconto c'è?** kōō·än'tō skōn'tō tshe?

LOSS & THEFT

How much do I owe?	**Quanto devo pagare?** kōō·än'tō de'vō pägä're?

EMERGENCIES & ACCIDENTS

Please call the police.	**Chiamate la polizia, per favore!** kyämä'te lä pōlētsē'ä, per fävō're!
Please call a doctor/an ambulance, quickly.	**Chiamate un dottore/un'ambulanza, presto!** kyämä'te ōōn dōtō're/ōōnämbōōlän'tsä, pre'stō!
Hurry!	**Fate presto!** fä'te pre'stō!
Danger!	**Pericolo!** perē'kōlō!
Someone has been hurt/robbed.	**Qualcuno è stato ferito/derubato.** kōō·älkōō'nō e stä'tō ferē'tō/derōōbä'tō.
I'm hurt.	**Sono ferito/ferita.** sō'nō ferē'tō/ferē'tä.
Where is the hospital?	**Dov'è l'ospedale?** dōve' lōspedä'le?
There's a fire.	**C'è un incendio.** tshe ōōn ēntshen' dē·ō
Help!/Thief!/Pick-pocket!	**Aiuto!/Al ladro!/Uno scippatore!** äyōō'tō!/äl lä'drō!/ōō'nō shēpätō're!
Police!	**Polizia!** pōlētsē'ä!
Stop that man/woman!	**Fermate quell'uomo/quella donna!** fermä'te kōō·elōō·ō'mō/kōō·e'lä dō'nä!

LOSS & THEFT

Can you help me, please?	**Mi può aiutare, per favore?** mē pōō·ō' äyōōtä're, per fävō're?
Where is the police station?	**Dov'è il commissariato?** dōve' ēl kōmēsäryä'tō?

Where is the American consulate/embassy?	**Dov'è il consolato americano/ l'ambasciata americana?** dōve' ēl kōnsōlä'tō ämerēkä'nō/lämbäshä'tä ämerēkä'nä?
Can you tell me where the lost and found is?	**Mi può dire dov'è l'ufficio «oggetti smarriti»?** mē pōō-o' dē're dōve' lōōfē'tshō «ōje'tē zmärē'tē»?
Someone has stolen my …	**Hanno rubato …** ä'nō rōōbä'tō …
I have lost my …	**Ho perso …** ō per'sō …
I left my … on the bus/ train.	**Ho dimenticato … sull'autobus/sul tre- no.** ō dēmentēkä'tō … sōōlou'tōbōōs/sōōl tre'nō.

backpack	**il mio zaino** ēl mē'ō dzī'nō
camera	**la mia macchina fotografica** lä mē'ä mä'kēnä fōtōgrä'fēkä
credit cards	**le mie carte di credito** le mē'e kär'te dē kre'dētō
glasses	**il miei occhiali** ēl mye'ē ōkyä'lē
luggage	**il mio bagaglio** ēl mē'ō bägä'lyō
money	**i miei soldi** ē mye'ē sōl'dē
passport	**il mio passaporto** ēl mē'ō päsäpōr'tō
railpass	**il mio biglietto ferroviario** ēl mē'ō bēlye'tō ferōvē·är'yō
traveler's checks	**i miei traveller's checks** ē mye'ē tre'velers sheks
wallet	**il mio borsellino** ēl mē'ō bōrselē'nō

DEALING WITH PROBLEM PEOPLE

Leave me alone or I'll call the police.	**Vattene, o chiamo la polizia.** vä'tene, ō kyä'mō lä pōlētsē'ä.
Stop following me.	**Smettila di seguirmi.** zme'tēlä dē segēr'mē.
I'm not interested.	**Non mi interessa.** nōn mē ēntere'sä.

ITALIAN

NUMBERS

I'm married.	**Sono sposato/sposata.** sō'nō spōzä'tō/spōzä'tä.
I'm waiting for my boyfriend/husband.	**Sto aspettando il mio ragazzo/mio marito.** stō äspetän'dō ēl mē'ō rägä'tsō/mē'ō märē'tō.
Enough!	**Basta!** bä'stä!
Go away!	**Sparisci!** spärē'shē!

NUMBERS

zero	**zero** dze'rō
one	**uno** ōō'nō
two	**due** dōō'e
three	**tre** tre
four	**quattro** kōō·ä'trō
five	**cinque** tshēn'kōō·e
six	**sei** se'ē
seven	**sette** se'te
eight	**otto** ō'tō
nine	**nove** nō've
ten	**dieci** dye'tshē
eleven	**undici** ōōn'dētshē
twelve	**dodici** dō'dētshē
thirteen	**tredici** tre'dētshē
fourteen	**quattordici** kōō·ätōr'dētshē
fifteen	**quindici** kōō·ēn'dētshē
sixteen	**sedici** se'dētshē
seventeen	**diciassette** dētshäse'te
eighteen	**diciotto** dētshō'tō
nineteen	**diciannove** dētshänō've
twenty	**venti** ven'tē
twenty-one	**ventuno** ventōō'nō
twenty-two	**ventidue** ventēdōō'e
twenty-three	**ventitré** ventētre!
twenty-four	**ventiquattro** ventēkōō·ä'trō

100

thirty	**trenta** tren'tä
forty	**quaranta** kōō·ärän'tä
fifty	**cinquanta** tshēnkōō·än'tä
sixty	**sessanta** sesän'tä
seventy	**settanta** setän'tä
eighty	**ottanta** ōtän'tä
ninety	**novanta** nōvän'tä
one hundred	**cento** tshen'tō
one thousand	**mille** mē'le
one million	**un milione** ōōn mēlyō'ne

ITALIAN

DAYS

What day is today?	**Che giorno è oggi?** ke jōr'nō e ō'jē?
It's Monday.	**È lunedì.** e lōōnedē'
... Tuesday	**... martedì** märtedē'
... Wednesday	**... mercoledì** merkōledē'
... Thursday	**... giovedì** jōvedē'
... Friday	**... venerdì** venerdē'
... Saturday	**... sabato** sä'bätō
... Sunday	**... domenica** dōme'nēkä

TIME

Time is told by the 24 hour clock. You can also reference the numbers section.

Excuse me. Can you tell me the time?	**Scusa, mi puoi dire che ore sono?** skōō'zä, mē pōō·oi' dē're ke ō're sōnō?
I'll meet you in ...	**Ci vediamo tra ...** tshē vedyä'mō trä ...
ten minutes.	**dieci minuti.** dye'tshē mēnōō'tē
a quarter of an hour.	**un quarto d'ora.** ōōn kōō·är'tō dō'rä
a half hour.	**mezz'ora.** medzō'rä

101

TIME

It is …	**È …** e …

    five past one.   **l'una e cinque.** lōō'nä e tshēn'kōō·e
    noon.   **mezzogiorno.** medzōjōr'nō
    midnight.   **mezzanotte.** medzänō'te

It is …	**Sono le …** sō'nō le …

    ten past two.   **due e dieci.** dōō'e e dye'tshē.
    a quarter past   **tre e un quarto.**
    three.   tre e ōōn kōō·är'tō.
    twenty past four.   **quattro e venti.** kōō·ä'trō e ven'tē.
    twenty-five past   **cinque e venticinque.**
    five.   tshēn'kōō·e e ventētshēn'kōō·e.
    half past six.   **sei e mezza.** se'ē e me'dzä.
    twenty-five to   **sette meno venticinque.**
    seven.   se'te me'nō ventētshēn'kōō·e.
    twenty to eight.   **otto meno venti.** ō'tō me'nō ven'tē.

It is …	**Manca …** män'kä …

    a quarter to nine.   **un quarto alle nove.**
                              ōōn kōō·är'tō ä'le nō've.
    ten to ten.   **dieci alle dieci.** dye'tshē ä'le dye'tshē.
    five to eleven.   **cinque alle undici.**
                                tshēn'kōō·e ä'le ōōn'dētshē.

yesterday	**ieri** ē·e'rē
last night	**ieri notte/ieri sera** ē·e'rē nō'te/ē·e'rē se'rä
today	**oggi** ō'jē
tonight	**stanotte/stasera** stänō'te/stäse'rä
tomorrow	**domani** dōmä'nē
morning	**mattina** mätē'nä
afternoon	**pomeriggio** pōmerē'jō
evening	**sera** se'rä
night	**notte** nō'te
day before yesterday	**l'altro ieri** läl'trō ē·e'rē
in two/three days	**tra due/tre giorni** trä dōō'e/trē jōr'nē

MONTHS

January	**gennaio** jenä'yō
February	**febbraio** febrä'yō
March	**marzo** mär'tsō
April	**aprile** äprē'le
May	**maggio** mä'jō
June	**giugno** jōō'nyō
July	**luglio** lōō'lyō
August	**agosto** ägōs'tō
September	**settembre** setem'bre
October	**ottobre** ōtō'bre
November	**novembre** nōvem'bre
December	**dicembre** dētshem'bre

Merry Christmas!	**Buon Natale!** bōō·ōn' nätä'le!
Happy Birthday!	**Buon compleanno!** bōō·ōn' kömple·ä'nō!
Happy Easter!	**Buona Pasqua!** bōō·ō'nä päs'kōō·ä!
Happy New Year!	**Buon anno!** bōō·önä'nō!

COLORS

beige	**beige** bezh
black	**nero** ne'rō
blue	**blu** blōō
brown	**marrone** märō'ne
gold	**oro/dorato** ō'rō/dōrä'tō
green	**verde** ver'de
gray	**grigio** grē'jō
yellow	**giallo** jä'lō
orange	**arancione** äräntshō'ne
pink	**rosa** rō'zä
purple	**viola** vyō'lä
red	**rosso** rō'sō
silver	**argento/argentato** ärjen'tō/ärjentä'tō
white	**bianco** byän'kō

ITALIAN

103

All words and phrases are accompanied by simplified pronunciation. The sound symbols you find in **Langenscheidt's European Phrasebook** are the symbols you are familiar with from your high-school or college dictionaries of the *English* language.

For German, these basic symbols are supplemented by seven symbols that have no equivalents in English. These seven are in italia – with the understanding that you may use the sound of the familiar symbol (the preceding symbol in the table below) until you have learned the specific German sound.

Symbol	Approximate Sound	Examples
	VOWELS	
ä	The *a* of *father*.	*Vater* fä'tər
ä	A sound that has to be learned by listening. (Pronounce the preceding vowel ä but much shorter.) *Until you have learned this sound, use the* u *of* up *or the* o *of* mother, *which will be understood.*	*Mann* män *ab* äp
ā	The *a* of *fate* (but without the "upglide").	*See* zā *Bär* bār
ā	A sound that has to be learned by listening. *Until you have learned this sound, use the* a *of* fate, *which will be understood.*	*schön* shān
e	The *e* of *met*.	*Fett* fet *Äpfel* ep'fəl

GERMAN

Symbol	Approximate Sound	Examples
e	A sound that has to be learned by listening. *Until you have learned this sound, use the e of met, which will be understood.*	*öffnen* eƒ′nən
ē	The *e* of *he*.	*sie* zē
ē̠	A sound that has to be learned by listening. *Until you have learned this sound, use the e of he, which will be understood.*	*Mühle* mē̠′lə
i	The *i* of *fit*.	*bitte* bit′ə
i̠	A sound that has to be learned by listening. *Until you have learned this sound, use the i of fit, which will be understood.*	*Müller* mi̠l′ər
ī	The *i* of *time*.	*nein* nīn
ō	The *o* of *nose* (but without the "upglide").	*holen* hō′lən
ô	The *o* of *often*.	*wollen* vôl′ən *morgen* môr′gən
oi	The *oi* of *voice*.	*heute* hoi′tə
ōō	The *u* of *rule*.	*Mut* mōōt
ŏŏ	The *u* of *book*.	*Mutter* mŏŏt′ər
ou	The *ou* of *house*.	*Raum* roum
ə	The neutral sound (unstressed): the *a* of *ago* or the *u* of *focus*.	*Mitte* mit′ə *genug* gənōōk′
N	This symbol does not stand for a sound but shows that the preceding vowel is nasal – is	(in words of French origin:) *Orange* ôräN′zhə

Symbol	Approximate Sound	Examples
	pronounced through nose and mouth at the same time. Nasal sounds have to be learned by listening. (Try not to use the *ng* of *sing* in their place.)	*Bonbon* bôNbôN′ *Terrain* tereN′

CONSONANTS

Symbol	Approximate Sound	Examples
b	The *b* of *boy*.	*bunt* bŏŏnt
d	The *d* of *do*.	*danke* däng′kə
f	The *f* of *fat*.	*fallen* fä′lən *vier* fēr
g	The *g* of *go*.	*gehen* gā′ən
h	The *h* of *hot*.	*hier* hēr
h	A sound that has to be learned by listening. This "guttural" sound resembles the *ch* of Scottish *loch*.	*suchen* zŏŏ′*h*ən *Bach* bä*h*
j	The *g* of *gem*.	*Dschungel* jŏŏng′əl
k	The *k* of *key*.	*kam* käm *Knie* knē
l	The *l* of *love* (not of *fall*).	*fallen* fä′lən
m	The *m* of *me*.	*mit* mit
n	The *n* of *no*.	*nie* nē
ng	The *ng* of *sing*.	*Junge* yŏŏng′ə
p	The *p* of *pin*.	*Plan* plän *gelb* gelp *Psalm* psälm

GERMAN

CONSONANTS

r	The *r* as spoken by most Germans has to be learned by listening. ***Until you have learned this sound, use the*** r ***of*** run ***or*** fairy.	*rufen* rōō'fən *viermal* fēr'mäl
s	The *s* of *sun* (not of *praise*).	*Glas* gläs *wissen* wis'ən
sh	The *sh* of *shine*.	*Schule* shōō'lə
sh	A sound that has to be learned listening. (It is somewhere between the *sh* of *shine* and the *h* of *huge*). ***Until you have learned this sound, use the*** sh ***of*** shine, ***which will be understood.***	*Reich* rīsh *lächeln* lesh'əln
t	The *t* of *toy*.	*Tag* täk *Theater* tā·ä'tər
tsh	The *ch* of *much*.	*deutsch* doitsh
ts	The *ts* of *its*.	*Zoll* tsôl *Platz* pläts
v	The *v* of English *vat*.	*November* nōvem'bər *Wasser* väs'ər
y	The *y* of *year*.	*ja* yä
z	The *z* of *zeal* or the *s* of *praise*.	*sind* zint *Eisen* ī'zən
zh	The *s* of *measure* or the *si* of *vision*.	*Jalousie* zhälōōzē' *Garage* gärä'zhə

Words of more than one syllable are given with a heavy stress mark (´) and, in many cases, with one or several light stress marks (´`): **Bremse** brem′zə, **Essenszeiten** es′əns·tsī̄tən

A raised dot separates two neighboring vowel symbols (and occasionally two consonant symbols): **ansehen** än′zā·ən, **Ruine** rōō·ē′nə. This dot is merely a convenience to the eye; it does not indicate a break in pronunciation.

EVERYDAY EXPRESSIONS

Yes.	**Ja.** yä.
No.	**Nein.** nīn.
Please.	**Bitte.** bi'tə.
Thank you.	**Danke.** däng'kə.
You're welcome.	**Keine Ursache.** kī'nə ŏŏr'zähə.
Excuse me.	**Entschuldigung.** entshŏŏl'digŏŏng.
I beg your pardon.	**Entschuldigen Sie./Entschuldige.** entshŏŏl'digən zē./entshŏŏl'digə.
Sorry.	**Tut mir Leid.** tŏŏt mēr līt.
How much is this/that?	**Wie viel kostet das?** vē fēl kôs'tət däs?
What time is it?	**Wie spät ist es?** vē shpät ist es?
At what time does the ... open/close?	**Wann öffnet .../schließt ...?** vän ef'nət .../shlēst ...?
Where can I find the/a restroom?	**Wo sind die Toiletten?** vō zint dē tô·äle'tən?
Is the water safe to drink?	**Kann man das Wasser trinken?** kän män däs vä'sər tring'kən?
Is this free? (city map, museum, etc.)	**Ist das umsonst?** ist däs ŏŏmzônst?

GERMAN

NOTEWORTHY SIGNS

Vorsicht! fôr'zisht! Caution

Wegen Renovierung geschlossen. vā'gən renōvē'rŏŏng gəshlô'sən Closed for Restoration

Berühren verboten. bərē'rən fərbō'tən Do Not Touch

111

GREETINGS

Notausgang nōťousgäng	Emergency Exit
Zutritt verboten tsŏŏ'trit ferbō'tən	Do Not Enter
Eintritt frei in'trit frī	Free Admission
Betreten verboten bətrā'tən ferbō'tən	Keep Out
Kein Zutritt kīn tsŏŏ'trit	No Entry
Rauchen verboten rou'hən ferbō'tən	No Smoking
Geöffnet von … bis … ge·ef'nət fôn … bis …	Open from … to …
Kein Trinkwasser kīn tringk'väsər	Undrinkable Water
Herren her'ən	Men
Damen dä'mən	Women

GREETINGS

Good morning.	**Guten Morgen.** gŏŏ'tən môr'gən.
Good afternoon.	**Guten Tag.** gŏŏ'tən täk.
Good night.	**Gute Nacht.** gŏŏ'tə nä*h*t.
Hello/Hi.	**Hallo/Hi.** hälō/hī.
What's your name?	**Wie heißen Sie?/Wie heißt du?** vē hī'sən zē?/vē hīst dŏŏ?
My name is …	**Ich heiße …** i*sh* hī'sə …
How are you?	**Wie geht es Ihnen/dir?** vē gāt es ē'nən/dēr?
Fine thanks. And you?	**Danke gut. Und Ihnen/dir?** däng'kə, gŏŏt. ŏŏnt ē'nən/dēr?
Where are you from?	**Wo kommen Sie her?/Wo kommst du her?** vō kô'mən zē här?/vō kômst dŏŏ här?
I'm from …	**Ich komme aus …** i*sh* kô'mə ous …

112

It was nice meeting you.	**Freut mich, Sie/dich kennen gelernt zu haben.** froit mi*sh*, zē/di*sh* ke'nən gəlernt' tsōō hä'bən.
Good-bye.	**Auf Wiedersehen.** ouf vē'dərzān.
Have a good trip.	**Gute Reise.** gōō'tə rī'zə.
Miss	**Frau** frou
Mrs.	**Frau** frou
Mr.	**Herr** her

CONVERSING & GETTING TO KNOW PEOPLE

Do you speak English/ French/Italian/ German/Spanish?	**Sprechen Sie Englisch/Französisch/Ita-lienisch/Deutsch/Spanisch?** shpre'*sh*ən zē eng'lish/fräntsā'zish/itälyä'nish/doitsh/shpä'nish?
I don't understand.	**Ich verstehe (Sie) nicht.** i*sh* fershtā'ə (zē) ni*sh*t.
Could you speak more slowly please?	**Könnten Sie bitte etwas langsamer sprechen?** kēn'tən zē bi'tə et'väs läng'zämər shpre'*sh*ən?
Could you repeat that please?	**Könnten Sie das bitte noch einmal wiederholen?** kēn'tən zē däs bi'tə nô*h* īn'mäl vēdərhō'lən?
I don't speak French/ Italian/German/ Spanish.	**Ich spreche kein Französisch/Italie-nisch/Deutsch/Spanisch.** i*sh* shpre'*sh*ə kīn fräntsā'zish/itälyä'nish/doitsh/shpä'nish.
Is there someone here who speaks English?	**Spricht hier jemand Englisch?** shpri*sh*t hēr yä'mänt eng'lish?
Do you understand?	**Verstehen Sie?/Verstehst du?** fershtā'ən zē? fershtāst' dōō?

GERMAN

113

Just a moment. I'll see if I can find it in my phrasebook.	**Einen Augenblick. Ich sehe einmal nach, ob das in meinem Sprachführer steht.** ī'nən ougənblik'. ish zā'ə īn'mäl nä*h*, ôp däs in mī'nəm shprä*h*'fērər shtāt.
Please point to your question/answer in the book.	**Zeigen Sie mir bitte Ihre Frage/Antwort im Sprachführer.** tsī'gən zē mēr bi'tə ē'rə frä'gə/änt'vôrt im shprä*h*'fērər.
My name is ... What's yours?	**Ich heiße ... Und wie heißen Sie/heißt du?** ish hī'sə ... ŏont vē hī'sən zē/hīst dōō?
It's nice to meet you.	**Freut mich, Sie/dich kennen zu lernen.** froit mi*sh*, zē/di*sh* ke'nən tsōō ler'nən.
This is my friend ...	**Das ist mein Freund/meine Freundin ...** däs ist mīn froint/mī'nə froin'din ...
This is my sister/ brother/wife/husband/ daughter/son ...	**Das ist meine Schwester/mein Bruder/ meine Frau/mein Mann/meine Tochter/ mein Sohn ...** däs ist mī'nə shves'tər/ mīn brōō'dər/mī'nə frou/mīn män/mī'nə tô*h*'tər/ mīn zōn ...
Where are you from?	**Wo kommen Sie her?/Wo kommst du her?** vō kô'mən zē hār?/vō kômst dōō hār?
What city?	**Aus welcher Stadt?** ous vel'shər shtät?
I'm from the United States/Canada/Austra- lia/England.	**Ich komme aus Amerika/Kanada/ Australien/England.** ish kô'mə ous ämā'rikä/ kä'nädä/oustrā'lē·ən/eng'länt.
Are you here on vaca- tion?	**Machen Sie/Machst du hier Urlaub?** mä'*h*ən zē/mä*h*st dōō hēr ōōr'loup?
Do you like it here?	**Gefällt es Ihnen/dir hier?** gəfelt es ē'nən/dēr hēr?
How long have you been here?	**Wie lange sind Sie/bist du schon hier?** vē läng'ə zint zē/bist dōō shōn hēr?

I just got here.	**Ich bin gerade erst angekommen.**
	i*sh* bin gərä′də erst *än*′gəkômən.
I've been here for … days.	**Ich bin seit … Tagen hier.**
	i*sh* bin zīt … tä′gən hēr.
I love it.	**Es gefällt mir sehr gut.**
	es gəfelt mēr zār gōōt.
It's okay.	**Na ja, es ist ganz nett.** nä yä es ist gänts net.
I don't like it.	**Es gefällt mir nicht.** es gəfelt mēr ni*sh*t.
It's too noisy/crowded/ dirty/boring.	**Es ist zu laut/voll/schmutzig/langweilig.**
	es ist tsōō lout/fôl/shmōō′tsi*sh*/läng′vīli*sh*.
Where are you staying?	**Wo wohnst du?** vō vônst dōō?
I'm staying at the youth hostel/camp- ground.	**Ich wohne in der Jugendherberge/ auf dem Campingplatz.** i*sh* vō′nə in där yōō′gənt·här′bärgə/ouf däm kem′pingpläts.
Where were you before you came here?	**Wo warst du vorher?** vō värst dōō fôr′hār?
Did you stay at a youth hostel/campground there?	**Hast du dort auch in der Jugendherber- ge/auf dem Campingplatz gewohnt?** häst dōō dôrt ou*h* in där yōō′gənt·här′bärgə/ouf däm kem′pingpläts gəvō′nt?
Did you like that city/ country/youth hos- tel/campground?	**Hat dir die Stadt/das Land/die Jugend- herberge/der Campingplatz gefallen?** hät dēr dē shtät/däs länt/dē yōō′gənt·här′bärgə/ där kem′pingpläts gəfä′lən?
Why not?	**Warum nicht?** värōōm′ ni*sh*t?
Where are you going from here?	**Wohin fährst du von hier aus?** vō′hin färst dōō fôn hēr ous?

USEFUL WORDS & EXPRESSIONS

Did you ever stay at the youth hostel in …?	**Warst du schon einmal in der Jugend-herberge in …?** värst dōō shōn īn'mäl in där yōō'gənt·här'bärgə in …?
I'm going there next.	**Da fahre ich als Nächstes hin.** dä fä'rə ish äls näsh'stəs hin.
It was nice meeting you.	**Es war schön, dich zu treffen.** es vär shān, dish tsōō 'trefən.
Here is my address. Write to me sometime.	**Hier ist meine Anschrift. Schreib mir doch einmal.** hēr ist mī'nə än'shrift. shrīb mēr dôh īn mäl'.
May I have your address? I'll write to you.	**Würdest du mir deine Adresse geben. Dann schreibe ich dir mal.** vir'dəst dōō mēr dī'nə ädre'sə gā'bən? dän schrī'bə ish dēr mäl.

USEFUL WORDS & EXPRESSIONS

Is it …?	**Ist es …?** ist es …?
Is it … or …?	**Ist es … oder …?** ist es … ō'dər …?
It is …	**Es ist …** es ist …
cheap/expensive	**billig/teuer** bi'lish/toi'ər
early/late	**früh/spät** frē/shpāt
near/far	**nah/weit** nä/vīt
open/closed	**geöffnet/geschlossen** ge·ef'nət/gəshlô'sən
right/left	**rechts/links** reshts/lingks
vacant/occupied	**frei/besetzt** frī/bəzetst'
entrance/exit	**Eingang/Ausgang** īn'gäng/ous'gäng
with/without	**mit/ohne** mit/ō'nə

116

ARRIVAL & DEPARTURE

Your passport, please.	**Ihren Pass bitte.** ē'rən päs, bi'tə.
I'm here on vacation/business.	**Ich mache hier Urlaub./Ich bin geschäftlich hier.** ish mä'hə hēr ōōr'loup./ish bin gəsheft'lish hēr.
I have nothing to declare.	**Ich habe nichts zu verzollen.** ish hä'bə nishts tsōō fertsô'lən.
I'll be staying …	**Ich bleibe …** ish blī'bə …
a week	**eine Woche** ī'nə vô'hə
two/three weeks	**zwei/drei Wochen** tsvī/drī vô'hən
a month	**einen Monat** ī'nən mō'nät
two/three months	**zwei/drei Monate** tsvī/drī mō'nätə
That's my backpack.	**Das ist mein Rucksack.** däs ist mīn rŏŏk'säk.
Where can I catch a bus/the subway into town?	**Wo fährt der Bus/die U-Bahn in Richtung Innenstadt ab?** vō fārt dār bŏŏs/dē ōō-bän in rish'tŏŏng in'ənshtät äp?
Which number do I take?	**Welche Linie muss ich nehmen?** vel'she lē'nē·ə mŏŏs ish nē'mən?
Which stop do I get off for the center of town?	**An welcher Haltestelle muss ich aussteigen?** än vel'shər häl'təshte'lə mŏŏs ish ous'shtīgən?
Can you let me know when we get to that stop?	**Würden Sie mir Bescheid sagen, wenn wir die Haltestelle erreichen?** vir'dən zē mēr bəshīt' zä'gən, ven vēr dē häl'təshte'lə erī'shən?
Where is gate number …?	**Wo ist Gleis …?** vō ist glīs …?

GERMAN

117

CHANGING MONEY

Excuse me, can you tell me where …	**Entschuldigung, können Sie mir sagen, wo …** entshōōl'digōōng, kēn'ən zē mēr zä'gən, vō …
the nearest bank is?	**die nächste Bank ist?** dē näsh'stə bängk ist?
the nearest money exchange is?	**die nächste Wechselstube ist?** dē näsh'stə vek'səlshtōōbə ist?
the nearest cash machine is?	**der nächste Geldautomat ist?** där näsh'tə gelt'outōmät ist?
I would like to exchange this currency.	**Ich möchte dieses Geld umtauschen.** ish mesh'tə dē'zəs gelt ŏŏm'toushən.
I would like to exchange these traveler's checks.	**Ich möchte diese Reiseschecks einlösen.** ish mesh'tə dē'zə rī'zəsheks īn'lāzən.
What is your exchange rate for U.S. dollars/traveler's checks?	**Wie ist der Wechselkurs für US-Dollar/Reiseschecks?** vē ist där vek'səlkŏŏrs fēr ōō·es·dô'lär/rī'zəsheks?
What is your commission rate?	**Wie hoch ist die Wechselgebühr?** vē hōh ist dē vek'səlgəbēr'?
Is there a service charge?	**Erheben Sie eine Bearbeitungsgebühr?** erhā'bən zē ī'nə be·är'bītigōōngs'gəbēr'?
I would like a cash advance on my credit card.	**Ich hätte gerne einen Barvorschuss auf meine Kreditkarte.** ish he'tə gern ī'nən bär'fôrshŏŏs ouf mī'nə krädit'kärtə.
I would like small/large bills.	**Geben Sie mir bitte kleine/große Scheine.** gä'bən zē mēr bi'tə klī'nə/grō'sə shī'nə.
I think you made a mistake.	**Ich glaube, Sie haben sich geirrt.** ish glou'bə, zē hä'bən zish ge·irt'.

YOUTH HOSTELS

Excuse me, can you direct me to the youth hostel?	**Entschuldigung, können Sie mir den Weg zur Jugendherberge erklären?** entshōōl'digōōng, ken'ən zē mēr dān vāk tsōōr yōō'gənt·härbər'gə erklä'rən?
Do you have any beds available?	**Haben Sie noch freie Plätze?** hä'bən zē nô*h* frī'ə ple'tsə?
For one/two.	**Für eine Person/zwei Personen.** fēr ī'nə perzōn'/tsvī perzō'nən?
… women	**… Frauen** frou'ən
… men	**… Männer** men'ər
We'd like to be in the same room.	**Wir würden gerne in einem Zimmer schlafen.** vēr vir'dən ger'nə in ī'nəm tsim'ər shlä'fən.
How much is it per night?	**Was kostet die Übernachtung?** vās kôs'tət dē ēbərnä*h*'tōōng?
Is there a limit on how many nights I/we can stay?	**Wie viele Nächte kann ich/können wir bleiben?** vē fē'lə nesh'tə kän ish/ken'ən vēr blī'bən?
I'll/We'll be staying …	**Ich bleibe …/Wir bleiben …** ish blī'bə …/vēr blī'bən …
tonight only	**nur über Nacht** nōōr ē'bər nä*h*t
two/three nights	**zwei/drei Tage** tsvī/drī tä'gə
four/five nights	**vier/fünf Tage** fēr/finf tä'gə
a week	**eine Woche** ī'ne vô'hə
Does it include breakfast?	**Ist das inklusive Frühstück?** ist d*ä*s inklōōzē'və frē'sht*i*k?
Do you serve lunch and dinner?	**Gibt es auch Mittag- und Abendessen?** gēpt es ou*h* mi'täk- ōōnt ä'bənt·e'sən?

GERMAN

119

HOTEL OR OTHER ACCOMMODATIONS

What are the hours for breakfast/lunch/dinner?

Wann gibt es Frühstück/Mittagessen/Abendessen?
vän gēpt es frē'shtĭk/mĭ'täk·e·sən/ä'bənt·es·ən?

What are the lockout hours?

Zu welchen Zeiten ist die Jugendherberge geschlossen? tsoō vel'shen tsī'tən ist dē yoō'gənt·härbär'gə geshlō'sən?

Can I leave my bags here during lockout?

Kann ich während dieser Zeit meine Taschen hier lassen? kän ish vā'rənt dē'zər tsīt mī'nə tä'shən hēr läs'ən?

Do I take my key with me or leave it with you when I go out?

Kann ich den Schlüssel mitnehmen, wenn ich weggehe, oder muss ich ihn abgeben? kän ish dān shlĭs'əl mĭt'nāmən, ven ish veg'gehə, ō'dər moōs ish ēn äb'gäbən?

Do you have lockers?

Haben Sie Schließfächer?
hä'bən zē shlēs'feshər?

What time is the curfew?

Um wie viel Uhr ist Nachtruhe?
oōm vē fēl oōr ist näht'roō·ə?

What time is checkout?

Um wie viel Uhr müssen die Zimmer geräumt werden? oōm vē fēl oōr mĭs'ən dē tsim'ər gəroimt' vär'dən?

Are there cooking/laundry facilities?

Kann man hier auch kochen/seine Wäsche waschen? kän män hēr ouh kô'hən/zī'nə ve'shə vä'shən?

Is there a reduction for children?

Gibt es Ermäßigung für Kinder?
gēpt es ermä'sigoōng fēr kin'dər?

HOTEL OR OTHER ACCOMMODATIONS

Zimmer frei/belegt tsim'ər frī/bəläkt   vacancy/no vacancy

Zimmer zu vermieten tsim'ər tsoō vermē'tən   Rooms for Rent

Wegen Urlaub geschlossen   Closed for Vacation
vā'gən ōōr'loup gəshlō'sən

I'm looking for …   **Ich suche …** ish zōō'hə …

    an inexpensive   **ein preiswertes Hotel.**
    hotel.   īn prīs'vārtəs hōtel'.
    a pension.   **eine Pension.** ī'nə päNsyōn'.
    a room.   **ein Zimmer.** īn tsìm'ər.

I have a reservation.   **Ich habe reserviert.** ish hä'bə rāzervērt'.

Do you have a room   **Haben Sie ein Zimmer für eine Nacht?**
for tonight?   hä'bən zē īn tsim'ər fēr ī'nə näht?

I'd like your cheapest   **Ich möchte das preiswerteste Zimmer.**
room.   ish mesh'tə däs prīs'vārtestə tsim'ər.

I'd like a single/double   **Ich möchte ein Einzelzimmer/**
room …   **Doppelzimmer.**
    ish mesh'tə īn īn'tsəltsim'ər/dô'pəltsim'ər.

    with a private bath   **mit eigenem Bad** mit ī'gənəm bät
    with a shared bath   **mit Gemeinschaftsbad**
    mit gəmīn'shäftsbät

    for … days/a week   **für … Tage/eine Woche**
    fēr … tä'gə/ī'nə vô'hə

How much is the   **Was kostet das Zimmer?**
room?   väs kôs'tət däs tsim'ər?

May I see the room?   **Kann ich mir das Zimmer ansehen?**
    kän ish mēr däs tsim'ər än'zā·ən?

Does it include break-   **Ist das mit Frühstück?**
fast?   ist däs mit frē'shtik?

I'll take it.   **Ich nehme es.** ish nā'mə es.

Do you have anything   **Haben Sie noch etwas Preiswerteres?**
cheaper?   hä'bən zē nôh et'väs prīs'vārtərəs?

GERMAN

121

What time is check-out?	**Um wie viel Uhr muss das Zimmer geräumt werden?** ŏŏm vē'fēl ōōr mŏŏs däs tsim'ər gəroimt vār'dən?

CAMPING ACCOMMODATIONS

Can you direct me to the nearest campground?	**Können Sie mir den Weg zum nächsten Campingplatz erklären?** ken'ən zē mēr dān vāk tsŏŏm nāsh'stən kem'pingpläts erklä'rən?
How much is it per night/per person/per tent?	**Was kostet das pro Tag/pro Person/pro Zelt?** väs kôs'tət däs prō täk/prō perzōn'/prō tselt?
Are showers included?	**Ist das mit Dusche?** ist däs mit dŏŏ'shə?
Where can I buy a shower token?	**Wo bekomme ich Münzen für die Dusche?** vō bəkô'mə ish min'tsən fēr dē dŏŏ'shə?
How much are they?	**Was kosten sie?** väs kôs'tən zē?
How many do I need?	**Wie viele brauche ich?** vē fē'lə brou'hə ish?
Are there cooking/laundry facilities?	**Gibt es eine Kochgelegenheit/eine Waschküche?** gēpt es ī'nə kôh'gəlāgənhīt/ī'nə väsh'kishə?
Can we rent a bed/mattress/tent?	**Können wir ein Bett/eine Luftmatratze/ein Zelt mieten?** ken'ən vēr īn bet/ī'nə lŏŏft'mäträ'tsə/īn tselt mē'tən?
May we light a fire?	**Darf man hier Feuer machen?** därf män hēr foi'ər mä'hən?
Where can I find ...	**Wo finde ich ...** vō fin'də ish ...
the drinking water?	**Trinkwasser?** tringk'väsər?
a camping equipment store?	**ein Geschäft für Campingbedarf?** īn gəsheft' fēr kem'pingbədärf?

a grocery store?	**ein Lebensmittelgeschäft?** īn lā'bənsmit'əlgəsheft?
a bank?	**eine Bank?** ī'ne bängk?
the laundry facilities?	**die Waschküche?** dē väsh'kishə?
a telephone?	**ein Telefon?** īn telefōn'?
a restaurant?	**ein Restaurant?** īn restōräN?
electric hook-ups?	**einen Stromanschluss?** ī'nən shtrōm'änshlŏŏs?

Is there a swimming pool?

Gibt es ein Schwimmbecken? gēpt es īn shvim'bekən?

How much does it cost?

Was kostet das? väs kôs'tət däs?

May we camp here/over there?

Darf man hier/dort drüben zelten? därf män hēr/dôrt drē'bən tsel'tən?

SIGNS

Zelten verboten tsel'tən fərbō'tən No Camping

Kein Durchgang kīn dōōrsh'gäng No Trespassing

Privatgrundstück privät'grōōntsht/k Private Property

CAMPING EQUIPMENT

I'd like to buy a/an/some …

Ich möchte … kaufen. ish mēsh'tə … kou'fən.

I'd like to rent a/an/some …

Ich möchte … mieten. ish mesh'tə … mē'tən.

air mattress/air mattresses	**eine Luftmatratze/Luftmatratzen** ī'nə lŏŏft'mäträ'tsə/lŏŏft'mäträ'tsən
butane gas	**eine Gasflasche** ī'nə gäs'fläshə
charcoal	**Holzkohle** hôlts'kōlə

GERMAN

CHECKING OUT

compass	**einen Kompass** īnən kôm'päs
eating utensils	**Essgeschirr** es'gəshir
flashlight	**eine Taschenlampe** īne tä"shənlämpə
folding chairs/ table	**Klappstühle/einen Klapptisch** kläp'shtēlə/īnən kläp'tish
ground sheet	**eine Regenplane** īnə rā'gənplänə
ice pack	**einen Kühlakku** īnən kēl'äkōō
insect spray	**Insektenspray** insek'tənshprā
kerosene	**Petroleum** petrō'lā·ŏŏm
lantern	**eine Lampe** īnə läm'pə
matches	**Streichhölzer** shtrīsh'heltsər
rope	**ein Seil** īn zīl
sleeping bag	**einen Schlafsack** īnən shläf'säk
soap	**Seife** zī'fə
tent	**ein Zelt** īn tselt
towel/towels	**ein Handtuch/Handtücher** īn hän'tōōh/händ'tēshər

CHECKING OUT

I'd like to check out. May I have my bill please?	**Ich reise ab. Machen Sie mir bitte die Rechnung fertig?** ish rī'zə äp. mä'hən zē mēr bi'tə dē resh'nŏŏng fēr'tish?
Could you give me a receipt?	**Geben Sie mir bitte eine Quittung.** gā'bən zē mēr bi'tə īnə kvi'tŏŏng.
Could you explain this item/charge?	**Könnten Sie mir diesen Posten erklären?** ken'tən zē mēr dē'zən pôs'tən erklä'rən?
Thank you.	**Danke.** däng'kə.
I enjoyed my stay.	**Ich hatte einen angenehmen Aufenthalt.** ish hä'tə īnən än'gənāmən ouf'ent·hält.
We enjoyed our stay.	**Wir hatten einen angenehmen Aufenthalt.** vēr hä'tən īnen än'gənāmən ouf'ent·hält.

124

TRANSPORTATION BY AIR

Is there a bus/train to the airport?	**Gibt es einen Bus/Zug zum Flughafen?** gēpt es īnən bŏŏs/tsōōk tsŏŏm flōōk'häfən?
At what time does it leave?	**Wann fährt er ab?** vän färt är äp?
How long does it take to get there?	**Wie lange fährt man dorthin?** vē läng'ə färt män dôrt·hin'?
Is there an earlier/later bus/train?	**Gibt es einen früheren/späteren Bus/ Zug?** gēpt es īnən frē'ərən/shpä'tərən bŏŏs/ tsōōk?
How much does it cost?	**Was kostet die Fahrt?** väs kôs'tət dē färt?
I'd like a flight to …	**Ich möchte einen Flug nach … buchen.** ish mesh'tə īnən flōŏk näh … bōŏ'hən.
a one-way/round trip ticket	**einfach/hin und zurück** īnfäh/hin ŏŏnt tsōŏr/k'
your cheapest fare	**den billigsten Tarif** dān bil'igstən tärēf
an aisle/window seat	**einen Platz am Gang/einen Fensterplatz** īnən pläts äm gäng/īnən fen'stərpläts
Is there a bus/train to the center of town?	**Fährt ein Bus/Zug in die Innenstadt?** färt īn bŏŏs/tsōōk in dē in'ənshtät?

RIDING THE BUS & SUBWAY

Could you tell me where the nearest bus/ subway station is?	**Können Sie mir sagen, wo die nächste Bushaltestelle/U-Bahnstation ist?** ken'ən zē mēr zä'gən, vō dē näsh'stə bŏŏs'hältəshte'lə/ōō'-bänshtätsyōn' ist?
Where can I buy a ticket?	**Wo bekomme ich einen Fahrschein?** vō bəkô'mə ish īnən fär'shīn?

125

TRAIN-STATION & AIRPORT SIGNS

How much does it cost?	**Was kostet die Fahrt?** väs kôs'tət dē färt?
Can I use this ticket for the subway and the bus?	**Gilt die Karte für Bus und U-Bahn?** gilt dē kär'tə fēr bōōs ōōnt ōō´-bän?
I'd like to buy ... tickets.	**Ich möchte ... Fahrscheine.** ish mesh'tə ... fär'shīnə.
I'd like to buy a book of tickets/weekly pass.	**Ich möchte eine Mehrfahrtenkarte/ Wochenkarte.** ish mesh'tə ī'nə mār'färtənkär'tə/vô'hənkärtə.
Which bus/train do I take to get to ...?	**Welchen Bus/Zug muss ich nach ... nehmen?** vel'shən bōōs/tsōōk mōōs ish näh ... nā'mən?
Do I have to change buses/trains to get to ...?	**Muss ich nach ... umsteigen?** mōōs ish näh ... ōōm'shtīgən?
When is the next/last bus/train to ...?	**Wann fährt der nächste Bus/Zug nach ...?** vän färt dār näsh'stə bōōs/tsōōk näh ...?
Can you tell me when we reach ...?	**Sagen Sie mir bitte, wenn wir in ... sind?** zä'gən zē mēr bi'tə, ven vēr in ... zint?
Do I get off here for ...?	**Muss ich hier aussteigen, um nach ... zu kommen?** mōōs ish hēr ous'shtīgən, ōōm näh ... tsōō kô'mən?
Please let me off here.	**Bitte lassen Sie mich hier aussteigen.** bi'tə lä'sən zē mish hēr ous'shtīgən.

TRAIN-STATION & AIRPORT SIGNS

Ankunft än'kōōnft	Arrival
Gepäckaufbewahrung gəpek'oufbəvärōōng	Baggage Check

Gepäckausgabe gəpek´ousgä bə	Baggage Pick-up
Geldwechsel gelt´veksəl	Change
Zoll tsôl	Customs
Abfahrt/Abflug äp´färt/äp´flōōk	Departure
Eingang īn´gäng	Entrance
Ausgang ous´gäng	Exit
Information in´fôrmätsyōn´	Information
Fundbüro fōōnt´bērō´	Lost & Found
Gepäckschließfächer gəpek´shlēs´feshər	Luggage Lockers
Rauchen verboten rou´hən fərbō´tən	No Smoking
Reservierungen räzervē´rōōngən	Reservations
Fahrkarten fär´kärtən	Tickets
Toiletten tô·äle´tən	Toilets
zu den Bahnsteigen/Zügen tsōō dän bän´shtī gən/tsē´gən	To the Platforms/ Trains
Wartesaal vär´təzäl	Waiting Room

GERMAN

TAKING THE TRAIN

Could you tell me where the train station is?	**Können Sie mir sagen, wie ich zum Bahnhof komme?** ken´ən zē mēr zä´gən, vē ish tsōōm bän´hōf kô´mə?
Could I have a train schedule to …	**Könnte ich bitte einen Fahrplan mit den Verbindungen nach … haben?** ken´tə ish bi´tə ī´nən fär´plän mit dän fərbin´dōōngən näh … hä´bən?

127

TAKING THE TRAIN

| When is the next/last train to …? | **Wann fährt der nächste/letzte Zug nach …?** |
| | vän färt där näsh'stə/lets'tə tsōōk näh …? |

| I would like to reserve a seat/couchette in 1st/2nd class. | **Ich möchte einen Sitzplatz/Liegewagen-platz in der 1./2. Klasse reservieren.** |
| | ish mesh'tə īnən zits'pläts/lē'gəvägənpläts' in där er'stən/tsvī'tən klä'sə räzervē'rən. |

| one-way/round trip | **einfache Fahrt/Hin- und Rückfahrt** |
| | īn'fähə färt/hin- ŏŏnt rik'färt |

| smoking/non-smoking | **Raucher/Nichtraucher** rou'hər/nisht'rouhər |

| aisle/window seat | **einen Platz am Gang/Fensterplatz** |
| | īnən pläts äm gäng/fen'stərpläts. |

| At what time does the night train to … leave? | **Wann geht der Nachtzug nach …?** |
| | vän gāt där näht'tsōōk näh …? |

| At what time does it arrive? | **Wann kommt er an?** vän kômt är än? |

| Do I have to change trains? At what stop? | **Muss ich umsteigen? An welchem Bahnhof?** |
| | mŏŏs ish ŏŏm'shtīgən? än vel'shəm bän'hōf? |

| I have a rail pass. Must I pay a supplement to ride this train? | **Ich habe einen Rail Pass. Muss ich für diesen Zug einen Zuschlag bezahlen?** |
| | ish hä'bə īnən räl päs. mŏŏs ish fēr dē'zən tsōōk īnən tsōō'shläk bəzä'lən? |

| Could you tell me where platform/track … is? | **Können Sie mir sagen, wo Bahnsteig/Gleis … ist?** |
| | ken'ən zē mēr zä'gən, vō bän'shtīk/glīs … ist? |

| Could you tell me where car number … is? | **Können Sie mir sagen, wo Wagen Nummer … ist?** ken'ən zē mēr zä'gən, vō vä'gən nŏŏ'mər … ist? |

128

Could you help me find my seat/couchette, please?	**Würden Sie mir helfen, meinen Sitzplatz/Liegewagenplatz zu finden?** vir'dən zē mēr hel'fən, mī'nən zits'pläts/lē'gəvägənpläts' tsoo fin'dən?
Is this seat taken?	**Ist dieser Platz noch frei?** ist dē'zər pläts nôh frī?
Excuse me, I think this is my seat.	**Entschuldigung. Ich glaube, das ist mein Platz.** entshool'digoong. ish glou'bə, däs ist mīn pläts.
Could you save my seat, please?	**Könnten Sie mir den Platz bitte frei-halten?** ken'tən zē mēr dän pläts bi'tə frī'hältən?
Where is the dining car?	**Wo ist der Speisewagen?** vō ist dār shpī'zəvägən?
Where are the toilets?	**Wo sind die Toiletten?** vō zint dē tô·äle'tən?

**For Europass and Flexipass users. With these passes you will only have access to certain countries. If your train goes through a country that is not on your pass, you will be required to pay an extra fare.

My rail pass only covers Spain/Portugal/France/Italy/Switzerland/Germany/Austria.	**Mein Rail Pass gilt nur für Spanien/Portugal/Frankreich/Italien/die Schweiz/Deutschland/Österreich.** mīn rāl pās gilt noor fēr shpä'nē·ən/pôr'tōogäl/frängk'rīsh/itä'lē·ən/dē shvīts/doitsh'länt/ā'stərish.
How much extra do I have to pay since my train goes through …?	**Was muss ich mehr bezahlen, da mein Zug durch … fährt?** väs moos ish mār bətsä'lən, dä mīn tsook doorsh … fārt?
Is there another way to get to … without having to go through …?	**Gibt es eine Möglichkeit, nach … zu gelangen, ohne durch … zu fahren?** gēpt es ī'nə mäg'lishkīt, näh … tsoo gəläng'ən, ō'nə doorsh … tsoo fä'rən?

GERMAN

129

BY BOAT

Is there a boat that goes to …?	**Gibt es ein Schiff nach …?** gēpt es īn shif näh …?
When does the next/ last boat leave?	**Wann geht das nächste/letzte Schiff?** vän gät däs näsh'stə/lets'tə shif?
I have a rail pass. Do I get a discount? How much?	**Ich habe einen Rail Pass. Bekomme ich Ermäßigung? Wie viel?** ish hä'be īnən räl päs. bəkô'mə ish ermä'sigōōng? vē fēl?
At what time does the boat arrive?	**Wann kommt das Schiff an?** vän kômt däs shif än?
How early must I get on board?	**Wann muss ich spätestens an Bord sein.** vän mōōs ish shpä'təstəns än bôrt zīn?
Can I buy seasickness pills nearby?	**Bekommt man hier in der Nähe Tabletten gegen Seekrankheit?** bəkômt' män hēr in där nä'ə täble'tən gä'gən zā'krängk'hīt?

GETTING AROUND BY CAR

I'd like to rent a car.	**Ich möchte einen Wagen mieten.** ish mesh'tə īnən vä'gən mē'tən.
for … days for a week	**für … Tage** fēr … tä'gə **für eine Woche** fēr īnə vô'hə
What is your daily/ weekly rate?	**Wie hoch ist die Tages-/Wochenpauschale?** vē hōh ist dē tä'gəs-/vô'hənpoushä'lə?
Do I need insurance?	**Brauche ich eine Versicherung?** brou'hə ish īnə ferzish'ərōōng?
Is mileage included?	**Gibt es eine Kilometerpauschale?** gēpt es īnə kēlōmä'tərpoushä'lə?
How much is it?	**Wie hoch ist sie?** vē hōh ist zē?

130

ROAD SIGNS

Stopp stôp   Stop

Einbahnstraße īn'bänshträ'sə   One Way

Einfahrt verboten īn'färt ferbō'tən   Do Not Enter

Vorfahrt gewähren fôr'färt gəwā'rən Yield

Parken verboten pär'kən ferbō'tən   No Parking

TAXI

I'd like to go to …   **Ich möchte nach …** ish mesh'tə näh …

What is the fare?   **Was macht das?** väs mäht däs?

Please stop here.   **Bitte halten Sie hier.** bi'tə häl'tən zē hēr.

Can you wait for me?   **Würden Sie bitte auf mich warten?**
                               vir'dən zē bi'tə ouf mish vär'tən?

GETTING AROUND ON FOOT

Excuse me, could you tell me how to get to …?	**Entschuldigung, wie komme ich nach …?** entshŏŏl'digŏŏng, vē kô'mə ish näh …?
Is it nearby/far?	**Ist das in der Nähe/weit?** ist däs in dār nä'ə/vīt?
Can I walk or should I take the bus/subway?	**Kann ich zu Fuß gehen oder nehme ich besser den Bus/die U-Bahn?** kän ish tsōō fōōs gä'ən ō'dər nä'mə ish be'sər dān bŏŏs/dē ōō'-bän?
Could you direct me to the nearest bus/subway station/stop?	**Können Sie mir den Weg zur nächsten Bushaltestelle/U-Bahnstation erklären?** ken'ən zē mēr dān vāk tsōōr näh'stən bŏŏs'häl'təshtelə/ōō'bänshtätsyon' erklä'rən?

131

EATING OUT

Straight ahead.	**Immer geradeaus.** im'ər gərä´də·ous`.
Go right/left.	**Nach rechts/links.** näh reshts/lingks.
At the corner/traffic light.	**An der Ecke/Ampel.** än dār e´kə/äm´pəl.
I'm lost.	**Ich habe mich verlaufen.** ish hä´bə mish ferlou´fən.
Could you show me where we are on this map?	**Können Sie mir auf der Karte zeigen, wo wir sind?** ken´ən zē mēr ouf dār kär´tə tsī´gən, vō vēr zint?

EATING OUT

Could we have a table outside/inside?	**Wir würden gerne draußen/drinnen essen.** vēr vir´dən ger´nə drou´sən/drin´ən es´ən.
Do you have a fixed-price menu?	**Haben Sie ein Menü?** hä´bən zē īn menē´?
Is service included?	**Ist das mit Bedienung?** ist däs mit bədē´nŏŏng?
Is there a cover charge?	**Muss man das Gedeck extra bezahlen?** mŏŏs män däs gədek´ eks´trä bətsä´lən?
Separate checks, please.	**Bitte getrennte Rechnungen.** bi´tə gətren´tə resh´nŏŏngən.
I'd like some apple/orange/grapefruit juice.	**Ich hätte gerne einen Apfelsaft/Orangensaft/Grapefruitsaft.** ish he´tə ger´nə ī´nən äp´fəlsäft/ôräN´zhənsäft/grāp´frŏŏtsäft`.
I'd like some coffee/tea with cream/lemon.	**Ich hätte gerne einen Kaffee/Tee mit Sahne/Zitrone.** ish he´tə ger´nə ī´nən kä´fā/tā mit zä´nə/tsitrō´nə.

I'd like a soda/beer/ mineral water.	**Ich möchte bitte ein Sodawasser/Bier/ Mineralwasser.** ish mesh'tə bi'tə īn zō'däväs'ər/bēr/minerä'väsər.

I'd like a glass/bottle of red/white/rose wine.
Ich möchte bitte ein Glas/eine Flasche Rotwein/Weißwein/Roséwein. ish mesh'tə bi'tə īn gläs/ī'nə flä'shə rōt'vīn/vīs'vīn/rōzā'vīn.

dry/sweet
trocken/lieblich trô'kən/lēp'lish

Cheers!
Prost!/Zum Wohl! prōst!/tsŏŏm vōl!

What is the special of the day?
Was können Sie heute besonders empfehlen? väs ken'ən zē hoi'tə bəzôn'dərs empfā'lən?

Do you have a tourist menu?
Haben Sie ein Touristenmenü? hä'bən zē īn tŏŏris'tənmenē'?

What is this? (pointing to item on menu)
Was ist das? väs ist däs?

I'll have this.
Ich nehme das. ish nā'mə däs.

I'd like some salt/pep-per/cheese/sugar/milk.
Ich hätte gerne Salz/Pfeffer/Käse/ Zucker/Milch. ish he'tə ger'nə zäls/pfe'fər/ kä'zə/tsŏŏ'kər/milsh.

More juice/coffee/tea/ cream/lemon/milk/ beer/wine.
Noch etwas Saft/Kaffee/Tee/Sahne/ Zitrone/Milch/Bier/Wein. nôh et'väs zäft/ kä'fā/tā/zä'nə/tsitrō'nə/milsh/bēr/vīn.

I cannot eat sugar/ salt/drink alcohol.
Ich vertrage keinen Zucker/kein Salz/ keinen Alkohol. ish ferträ'gə kī'nən tsŏŏ'kər/ kīn zäls/kī'nən äl'kōhōl.

I am a diabetic.
Ich bin Diabetiker/Diabetikerin. ish bin dē·äbā'tikər/dē·äbā'tikərin.

I am a vegetarian.
Ich bin Vegetarier/Vegetarierin. ish bin vägätä'rē·ər/vägätä'rē·ərin.

GERMAN

133

FOOD SHOPPING

May I have the check, please.	**Die Rechnung bitte.** dē re*sh*'nŏŏng, bĭ'tə.
Keep the change.	**Das Wechselgeld ist für Sie.** däs vek'səlgelt ist fēr zē.

FOOD SHOPPING & PICNIC FOOD

Can you make me a sandwich.	**Ich hätte gerne ein Sandwich.** i*sh* he'tə ger'nə īn zent'vitsh.
To take out.	**Zum Mitnehmen.** tsŏŏm mĭt'nāmən.
I'd like some …	**Ich möchte …** i*sh* me*sh*'tə …
I'll have a little more.	**Ich nehme noch etwas.** i*sh* nā'mə nôh et'väs.
That's too much.	**Das ist zu viel.** däs ist tsŏŏ fēl.
Do you have …	**Haben Sie …** hä'bən zē …
I'd like …	**Ich möchte …** i*sh* me*sh*'tə …

a box of	**eine Schachtel** ī'nə *sh*ä*h*'təl
a can of	**eine Dose** ī'nə dō'zə
a jar of	**ein Glas** īn gläs
a half kilo of	**ein halbes Kilo** īn häl'bəs kē'lō
a kilo of	**ein Kilo** īn kē'lō
a half liter	**einen halben Liter** ī'nən häl'bən lē'tər
a liter	**einen Liter** ī'nən lē'tər
a packet of	**ein Päckchen** īn pek'*sh*ən
a slice of	**eine Scheibe** ī'nə *sh*ī'bə
a bottle opener	**einen Flaschenöffner** ī'nən flä'*sh*ənefnər
a can opener	**einen Dosenöffner** ī'nən dō'zənefnər
a cork screw	**einen Korkenzieher** ī'nən kôr'kəntsē'ər
it sliced	**in Scheiben** in *sh*ī'bən

Do you have any plastic forks/spoons/knives and napkins?	**Haben Sie Plastikgabeln/Plastiklöffel/ Plastikmesser und Servietten?** hä'bən zē pläs'tikgä'bəln/pläs'tikleføl/pläs'tikme'sər ŏŏnt zervē·e'tən?
May I have a bag?	**Geben Sie mir bitte eine Tüte?** gä'bən zē mēr bi'tə ī'nə tē'tə?
Is there a park nearby?	**Ist hier in der Nähe ein Park?** ist hēr in dār nä'ə īn pärk?
May we picnic there?	**Kann man dort ein Picknick machen?** kän män dôrt īn pik'nik mä'hən?
May we picnic here?	**Können wir hier ein Picknick machen?** kēn'ən vēr hēr īn pik'nik mä'hən?

Fruits

apples	**Äpfel** ep'fəl
apricots	**Aprikosen** äprikō'zən
bananas	**Bananen** bänä'nən
blueberries	**Blaubeeren** blou'bärən
cantaloupe	**Melonen** melō'nən
cherries	**Kirschen** kir'shən
dates	**Datteln** dä'təln
figs	**Feigen** fī'gən
grapefruits	**Grapefruits** gräp'frŏŏts
grapes	**Trauben** trou'bən
lemons	**Zitronen** tsitrō'nən
nectarines	**Nektarinen** nektärē'nən
oranges	**Orangen** ôräN'zhən
peaches	**Pfirsiche** pfir'sishə
pears	**Birnen** bir'nən
pineapple	**Ananas** ä'nänäs
plums	**Pflaumen** pflou'mən
raisins	**Rosinen** rōzē'nən
raspberries	**Himbeeren** him'bärən

135

strawberries	**Erdbeeren** ārt'bārən
tangerines	**Mandarinen** mändärē'nən
watermelon	**Wassermelone** vä'sərmelō'nə

Vegetables

artichokes	**Artischocken** ärtishô'kən
asparagus	**Spargel** shpär'gəl
green/kidney beans	**grüne Bohnen/Kidneybohnen** grē'nə bō'nən/kid'nēbō'nən
broccoli	**Brokkoli** brô'kōlē
red cabbage	**Rotkohl** rōt'kōl
carrots	**Möhren** mā'rən
cauliflower	**Blumenkohl** blōō'mənkōl
celery	**Staudensellerie** shtou'dənsel'ərē
corn	**Mais** mīs
cucumber	**Gurke** gōōr'kə
eggplant	**Aubergine** ōberzhē'nə
fennel	**Fenchel** fen'shəl
french fries	**Pommes frites** pôm frit
garlic	**Knoblauch** knōb'louh
leeks	**Lauch** louh
lentils	**Linsen** lin'zən
lettuce	**Kopfsalat** kôpf'sälät'
mushrooms	**Champignons** shäm'pinyôNs
black/green olives	**schwarze/grüne Oliven** shvär'tsə/grēnə ôlē'vən
onions	**Zwiebeln** tsvē'bəln
peas	**Erbsen** erp'sən
hot/sweet peppers	**Chilischoten/Paprikaschoten** tshēl'ēshōtən/päp'rikäshō'tən
pickles	**Gewürzgurken** gəvirts'gōōrkən
potatoes	**Kartoffeln** kärtô'fəln
radish	**Rettich** re'tish
rice	**Reis** rīs
sauerkraut	**Sauerkraut** zou'ərkrout

spinach	**Spinat** shpinät′
tomatoes	**Tomaten** tōmä′tən
zucchini	**Zucchini** tsŏŏ′kēnē

Meats/Cold Cuts

beef	**Rindfleisch** rint′flish
bologna	**Mortadella** môrtäde′lä
chicken	**Hähnchen** hān′*shə*n
fish	**Fisch** fish
ham	**Schinken** shing′kən
hamburger/ground beef	**Hackfleisch** häk′flish
hot dogs/frankfurters	**Hot Dogs/Würstchen** hôt dôgs/virst′*shə*n
lamb	**Lamm** läm
pork	**Schweinefleisch** shvī′nəflish
roast beef	**Roastbeef** rōst′bēf
salami	**Salami** zälä′mē
sausage	**Wurst** vŏŏrst
turkey	**Truthahn** trōōt′hän
veal	**Kalbfleisch** kälp′flish

Nuts

almonds	**Mandeln** män′dəln
brazil nuts	**Paranüsse** pä′rän*i*sə
cashews	**Cashewkerne** ke′shōōker′nə
chestnuts	**Kastanien** kästä′nē-ən
hazelnuts	**Haselnüsse** hä′zəln*i*sə
peanuts	**Erdnüsse** ārt′n*i*sə
walnuts	**Walnüsse** väl′n*i*sə

Condiments

butter	**Butter** bŏŏ′tər
honey	**Honig** hō′nish

GERMAN

137

FOOD SHOPPING

horseradish	**Meerrettich** mār'etish
jam/jelly	**Marmelade/Gelee** märmelä'də/zhəlā'
ketchup	**Ketchup** ke'tshäp
margarine	**Margarine** märgärē'nə
mayonnaise	**Majonäse** mäyônā'zə
mustard	**Senf** zenf
vegetable/olive oil	**Pflanzenöl/Olivenöl** pflän'tsənāl/ôlē'vənāl'
pepper	**Pfeffer** pfe'fər
mild/hot salsa	**milde/scharfe Sauce** mil'də/shär'fə zō'sə
salt	**Salz** zäls
sugar	**Zucker** tsŏŏ'kər
tabasco/hot sauce	**Tabasco/scharfe Sauce** täbäs'kō/shär'fə zō'se
vinegar	**Essig** e'sish

Miscellaneous

bread	**Brot** brōt
cake	**Kuchen** kōō'hən
candy	**Süßigkeiten** zē'sishkī'tən
cereal	**Getreideflocken** gətrī'dəflô'kən
cheese	**Käse** kä'zə
chocolate	**Schokolade** shôkōlä'də
cookies	**Kekse** kāk'sə
crackers	**Kräcker** kre'kər
eggs	**Eier** ī'ər
ice cream	**Eiscreme** īs'krām
popcorn	**Popcorn** pôp'kôrn
potato chips	**Kartoffelchips** kärtô'fəltships'
rolls	**Brötchen** brāt'shən
spaghetti	**Spagetti** shpäge'tē
yogurt	**Jogurt** yō'gōōrt

Drinks

beer	**Bier** bēr
coffee	**Kaffee** kä'fā
hot chocolate	**heiße Schokolade** hī'sə shôkōlä'də
apple juice	**Apfelsaft** äp'fəlzäft
cranberry juice	**Preiselbeersaft** prī'zəlbārzäft
grapefruit juice	**Grapefruitsaft** grā'pfrōōtzäft
orange juice	**Orangensaft** ôräNzhənzäft
tomato juice	**Tomatensaft** tōmä'tənzäft
milk	**Milch** milsh
soft drinks	**alkoholfreie Getränke** ä'kōhōlfrī'ə gətreng'kə
tea	**Tee** tā
sparkling/mineral water	**Mineralwasser mit Kohlensäure/ Mineralwasser** minəräl'väsər mit kō'lənzoirə/minəräl'väsər
red/white/rose wine	**Rotwein/Weißwein/Rosé(wein)** rōt'vīn/vīs'vīn/rōzā'(vīn)
dry/sweet	**trocken/lieblich** trô'kən/lēp'lish

USING THE TELEPHONE

GERMAN

Can I use local currency to make a local/long-distance call or do I need to buy a phone card?	**Ich möchte ein Orts-/Ferngespräch führen. Kann ich mit Münzen telefonieren oder brauche ich eine Telefonkarte?** ish mesh'tə īn ôrts'-/fern'gəshpräsh fē'rən. Kän ish mit min'tsən tāläfōnē'rən ō'dər brou'hə ish ī'nə tāläfōn'kärtə?
Do I need to buy tokens?	**Muss ich Telefonmünzen kaufen?** mōōs ish tāläfōn'mintsən kou'fən?
Where can I buy tokens?/a phone card?	**Wo bekomme ich Telefonmünzen/eine Telefonkarte?** vō bəkô'mə ish tāläfōn'mintsən/ ī'nə tāläfōn'kärtə?
... tokens, please. How much?	**... Telefonmünzen bitte. Was macht das?** ... tāläfōn'mintsən bi'tə. väs mäht däs?

POST OFFICE

I'd like to buy phone card. How much does it cost?	**Ich bekomme eine Telefonkarte. Was kostet sie?** ish bəkô'mə īnə tālāfôn'kärtə. väs kôs'tət zē?
How do you use the phone card?	**Wie benutzt man die Telefonkarte?** vē bənŏŏtst män dē tālāfôn'kärtə?
Excuse me, where is the nearest phone?	**Entschuldigung, wo ist die nächste Telefonzelle?** entshŏŏl'digŏŏng, vō ist dē näsh'stə tālāfôn'tselə?
I'd like to make a collect call.	**Ich möchte ein R-Gespräch führen.** ish mësh'tə īn er'-gəshpräsh fē'rən
The number is …	**Die Nummer lautet …** dē nŏŏ'mər lou'tət …
Hello. This is …	**Hallo. Hier ist …** hälô'. hēr ist …
May I speak to …	**Kann ich mit … sprechen?** kän ish mit … shpre'shən?

POST OFFICE

Can you direct me to the nearest post office?	**Können Sie mir den Weg zum nächsten Postamt erklären?** ken'ən zē mēr dān väk tsŏŏm näsh'stən pôst'ämt erklā'rən?
Which window is for …	**An welchem Schalter kann ich …** än vel'shəm shäl'tər kän ish …
stamps?	**Briefmarken kaufen?** brēf'märkən kou'fən?
sending/cashing a money order? airmail writing paper?	**eine Geldanweisung aufgeben/einlösen?** īnə gelt'änvī'zŏŏng ouf'gābən/īn'lāzən? **Luftpostpapier kaufen?** lŏŏft'pôstpäpēr' kou'fən?

140

I'd like ... stamps for postcards/letters to America.

Ich hätte gerne ... Briefmarken für Postkarten/Briefe nach Amerika.
i*sh* he'tə ger'nə ... brēf'märkən fēr pôst'kärtən/ brē'fə näh ämä'rikä.

I'd like to send this airmail.

Ich möchte das per Luftpost verschicken.
i*sh* m*e*sh'tə däs per lõõft'pôst fershi'kən.

How much does it cost?

Was kostet das?
väs kôs'tət däs?

PHARMACY & DRUGSTORE

Can you direct me to the nearest pharmacy?

Können Sie mir den Weg zur nächsten Apotheke erklären? ken'ən zē mēr dān vāk tsōōr nä*sh*'stən äpōtā'kə erklā'rən?

I'd like a/an/some ...

Ich brauche ... i*sh* brou'hə ...

    aspirin

        Kopfschmerztabletten
        kôpf'shmertstäble'tən

    Band-Aids

        Pflaster pfläs'tər

    cough medicine

        Hustensaft hōōs'tənzäft

    contraceptives

        ein Verhütungsmittel
        īn ferh*ē*'tōōngsmi'təl

    eye drops

        Augentropfen ou'gəntrôpfən

    insect repellant

        Insektenspray insek'tənshprā

    sanitary napkins

        Damenbinden dä'mənbindən

Could you give me something for ...

Haben Sie etwas gegen ... hä'bən zē et'väs gā'gən ...

    constipation

        Verstopfung fershtôp'fōōng

    diarrhea

        Durchfall dōōr*sh*'fäl

    a headache

        Kopfschmerzen kôpf'shmertsən

    hay fever

        Heuschnupfen hoi'shnōōpfən

    indigestion

        Verdauungsstörungen
        ferdou'ōōngs·sht*ā*'rōōngən

GERMAN

141

itching	**Juckreiz** yŏŏk'rīts
nausea/travel sickness	**Übelkeit/Reisekrankheit** ē'bəlkīt/rī'zəkrängk'hīt
a rash	**Ausschlag** ous'shläk
sore throat	**Halsschmerzen** häls'shmertsən
sunburn	**Sonnenbrand** zôn'ənbränt

May I have a/an/some … **Ich bekomme …** ish bəkô'mə …

deodorant	**ein Deodorant** īn dā·ōdôränt'
razor	**einen Rasierapparat** ī'nən räzēr'äpärät'
razor blades	**Rasierklingen** räzēr'klingən
shampoo/conditioner	**ein Shampoo/einen Haarfestiger** īn shempōō'/ī'nən här'festigər
soap	**Seife** zī'fə
suntan oil/cream/lotion	**Sonnenöl/Sonnencreme/Sonnenmilch** zôn'ən·āl/zôn'ənkräm/zôn'ənmilsh
tissues	**Papiertaschentücher** päpēr'täsh'entēshər
toilet paper	**Toilettenpapier** tô·äle'tənpäpēr'
toothbrush	**eine Zahnbürste** ī'nə tsän'bırstə
toothpaste	**eine Zahncreme** ī'nə tsän'kräm
cleaning/soaking solution for contact lenses	**Reinigungslösung/Aufbewahrungslösung für Kontaktlinsen** rī'nigōōngs·lā'zōōng/ouf'bəvärōōngs-la'zōōng fēr kôntäkt'/linzən

How much does it cost? **Was macht das?** väs mäht däs?

TOBACCO SHOP

I'd like to buy … **Ich bekomme …** ish bəkô'mə …

a pack/carton of cigarettes.	**ein Päckchen/eine Stange Zigaretten.** īn pek'shən/ī'nə shtäng'ə tsēgäre'tən.

a cigarette lighter.	**ein Feuerzeug.** īn foi'ərtsoik.
a cigar.	**eine Zigarre.** ī'nə tsēgä'rə.
May I have some matches?	**Kann ich ein paar Streichhölzer haben?** kän ish īn pär shtrīsh'heltsər hä'bən?

PHOTOGRAPHY

I'd like to buy a roll of film.	**Ich hätte gerne einen Film.** ish he'tə ger'nə ī'nən film.
Black and white./ Color.	**Schwarzweißfilm./Farbfilm.** shvärtsvīs'film./färp'film.
How much are they?	**Was macht das?** väs mäht däs?
I'd like to buy batteries for this camera.	**Ich brauche Batterien für diese Kamera.** ish brou'hə bätərē'ən fēr dē'zə kä'merä.

HEALTH

The Doctor

I don't feel well.	**Es geht mir nicht gut.** es gāt mēr nisht gōōt.
Could you direct me to a doctor that speaks English.	**Kennen Sie einen Arzt, der Englisch spricht?** ke'nən zē ī'nən ärtst, dār eng'lish shprisht?
I have (a) ...	**Ich habe ...** ish hä'bə ...
burn	**eine Verbrennung** ī'nə ferbre'nŏŏng
chest pains	**Schmerzen in der Brust** shmer'tsən in dār brŏŏst
cold	**eine Erkältung** ī'nə erkel'tŏŏng
cough	**Husten** hŏŏs'tən
cramps	**Krämpfe** krem'pfə
cut	**eine Schnittwunde** ī'nə shnit'vŏŏndə
diarrhea	**Durchfall** dōōrsh'fäl
fever	**Fieber** fē'bər

GERMAN

143

flu	**Grippe** gri'pə
infection	**eine Infektion** ī'nə infektsyōn'
nausea	**Übelkeit** ē'bəlkīt
rash	**Ausschlag** ous'shläk
sore throat	**Halsschmerzen** häls'shmertsən
sprained ankle	**einen verstauchten Knöchel**
	ī'nən fershtouh'tən kne'shəl
stomach ache	**Magenschmerzen** mä'gənshmertsən

It hurts here.   **Hier tut es weh.** hēr tōōt es vā.

I've been vomiting.   **Ich musste mich übergeben.**
ish mŏŏs'tə mish ē̄bərgā'bən.

I'm having difficulty breathing.   **Ich habe Schwierigkeiten beim Atmen.**
ish hä'bə shvē'rishkī'tən bīm ät'mən.

I'm allergic to penicillin.   **Ich bin allergisch gegen Penicillin.**
ish bin älär'gish gā'gən pen'itsilēn'.

I'm diabetic.   **Ich bin Diabetiker/Diabetikerin.**
ish bin dē-äbā'tikər/dē-äbā'tikərin.

I don't smoke/drink.   **Ich rauche nicht/trinke keinen Alkohol.**
ish rou'hə nisht/tring'kə kī'nən älkōhōl'.

The Dentist

Could you direct me to a dentist that speaks English?   **Kennen Sie einen Zahnarzt, der Englisch spricht?** ke'nən zē ī'nən tsän'ärtst, dār eng'lish shprisht?

I have a toothache. This tooth.   **Ich habe Zahnschmerzen. Dieser Zahn.**
ish hä'bə tsän'shmertsən. dē'zər tsän.

My tooth is loose.   **Mein Zahn wackelt.** mīn tsän vä'kəlt.

My tooth is broken.   **Mein Zahn ist abgebrochen.**
mīn tsän ist äp'gəbrôhən.

144

I've broken/lost a filling.	**Mir ist eine Füllung zerbrochen./Ich habe eine Füllung verloren.** mēr ist ī'nə f/l'ōōng tserbrō'hən./ish hä'bə ī'nə f/l'ōōng ferlô'rən.

Paying

How much does this cost?	**Was kostet das?** väs kôs'tət däs?
I have health insurance.	**Ich bin krankenversichert.** ish bin kräng'kənferzi'shərt.
I'm supposed to call this number.	**Ich muss diese Nummer anrufen.** ish mōōs dē'zə nōō'mər än'rōōfən.
How much do I owe you?	**Was bin ich Ihnen schuldig?** väs bin ish ē'nən shōōl'dish?

SIGHTSEEING

Can you recommend a good, inexpensive restaurant?	**Können Sie mir ein gutes, preiswertes Restaurant empfehlen?** ken'ən zē mēr in gōō'təs, pris'värtəs restōräN' empfā'lən?
a fun nightclub?	**ein Nachtlokal, in dem man sich gut amüsieren kann** in näht'lōkäl', in däm män zish gōōt ämēzē'rən kän?
a good place to dance?	**ein gutes Tanzlokal** in gōō'təs tänts'lōkäl?
Can you tell me where the tourist office is?	**Können Sie mir sagen, wo das Fremdenverkehrsbüro ist?** ken'ən zē mēr zä'gən, vō däs frem'dənferkärs'bērō' ist?
What are the main points of interest here?	**Welches sind die wichtigsten Sehenswürdigkeiten?** vel'shəs zint dē vish'tishstən zā'əns·vir'tish·kī'tən?
What time does it open/close?	**Wann öffnet/schließt es?** vän ef'nət/shlēst es?

145

SIGHTSEEING

What time is the last entry?

Wann ist der letzte Einlass?
vän ist dār lets'tə īn'läs?

How much is the admission? Free.

Was kostet der Eintritt? Der Eintritt ist frei. väs kôs'tət dār īn'trit? dār īn'trit ist frī.

Is there a discount for students/children/teachers/senior citizens?

Gibt es Ermäßigung für Studenten/ Kinder/Lehrer/Senioren?
gēpt es ermä'sigŏŏng fēr shtŏŏden'tən/kin'dər/lä'rər/zānyō'rən?

Is the ticket good all day?

Gilt die Karte den ganzen Tag?
gilt dē kär'tə dān gän'tsən täk?

Is there a sightseeing tour?

Kann man eine Besichtigung machen?
kän män ī'nə bəzish'tigŏŏng mä'hən?

What time does it start?

Wann beginnt sie?
vän bəgint' zē?

How much does it cost?

Was kostet sie?
väs kôs'tət zē?

How long is it?

Wie lange dauert sie? vē läng'ə dou'ərt zē?

Does the guide speak English?

Spricht der Fremdenführer Englisch?
shprisht dār frem'dənfē'rər eng'lish?

Am I allowed to take pictures/a video?

Darf ich hier fotografieren/filmen?
därf ish hēr fōtōgräfē'rən/fil'mən?

Can you direct me to the …?

Können Sie mir den Weg … erklären?
ken'ən zē mēr dān vāk … erklä'rən?

art gallery   **zur Kunstgalerie** tsŏŏr kŏŏnst'gälərē
beach   **zum Strand** tsŏŏm shtränt
castle   **zum Schloss** tsŏŏm shlôs
cathedral   **zur Kathedrale** tsŏŏr kätädrä'lə
cemetery   **zum Friedhof** tsŏŏm frēt'hōf
church   **zur Kirche** tsŏŏr kēr'shə
fountain   **zum Brunnen** tsŏŏm brŏŏ'nən

gardens	**zum Park** tsŏŏm pärk
harbor	**zum Hafen** tsŏŏm hä'fən
lake	**zum See** tsŏŏm zā
monastery	**zum Kloster** tsŏŏm klōs'tər
mountains	**in die Berge** in dē bär'gə
movies	**zum Kino** tsŏŏm kē'nō
museum	**zum Museum** tsŏŏm mōōzā'ŏŏm
old city	**in die Altstadt** in dē ält'shtät .
palace	**zum Schloss** tsŏŏm shlôs
ruins	**zur Ruine** tsŏŏr rōō·ē'nə
shops/bazaar	**zu den Geschäften/zum Einkaufszentrum** tsŏŏ dän gəshef'tən/ tsŏŏm ī'nkoufs·tsen'trōōm
statue	**zum Denkmal** tsŏŏm dengk'mäl
tomb	**zum Grabmal** tsŏŏm gräp'mäl
trails (for hiking)	**zum Wanderweg** tsŏŏm vän'dərvāk
university	**zur Universität** tsŏŏr ŏŏ'nēversētät'
zoo	**zum Zoo** tsŏŏm tsō

Is it far from here?	**Ist das weit von hier?** ist däs vīt fôn hēr?
Can we walk there?	**Können wir zu Fuß dahin gehen?** kēn'ən vēr tsŏŏ fŏŏs dähin' gā'ən?
Straight ahead.	**Immer geradeaus.** i'mər gərä'də·ous'.
Go right/left.	**Nach rechts/links.** näh rech/ts/lingks.
At the corner/traffic light.	**An der Ecke/Ampel.** än dār e'kə/äm'pəl.

DISCOUNT INFORMATION

| Do I get a discount with my student/ teacher's/senior citizens card? | **Gibt es Ermäßigung für Studenten/ Lehrer/Senioren?** gēpt es ermä'sigŏŏng fēr shtŏŏden'tən/lä'rər/ zenyô'rən? |

GERMAN

147

EMERGENCIES

Do I get a discount with my Eurailpass/Europass/Flexipass?	**Bekomme ich mit meinem Eurailpass/Europass/Flexipass Ermäßigung?** bəkô′mə ish mit mī′nəm yōōrāl′päs/yōōrōpäs/flek′sēpäs′ ermä′sigŏŏng?
How much of a discount?	**Wie hoch ist die Ermäßigung?** vē hōh ist dē ermä′sigŏŏng?
How much do I owe?	**Was muss ich noch bezahlen?** väs mŏŏs ish nôh bətsä′lən?

EMERGENCIES & ACCIDENTS

Please call the police.	**Bitte rufen Sie die Polizei.** bi′tə rōō′fən zē dā pōlētsī′.
Please call a doctor/an ambulance, quickly.	**Rufen Sie bitte schnell einen Arzt/Krankenwagen.** rōō′fən zē bi′tə shnel ī′nən ärtst/kräng′kənvägən.
Hurry!	**Beeilen Sie sich bitte!** be·ī′lən zē zish bi′tə!
Danger!	**Gefahr!** gəfär′!
Someone has been hurt/robbed.	**Jemand wurde verletzt/überfallen.** yā′mänt vŏŏr′də ferletst′/ēbərfä′lən.
I'm hurt.	**Ich bin verletzt.** ish bin ferletst′.
Where is the hospital?	**Wo ist das Krankenhaus?** vō ist däs kräng′kənhous?
There's a fire.	**Es brennt.** es brent.
Help!/Thief!/Pickpocket!	**Hilfe!/Ein Dieb!/Taschendieb!** hil′fə! īn dēp!/tä′shəndēp!
Police!	**Polizei!** pōlētsī′!
Stop that man/woman!	**Halten Sie diesen Mann/diese Frau!** häl′tən zē dē′zən män/dē′zə frou!

148

LOSS & THEFT

Can you help me, please?	**Können Sie mir bitte helfen?** ken'ən zē mēr bi'tə hel'fən?
Where is the police station?	**Wo ist die Polizeiwache?** vō ist dē pōlētsī'vähə?
Where is the American consulate/embassy?	**Wo ist das amerikanische Konsulat/ die amerikanische Botschaft?** vō ist däs ämärikä'nishə kônzōōlät'/dē ämärikä'nishə bōt'shäft?
Can you tell me where the lost and found is?	**Wo ist das Fundbüro?** vō ist däs fōōnt'bērō'?
Someone has stolen ...	**Man hat mir ... gestohlen.** män hät mēr ... gəshtō'lən.
I have lost ...	**Ich habe ... verloren.** ish hä'bə ... ferlō'rən.
I left ... on the bus/ train.	**Ich habe ... im Bus/Zug liegen gelassen.** ish hä'bə ... im bōōs/tsōōk lē'gən gəlä'sən.
my backpack	**meinen Rucksack** mī'nən rŏŏk'säk
my camera	**meine Kamera** mī'nə kä'merä
my credit cards	**meine Kreditkarten** mī'nə krädit'kärtən
my glasses	**meine Brille** mī'nə bri'lə
my luggage	**mein Gepäck** mīn gəpek'
my money	**mein Geld** mīn gelt
my passport	**meinen Pass** mī'nən päs
my rail pass	**meinen Fahrausweis** mī'nən fär'ousvīs
my traveler's checks	**meine Reiseschecks** mī'nə rī'zəsheks
my wallet	**meine Brieftasche** mī'nə brēf'täshə

GERMAN

149

DEALING WITH PROBLEM PEOPLE

Leave me alone or I'll call the police.	**Lassen Sie mich in Ruhe oder ich rufe die Polizei!** lä'sən sē mish in rōō'e ō'dər ish rōō'fə dē pōlētsī!
Stop following me.	**Hören Sie auf, mich zu verfolgen.** hä'rən zē ouf, mish tsōō ferfôl'gən!
I'm not interested.	**Ich bin nicht interessiert.** ish bin nisht intəresērt'.
I'm married.	**Ich bin verheiratet.** ish bin ferhī'rätət.
I'm waiting for my boyfriend/husband.	**Ich warte auf meinen Freund/Mann.** ish vär'tə ouf mī'nən froint/män.
Enough!	**Schluss jetzt!** shlōōs yetst!
Go away!	**Verschwinden Sie!** fershvin'dən zē!

NUMBERS

zero	**null** nŏŏl
one	**eins** īns
two	**zwei** tsvī
three	**drei** drī
four	**vier** fēr
five	**fünf** fînf
six	**sechs** zeks
seven	**sieben** zē'bən
eight	**acht** äht
nine	**neun** nŏin
ten	**zehn** tsān
eleven	**elf** elf
twelve	**zwölf** tsvelf
thirteen	**dreizehn** drī'tsān
fourteen	**vierzehn** fir'tsān
fifteen	**fünfzehn** fînf'tsān

sixteen	**sechzehn** ze*sh*'tsän
seventeen	**siebzehn** zēp'tsän
eighteen	**achtzehn** ä*h*'tsän
nineteen	**neunzehn** noin'tsän
twenty	**zwanzig** tsvän'tsi*sh*
twenty-one	**einundzwanzig** īn'o͝ontsvän'tsi*sh*
twenty-two	**zweiundzwanzig** tsvī'o͝ontsvän'tsi*sh*
twenty-three	**dreiundzwanzig** drī'o͝ontsvän'tsi*sh*
twenty-four	**vierundzwanzig** fēr'o͝ontsvän'tsi*sh*
thirty	**dreißig** drī'si*sh*
forty	**vierzig** fir'tsi*sh*
fifty	**fünfzig** fünf'tsi*sh*
sixty	**sechzig** ze*sh*'tsi*sh*
seventy	**siebzig** zēp'tsi*sh*
eighty	**achtzig** ä*h*'tsi*sh*
ninety	**neunzig** noin'tsi*sh*
one hundred	**(ein)hundert** (īn) ho͝on'dərt
one thousand	**(ein)tausend** (īn) tou'zənt
one million	**eine Million** ī'nə milyōn'

DAYS

What day is today?	**Welcher Tag ist heute?** vel'*sh*ər täk ist hoi'tə?
It's Monday.	**Heute ist Montag.** hoi'tə ist mōn'täk.
... Tuesday.	**... Dienstag.** ... dēn'stäk.
... Wednesday.	**... Mittwoch.** mit'vô*h*.
... Thursday.	**... Donnerstag.** dôn'ərstäk.
... Friday.	**... Freitag.** frī'täk.
... Saturday.	**... Samstag.** zäms'täk.
... Sunday.	**... Sonntag.** zôn'täk.

GERMAN

151

TIME

Time is told by the 24-hour clock. You can also reference the numbers section.

Excuse me. Can you tell me the time?	**Entschuldigung. Können Sie mir sagen, wie spät es ist?** entschōōl'digŏŏng. ken'ən zē mēr zä'gən, vē shpāt es ist?
I'll meet you in …	**Wir treffen uns in …** vēr tre'fən ŏŏns in …

    ten minutes   **zehn Minuten** tsān minōō'tən

    a quarter of an hour   **einer Viertelstunde** ī'nər vir'təlshtōōn'də

    a half hour   **einer halben Stunde** ī'nər häl'bən shtōōn'də

    three quarters of an hour   **einer Dreiviertelstunde** ī'nər drī'firtəlshtōōn'də

It is …   **Es ist …** es ist …

    five past one.   **fünf nach eins.** fínf näh īns.

    ten past two.   **zehn nach zwei.** tsān näh tsvī.

    a quarter past three.   **Viertel nach drei.** fir'təl näh drī.

    twenty past four.   **zwanzig nach vier.** tsvän'tsisih näh fēr.

    twenty-five past five.   **fünf vor halb sechs.** fínf fôr hälp zeks.

    half past six.   **halb sieben.** hälp zē'bən.

    twenty-five to seven.   **fünf nach halb sieben.** fínf näh hälp zē'bən.

    twenty to eight.   **zwanzig vor acht.** tsvän'tsisih fôr äht.

    a quarter to nine.   **Viertel vor neun.** fir'təl fôr noin.

    ten to ten.   **zehn vor zehn.** tsān fôr tsān.

    five to eleven.   **fünf vor elf.** fínf fôr elf.

    noon.   **zwölf Uhr mittags.** tsvelf ōōr mi'täks.

    midnight.   **zwölf Uhr nachts.** tsvelf ōōr nähts.

yesterday	**gestern** ges'tərn
last night	**gestern Abend** ges'tərn ä'bənt
today	**heute** hoi'tə
tonight	**heute Abend** hoi'tə ä'bənt
tomorrow	**morgen** môr'gən
morning	**der Morgen** där môr'gən
afternoon	**der Nachmittag** där nä*h*'mitäk
evening	**der Abend** där ä'bənt
night	**die Nacht** dē nä*h*t
day before yesterday	**vorgestern** fôr'gestərn
in two/three days	**in zwei/drei Tagen** in tsvī/drī tä'gən

MONTHS

January	**Januar** yän'ōō·är
February	**Februar** fä'brōō·är
March	**März** merts
April	**April** äpril'
May	**Mai** mī
June	**Juni** yōō'nē
July	**Juli** yōō'lē
August	**August** ougŏōst'
September	**September** septem'bər
October	**Oktober** ŏktō'bər
November	**November** nŏvem'bər
December	**Dezember** dātsem'bər

Merry Christmas!	**Frohe Weihnachten!** frō'ə vī'nä*h*tən!
Happy Easter!	**Frohe Ostern!** frō'ə ōs'tərn!
Happy New Year!	**Ein gutes neues Jahr!** īn gōō'təs noi'əs yär!
Happy Birthday!	**Alles Gute zum Geburtstag!** ä'ləs gōō'tə tsŏōm gəbōōrts'täk!

GERMAN

153

COLORS

COLORS

beige	**beige** bāzh
black	**schwarz** shvärts
blue	**blau** blou
brown	**braun** broun
gold	**golden** gôl'dən
green	**grün** grēn
gray	**grau** grou
yellow	**gelb** gelp
orange	**orange** ôräNzh'ə
pink	**rosa** rō'zä
purple	**purpurrot** pŏŏr'pŏŏrōt
red	**rot** rōt
silver	**silbern** zil'bərn
white	**weiß** vīs

HOW DO YOU PRONOUNCE IT?

All words and phrases are accompanied by simplified pronunciation. The sound symbols are the ones you are familiar with from your high-school or college dictionaries of the *English* language, but applied here to foreign languages – a unique feature of **Langenscheidt's European Phrasebook**.

Symbol	Approximate Sound	Examples
	VOWELS	
ä	The *a* of *father*.	*casa* kä′sä
e	The *e* of *met* (but tending toward the *a* of *fate*).	*meses* me′ses
ē	The *e* of *he*.	*camino* kämē′nō *ir* ēr
ī	The *i* of *time*.	*hai* ī *mosaico* mōsī′kō
ō	The *o* of *nose* (but without the "upglide").	*como* cō′mō *norte* nōr′te
oi	The *oi* of *voice*.	*estoy* estoi′
ōō	The *u* of *rule* (but without the "upglide").	*agudo* ägōō′dō
ou	The *ou* of *house*.	*causa* kou′sä
	CONSONANTS	
b	A sound that has to be learned by listening (and which differs from country to country). Until you have learned this sound, use the *b* of *bed*. See also v, below.	*hablar* äblär′ *beber* beber′
g	The *d* of *do*.	*rendir* rendēr′

SPANISH

155

Symbol	Approximate Sound	Examples
f	The *f* of *far*.	*efecto* efek'tō
g	The *g* of *go*.	*gato* gä'tō
h	A sound that has to be learned by listening. (This "guttural" sound resembles the *ch* of Scottish *loch* and of German *Bach*.) *Until you have learned this sound, use the* h *of* hot.	*Juan* hōōän' *gente* hen'te
k	The *k* of *key*, the *c* of *can*.	*cubo* kōō'bō
l	The *l* of *love* (not of *fall*). (See also the combination ly, below.)	*lado* lä'dō
m	The *m* of *me*.	*mesa* me'sä
n	The *n* of *no*. (See also the combination ny, below.)	*andar* ändär'
ng	The *ng* of *sing*.	*banco* bäng'kō
p	The *p* of *pin*.	*poco* pō'kō
r	The *r* of *run*, but with a stronger "trill" in many words, especially words with *rr*.	*rico* rē'kō *grande* grän'de *perro* pe'rō
s	The *s* of *sun*. (See also z, below.)	*servir* servēr'
t	The *t* of *toy*.	*tiempo* tyem'pō
tsh	The *ch* of *much*.	*muchacha* mōōtshä'tshä
v	A sound that is usually identical to the b, above. But the pronunciation varies greatly; and for the sake of simplicity the letter v is represented here by v.	*vida* vē'dä *huevo* ōō·e'vō

Symbol	Approximate Sound	Examples
y	The *y* of *year*. (See also the combinations ly and ny, below.)	*yo* yō *hielo* ye'lō
z	The *z* of *zeal*. (Note: Spanish *s* is pronounced z before *b, d, g, l, m, n,* and *r.*)	*mismo* mēz'mō *desde* dez'de

Note these frequent combinations:

ly	as in **caballo** käbä'lyo or **julio** hōō'lyō
ny	as in **ano** ä'nyō or **junio** hōō'nyō
ōō·e	as in **bueno** bōō·e'nō
ōō·ä	as in **cuanto** kōō·än'tō
ōō'ē	as in **muy** mōō'ē
ōō·ō	as in **cuota** kōō·ō'tä
e'ē	as in **rey** re'ē
e·ōō	as in **neumático** ne·ōōmä'tēkō
ä·ē	as in **caída** kä·ē'dä

Words of more than one syllable are given with a stress mark.

A raised dot separates two neighboring vowel symbols, and occasionally two consonant symbols: *ahora* ä·ō'ra, *sangría* säng·grē'a. This dot is merely a convenience to the eye; it does not indicate a break in pronunciation.

EVERYDAY EXPRESSIONS

Yes.	**Sí.** sē.
No.	**No.** nō.
Please.	**Por favor.** pōr fävōr'.
Thank you.	**Gracias.** grä'syäs.
You're welcome.	**De nada.** de nä'dä.
Excuse me.	**Disculpa.** dēskōōl'pä.
I beg your pardon.	**Perdona.** perdō'nä.
Sorry.	**Perdón.** perdōn'.
How much is this/that?	**¿Cuánto cuesta esto/eso?** ¿kōō·än'tō kōō·es'tä es'tō/e'sō?
What time is it?	**¿Qué hora es?** ¿ke ō'rä es?
At what time does the … open/close?	**¿A qué hora abre/cierra …?** ¿ä ke ō'rä ä'bre/sye'rä …?
Where can I find the/ a restroom?	**¿Dónde hay un baño?** ¿dōn'de ī ōōn bä'nyō?
Is the water safe to drink?	**¿Se puede beber el agua?** ¿se pōō·e'de beber' el ä'gōō·ä?
Is this free? (city map, museum, etc.)	**¿Es gratis?** ¿es grä'tēs?

NOTEWORTHY SIGNS

Cuidado kōō·ēdä'dō	Caution
Cerrado por obras serä'dō pōr ō'bräs	Closed for Restoration
No tocar nō tōkär'	Do Not Touch

SPANISH

159

GREETINGS

Salida de emergencia sälē'dä de emer*hen*'syä	Emergency Exit
No entre nō en'tre	Do Not Enter
Entrada libre enträ'dä lē'bre	Free Admission
No entrar no enträr'	Keep Out
Prohibido entrar prō-ēbē'dō enträr'	No Entry
Prohibido fumar prō-ēbē'dō fōōmär'	No Smoking
Abierto de … a … äbyer'tō de … ä …	Open from … to …
Agua no potable ä'gōō-ä nō pōtä'ble	Undrinkable Water
Señores/Caballeros senyō'res/käbälye'rōs	Men
Señoras/Damas senyō'räs/dä'mäs	Women

GREETINGS

Good morning.	**Buenos días.** bōō-e'nōs dē'äs.
Good afternoon.	**Buenas tardes.** bōō-e'näs tär'des.
Good night.	**Buenas noches.** bōō-e'näs nō'tshes.
Hello/Hi.	**¡Hola!** ¡ō'lä!
What's your name?	**¿Cómo te llamas?** ¿kō'mō te lyä'mäs?
My name is …	**Me llamo …** me lyä'mō …
How are you?	**¿Cómo estás?** ¿kō'mō estäs'?
Fine thanks. And you?	**Bien, gracias. ¿Y tú?** byen', grä'syäs. ¿ē tōō?
Where are you from?	**¿De dónde eres?** ¿de dōn'de e'res?
I'm from …	**Soy de …** soi de …
It was nice meeting you.	**Mucho gusto de haberte conocido.** mōō'tshō gōōs'tō de äber'te kōnōse'dō.

Good-bye.	**Adiós.** ädyōs'.
Have a good trip.	**Buen viaje.** bōō·en' vē·ä'he.
Miss	**Señorita** senyōrē'tä
Mrs./Madam	**Señora** senyō'rä
Mr./Sir	**Señor** senyōr'

CONVERSING & GETTING TO KNOW PEOPLE

Do you speak English/French/Italian/German/Spanish?	**¿Hablas inglés/francés/italiano/alemán/español?** ¿ä'bläs ēng·gles'/fränses'/ētälyä'nō/älemän'/espänyōl'?
I don't understand.	**No entiendo.** no entyen'do.
Could you speak more slowly please?	**¿Podrías hablar más despacio, por favor?** ¿pōdrē'äs äblär' mäs despä'syō, pōr fävōr?
Could you repeat that please?	**¿Podrías repetir eso, por favor?** ¿pōdrē'äs repetēr' e'sō, pōr fävōr?
I don't speak French/Italian/German/Spanish.	**No hablo francés/italiano/alemán/español.** no ä'blō franses'/ētälyä'nō/älemän'/espänyōl.
Is there someone here who speaks English?	**¿Hay alguien aquí que hable inglés?** ¿ī älgyen' äkē' ke ä'ble ēng·gles'?
Do you understand?	**¿Entiendes?** ¿entyen'des?
Just a moment. I'll see if I can find it in my phrasebook.	**Un momento. Voy a ver si lo encuentro en mi manual de conversación.** ōōn mōmen'tō. voi ä ver sē lō enkōō·en'trō en mē mänōō·äl' de kōnversäsyōn'.
Please point to your question/answer in the book.	**Por favor, señala tu pregunta/respuesta en el libro.** pōr fävōr, senyä'lä tōō pregōōn'tä/respōō·es'tä en el lē'brō.

CONVERSING

My name is … What's yours?	**Me llamo… ¿Y tú, cómo te llamas?** me lyä'mō … ¿ē tōō, kō'mō te lyä'mäs?
It's nice to meet you.	**Mucho gusto de conocerte.** mōō'tshō gōōs'tō de kōnōser'te.
This is my friend (female)/sister/wife/daughter …	**Ésta es mi amiga/hermana/mujer/hija …** es'tä es mē ämē'gä/ermä'nä/mōō*her*'/ē'*hä* …
This is my friend (male)/brother/husband/son …	**Éste es mi amigo/hermano/marido/hijo …** es'te es mē ämē'gō/ermä'nō/märē'dō/ē'*hō* …
Where are you from?	**¿De dónde eres?** ¿de dōn'de e'res?
What city?	**¿De qué ciudad?** ¿de ke syōōdäd?
I'm from the United States/Canada/Australia/England.	**Soy de Estados Unidos/Canadá/Australia/Inglaterra.** soi de estä'dōs ōōnē'dōs/känädä'/ousträ'lyä/ēng·glä·te'rä.
Are you here on vacation?	**¿Estás aquí de vacaciones?** ¿estäs' äkē' de väkäsyō'nes?
Do you like this country/this city/this place?	**¿Te gusta este país/esta ciudad/este lugar?** ¿te gōōs'tä es'te pä·ēs'/es'tä syōōdäd'/es'te lōōgär'?
How long have you been here?	**¿Cuánto tiempo llevas aquí?** ¿kōō·än'to tyem'pō lye'väs äkē'?
I just got here.	**Acabo de llegar.** äkä'bō de lyegär'.
I've been here for … days.	**Llevo aquí … días.** lye'vō äkē' … dē'äs.
I love it.	**Me gusta mucho.** me gōōs'tä mōō'tshō.
It's okay.	**Está bien.** estä' byen'.
I don't like it.	**No me gusta.** no me gōōs'tä.

It's too noisy/boring. **Es demasiado ruidoso/aburrido.**
es demäsyä'dō rōō·ēdō'sō/äbōōrē'dō.

It's too crowded/dirty. **Está demasiado lleno/sucio.**
estä' demäsyä'dō lye'nō/sōō'syō.

Where are you staying? **¿Dónde te alojas?** ¿dōn'de te älō'häs?

I'm staying at the … youth hostel/campground. **Estoy en el albergue juvenil/camping …**
estoi en el älber'ge *h*ōōvenēl'/kämpēng' …

Where were you before you came here? **¿Dónde has estado antes de venir aquí?**
¿dōn'de äs estä'dō än'tes de venēr' äkē'?

Did you stay at a youth hostel/campground there? **¿Te quedaste allí en un albergue juvenil/camping?** ¿te kedäs'te älyē' en ōōn älber'ge *h*ōōvenēl'/kämpēng'?

Did you like that city/country/youth hostel/campground? **¿Te gustó esa ciudad/ese país/ese albergue juvenil/ese camping?**
¿te gōōstō' e'sä syōōdäd/e'se pä·ēs'/e'se älber'ge *h*ōōvenēl'/e'se kämpēng'?

Why not? **¿Por qué no?** ¿pōr ke nō?

Where are you going from here? **¿Adónde vas a ir desde aquí?**
¿ädōn'de väs ä ēr dez'de äkē'?

Did you ever stay at the youth hostel in …? **¿Te has quedado alguna vez en el albergue juvenil de …?** ¿te äs kedä'dō älgōō'nä ves en el älber'ge *h*ōōvenēl' de …?

I'm going there next. **Voy a ir allí.** voi ä ēr älyē'.

It was nice meeting you. **Mucho gusto de conocerte.**
mōō'tshō gōōs'tō de kōnōser'te.

Here is my address. Write to me sometime. **Aquí está mi dirección. ¡Escríbeme algún día!** äkē estä' mē dēreksyōn'. eskrē'beme älgōōn' dē·ä.

SPANISH

ARRIVAL & DEPARTURE

May I have your address? I'll write to you.	**¿Me podrías dar tu dirección? Yo te escribiré.** ¿me pōdrē'äs där tōō dēreksyōn'? yō te eskrēbēre'.

USEFUL WORDS & EXPRESSIONS

Is it ...?	**¿Es ...?** ¿es ...?
Is it ... or ...?	**¿Es ... o ...?** ¿es ... ō ...?
It is cheap/expensive.	**Es barato/caro.** es bärä'tō/kä'rō.
It is early/late.	**Es temprano/tarde.** es temprä'nō/tär'de.
It is near/far.	**Está cerca/lejos.** estä' ser'kä/le'hos.
It is open/closed.	**Está abierto/cerrado.** estä' äbyer'tō/serä'dō.
It is right/left.	**Está a la derecha/a la izquierda.** estä' ä lä dere'tshä/ä lä ēskyer'dä.
vacant/occupied	**libre/ocupado** lē'bre/ōkōōpä'dō.
entrance/exit	**la entrada/la salida** lä enträ'dä/lä säle'dä
with/without	**con/sin** kōn/sēn

ARRIVAL & DEPARTURE

Your passport please.	**Su pasaporte, por favor.** sōō päsäpōr'te, pōr fävōr'.
I'm here on vacation/business.	**Estoy aquí de vacaciones/por trabajo.** estoi' akē' de väkäsyō'nes/pōr träbä'hō.
I have nothing to declare.	**No tengo nada que declarar.** nō teng'gō nä'dä ke deklärär'.
I'll be staying ...	**Voy a quedarme ...** voi ä kedär'me ...
a week	**una semana** ōō'nä semä'nä
two/three weeks	**dos/tres semanas** dōs/tres semä'näs

| a month | **un mes** ōōn mes |
| two/three months | **dos/tres meses** dōs/tres mē'ses. |

| That's my backpack. | **Ésta es mi mochila.** es'tä es mē mōtshē'lä. |

| Where can I catch a bus/the subway into town? | **¿Dónde puedo coger un autobús/el metro para ir al centro?** ¿dōn'de pōō·e'dō kōher' ōōn outobōōs'/el me'trō pä'rä ēr äl sen'trō? |

| Which number do I take? | **¿Qué número tengo que coger?** ¿ke nōō'merō teng'gō ke kōher'? |

| Which stop do I get off for the center of town? | **¿En qué parada tengo que bajarme para llegar al centro de la ciudad?** ¿en ke pä'rä'dä teng'gō ke bähär'me pä'rä lyegär' äl sen'trō de lä syōōdäd'? |

| Can you let me know when we get to that stop? | **¿Podría avisarme cuando lleguemos a esa parada?** ¿pōdrē'ä avēsär'me kōō·än'dō lyege'mōs ä e'sä pä'rä'dä? |

| Where is gate number ...? | **¿Dónde está la puerta de salida número ...?** ¿dōn'de estä' lä pōō·er'tä de sälē'dä nōō'merō ...? |

CHANGING MONEY

| Excuse me, can you tell me where the nearest bank is? | **Disculpe, ¿puede decirme dónde está el banco más cercano?** dēskōōl'pe, ¿pōō·e'de desēr'me dōn'de estä' el bäng'kō mäs serkä'nō? |

| ... money exchange is? | **... la oficina de cambio?** ... lä ōfēsē'nä de käm'byō? |

| ... cash machine is? | **... el cajero automático?** ... el kähe'rō outōmä'tēkō? |

| I would like to exchange this currency. | **Quisiera cambiar este dinero.** kēsye'rä kämbyär' es'te dēne'rō. |

SPANISH

165

YOUTH HOSTELS

I would like to exchange these traveler's checks.	**Quisiera cambiar estos cheques de viaje.** kēsye'rä kämbyär' es'tōs tshe'kes de vyä*he*.
What is your exchange rate for U.S. dollars/traveler's checks?	**¿Cuál es su valor de cambio para dólares norteamericanos/cheques de viaje?** ¿kōō·äl es sōō välōr' de käm'byō pärä dō'läres nōrte·ämerēkä'nōs/tshe'kes de vyä*he*?
What is your commission rate?	**¿Cuánto es la tasa de comisión?** ¿kōō·än'tō es lä tä'sä de kōmēsyōn?
Is there a service charge?	**¿Hay que pagar por el servicio?** ¿ī ke pägär' pōr el servē'syō?
I would like a cash advance on my credit card.	**Quisiera un adelanto en efectivo de mi tarjeta de crédito.** kēsye'rä ōōn ädelän'tō en efektē'vō de mē tär*he*'tä de kre'dētō.
I would like small/large bills.	**Quisiera billetes pequeños/grandes.** kēsye'rä bēlye'tes peke'nyōs/grän'des.
I think you made a mistake.	**Creo que usted ha cometido un error.** kre'ō ke ōōste' ä kōmetē'dō ōōn erōr'.

YOUTH HOSTELS

Excuse me, can you direct me to the youth hostel?	**Disculpe, ¿podría decirme cómo llegar al albergue juvenil?** ¿dēskōōl'pe, pōdrē'ä desēr'me kō'mō lyegär' äl älber'ge *h*ōōvenēl'?
Do you have any beds available? For one/two.	**¿Tiene usted camas libres? Para una persona/dos personas.** ¿tye'ne ōōste' kä'mäs lē'bres? pärä ōō'nä persō'nä/dōs persō'näs?
… women	**… señoras** … senyō'räs
… men	**… señores** … senyō'res

166

We'd like to be in the same room.	**Nos gustaría estar en la misma habitación.** nōs gōōstärē'ä estär' en lä mēz'mä äbētäsyōn'.
How much is it per night?	**¿Cuánto cuesta una noche?** ¿kōō·än'tō kōō·es'tä ōō'nä nō'tshe?
Is there a limit on how many nights I/we can stay?	**¿Hay un límite de cuántas noches puedo quedarme/podemos quedarnos?** ¿ī ōōn lē'mēte de kōō·än'täs nō'tshes pōō·e'dō kedär'me/pōde'mōs kedär'nōs?
I'll/We'll be staying …	**Voy a quedarme/Vamos a quedarnos …** voi ä kedär'me/vä'mōs ä kedär'nōs …
tonight only two/three nights four/five nights	**sólo esta noche** sō'lō es'tä nō'tshe **dos/tres noches** dōs/tres nō'tshes **cuatro/cinco noches** kōō·ät'rō/sēng'kō nō'tshes
a week	**una semana** ōō'nä semä'nä
Does it include breakfast?	**¿Está incluido el desayuno?** ¿estä' ēnklōō·ē'dō el desäyōō'nō?
Do you serve lunch and dinner?	**¿Sirven ustedes comida y cena?** ¿sēr'ven ōōste'des kōmē'dä ē se'nä?
What are the hours for breakfast/lunch/dinner?	**¿A qué hora es el desayuno/la comida/la cena?** ¿ä ke ō'rä es el desäyōō'nō/lä kōmē'dä/lä se'nä?
What are the lockout hours?	**¿A qué hora se cierra?** ¿ä ke ō'rä se sye'rä?
Can I leave my bags here during lockout?	**¿Puedo dejar mis maletas aquí mientras esté cerrado?** ¿pōō·e'dō dehär' mēs mäle'täs äkē' myen'träs este' serä'dō?
Do I take my key with me or leave it with you when I go out?	**¿Me llevo la llave o la dejo aquí cuando salga?** ¿me lye'vō lä lyä've ō lä de'hō äkē' kōō·än'dō säl'gä?

SPANISH

HOTEL OR OTHER ACCOMMODATIONS

| Do you have lockers? | **¿Tiene usted armarios con llave?** |
| | ¿tye'ne ōōste' ärmär'yōs kōn lyä've? |

| What time is the curfew? | **¿A qué hora se prohíbe entrar y salir?** |
| | ¿ä ke ō'rä se prohē'be enträr' ē sälēr'? |

| What time is checkout? | **¿A qué hora hay que desocupar la habitación?** ¿ä ke ō'rä ī ke desōkōōpär' lä äbētäsyōn'? |

| Are there cooking/laundry facilities? | **¿Hay lugares para cocinar/lavar?** |
| | ¿ī lōōgä'res pä'rä kōsēnär'/lävär'? |

| Is there a reduction for children? | **¿Hay reducción de precio para niños?** |
| | ¿ī redōōksyōn' de pre'syō pä'rä nē'nyōs? |

HOTEL OR OTHER ACCOMMODATIONS

libre/ocupado lē'bre/ōkōōpä'dō	vacancy/no vacancy
Habitaciones de alquiler äbētäsyō'nes de älkēler'	Rooms for Rent
Cerrado por vacaciones serä'dō pōr väkäsyō'nes	Closed for Vacation

I'm looking for …	**Estoy buscando …** estoi' bōōskän'dō …
an inexpensive hotel.	**un hotel económico.** ōōn ōtel' ekōnō'mēkō.
a pension.	**una pensión.** ōō'nä pensyōn'.
a room.	**una habitación.** ōō'nä äbētäsyōn'.
I have a reservation.	**Tengo una reserva.** teng'gō ōō'nä reser'vä.
Do you have a room for tonight?	**¿Tiene una habitación para esta noche?** ¿tye'ne ōō'nä äbētäsyōn' pä'rä es'tä nō'tshe?
I'd like your cheapest room.	**Quisiera la habitación más barata.** kēsye'rä lä äbētäsyōn' mäs bärä'tä.

I'd like a single/double room	**Quisiera una habitación sencilla/doble** kēsye'rä ōō'nä äbētäsyōn' sensē'lyä/dō'ble
with a private bath.	**con baño privado.** kōn bä'nyō prēvä'dō
with a shared bath.	**con baño compartido.** kōn bä'nyō kōmpärtē'dō
for … days, a week.	**para … días, una semana.** pä'rä … dē'äs, ōō'nä semä'nä
How much is the room?	**¿Cuánto cuesta esta habitación?** ¿kōō·än'tō kōō·es'tä es'tä äbētäsyōn'?
May I see the room?	**¿Podría ver la habitación?** ¿pōdrē'ä ver lä äbētäsyōn'?
Does it include breakfast?	**¿Está incluido el desayuno?** ¿estä' ēnklōō·e'dō el desäyōō'nō?
I'll take it.	**La tomaré.** lä tōmäre'.
Do you have anything cheaper?	**¿Tiene algo más barato?** ¿tye'ne äl'gō mäs bärä'tō?
What time is check-out?	**¿A qué hora hay que desocupar la habitación?** ¿ä ke ō'rä ī ke desōkōōpär' lä äbētäsyōn'?

CAMPING ACCOMMODATIONS

Can you direct me to the nearest campground?	**¿Podría decirme cómo llegar al camping más cercano?** ¿pōdrē'ä desēr'me kō'mō lyegär' äl kämpēng' mäs serkä'nō?
How much is it per night/per person/per tent?	**¿Cuánto cuesta por noche/por persona/por tienda?** ¿kōō·än'tō kōō·es'tä pōr nō'tshe/pōr persō'nä/pōr tyen'dä?
Are showers included?	**¿Están incluidas las duchas?** ¿estän' ēnklōō·e'däs läs dōō'tshäs?

CAMPING ACCOMMODATIONS

Where can I buy a shower token?	**¿Dónde puedo comprar una ficha para la ducha?** ¿dōn'de pōō·e'dō kōmprär' ōō'nä fē'tshä pä'rä lä dōō'tshä?
How much are they?	**¿Cuánto cuestan?** ¿kōō·än'tō kōō·es'tän?
How many do I need?	**¿Cuántas necesito?** ¿kōō·än'täs nesesē'tō?
Are there cooking/laundry facilities?	**¿Hay lugares para cocinar/lavar?** ¿ī lōōgä'res pä'rä kōsēnär'/lävär'?
Can we rent a bed/mattress/tent?	**¿Podemos alquilar una cama/un colchón/una tienda de campaña?** ¿pōde'mōs älkēlär' ōō'nä kä'mä/ōōn kōltshōn'/ōō'na tyen'dä de kämpä'nyä?
May we light a fire?	**¿Podemos hacer fuego?** ¿pōde'mōs äser' fōō·e'gō?
Where can I find ...	**¿Dónde hay ...** ¿dōn'de ī ...?
the drinking water?	**agua potable?** ä'gōō·ä pōtä'ble?
a camping equipment store?	**una tienda de artículos para camping?** ōō'nä tyen'dä de ärtē'kōōlōs pä'rä kämpēng'?
a grocery store?	**una tienda de comestibles?** ōō'nä tyen'dä de kōmestēbles?
a bank?	**un banco?** ōōn bäng'kō?
the laundry facilities?	**una lavandería/un lavadero?** ōō'nä lävänderē'ä/ōōn läväde'rō?
a telephone?	**un teléfono?** ōōn tele'fōnō?
a restaurant?	**un restaurante?** ōōn restourän'te?
electric hook-ups?	**tomas de electricidad?** tō'mäs de elektrēsēdäd'?
Is there a swimming pool?	**¿Hay una piscina?** ¿ī ōō'nä pēsē'nä?

How much does it cost?	**¿Cuánto cuesta?** ¿kōō·än'tō kōō·es'tä?
May we camp here/over there?	**¿Podemos acampar aquí/allí?** ¿pōde'mōs äkämpär' äkē'/älyē'?

SIGNS

Prohibido acampar prō·ēbē'dō äkämpär'	No Camping
Prohibido pasar prō·ēbē'dō päsär'	No Trespassing
Propiedad privada prōpyedäd' prēvä'dä	Private Property

CAMPING EQUIPMENT

I'd like to buy a/an/some …	**Quisiera comprar un/una/algunos/algunas …** kēsye'rä kōmprär' ōōn/ōō'nä/älgōō'nōs/älgōō'näs…
I'd like to rent a/an/some …	**Quisiera alquilar …** kēsye'rä älkēlär' …
air mattress/air mattresses.	**un colchón de aire/colchones de aire.** ōōn kōltshōn' de ī're/kōltshō'nes de ī're
butane gas.	**gas butano.** gäs bōōtä'nō
charcoal.	**carbón.** kärbōn'
compass.	**una brújula.** ōō'na brōō'hōōlä
eating utensils.	**cubiertos.** kōōbyer'tōs
flashlight.	**una linterna de bolsillo.** ōō'nä lēnter'nä de bōlsē'lyō
folding chairs/table.	**una silla/mesa plegable.** ōō'nä sē'lyä/me'sä plegä'ble
ground sheet.	**una colchoneta para el suelo.** ōō'nä kōltshōne'tä pä'rä el sōō·e'lō
ice pack.	**un paquete de hielo.** ōōn päke'te de ye'lō
insect spray.	**un spray contra insectos.** ōōn spre'ē kōn'trä ēnsek'tōs

SPANISH

171

kerosene.	**petróleo.** petrō'le·ō
lantern.	**una lámpara.** ōō'nä läm'pärä
matches.	**cerillas.** serē'lyäs
rope.	**una cuerda.** ōō'nä kōō·er'dä
sleeping bag.	**un saco de dormir.** ōōn sä'kō de dōrmēr'
soap.	**jabón.** /äbōn'
tent.	**una tienda de campaña.** ōō'nä tyen'dä de kämpä'nyä
towel/towels.	**una toalla/toallas.** ōō'nä tō·ä'lyä/tō·ä'lyäs

CHECKING OUT

I'd like to check out. May I have my bill please?	**Quisiera desocupar la habitación. ¿Me podría dar la cuenta, por favor?** kēsye'rä desōkōōpär lä äbētäsyōn'. ¿me pōdrē'ä där lä kōō·en'tä, pōr fävōr'?
Could you give me a receipt.	**¿Me podría dar un recibo?** ¿me pōdrē'ä där ōōn resē'bō?
Could you explain this item/charge?	**¿Podría explicarme este cargo?** ¿pōdrē'ä eksplēkär'me es'te kär'gō?
Thank you. I enjoyed my stay.	**Gracias. He estado muy a gusto aquí.** grä'syäs. e estä'dō mōō'ē ä gōōs'tō äkē'.
We enjoyed our stay.	**Hemos estado muy a gusto aquí.** e'mōs estä'dō mōō'ē ä gōōs'tō äkē'.

TRANSPORTATION BY AIR

Is there a bus/train to the airport?	**¿Hay un autobús/tren al aeropuerto?** ¿ī ōōn outōbōōs'/tren äl ä·erōpōō·er'tō?
At what time does it leave?	**¿A qué hora sale?** ¿ä ke ō'rä sä'le?

172

How long does it take to get there?	**¿Cuánto tiempo tarda en llegar allí?** ¿kōō·än'tō tyem'pō tär'dä en lyegär' älyē'?
Is there an earlier/later bus/train?	**¿Hay un autobús/tren antes/más tarde?** ¿ī ōōn outōbōōs'/tren än'tes/mäs tär'de?
How much does it cost?	**¿Cuánto cuesta?** ¿kōō·än'tō kōō·es'tä?
I'd like a flight to …	**Quisiera un vuelo a …** kēsye'rä ōōn vōō·e'lō ä …
a one-way/round trip ticket	**un billete sencillo/de ida y vuelta** ōōn bēlye'te sensē'lyō/de ē'dä ē vōō·el'tä
your cheapest fare	**el viaje más barato** el vyä'he mäs bärä'tō
an aisle/window seat	**un asiento de pasillo/ventana** ōōn äsyen'tō de päsē'lyō/ventä'nä
Is there a bus/train to the center of town?	**¿Hay un autobús/tren al centro de la ciudad?** ¿ī ōōn outōbōōs'/tren äl sen'trō de lä syōōdäd'?

RIDING THE BUS & SUBWAY

Could you tell me where the nearest bus/subway station is?	**¿Me podría decir dónde está la estación de autobuses/la estación de metro más cercana?** ¿me pōdrē'ä desēr' dōn'de estä' lä estäsyōn' de outōbōō'ses/lä estäsyōn' de me'trō mäs serkä'nä?
Could you tell me where the nearest bus/subway stop is?	**¿Me podría decir dónde está la parada de autobús/la estación de metro más cercana?** ¿me pōdrē'ä desēr' dōn'de estä' lä pärä'dä de outōbōōs'/lä estäsyōn' de me'trō mäs serkä'nä?
Where can I buy a ticket?	**¿Dónde puedo comprar un billete?** ¿dōn'de pōō·e'dō kōmprär' ōōn bēlye'te?

SPANISH

173

| How much does it cost? | **¿Cuánto cuesta?** |
| | ¿kōō·än'tō kōō·es'tä? |

| Can I use this ticket for the subway and the bus? | **¿Puedo usar este billete para el metro y el autobús?** ¿pōō·e'dō ōōsär' es'te bēlye'te pä'rä el me'trō ē el outōbōōs'? |

| I'd like to buy … tickets. | **Quisiera comprar … billetes.** |
| | kēsye'rä kōmprär' … bēlye'tes. |

| I'd like to buy a book of tickets/weekly pass. | **Quisiera comprar un taco de billetes/un billete semanal/un bonobús.** |
| | kēsye'rä kōmprär' ōōn tä'kō de bēlye'tes/ōōn bē' lye'te semänäl'/ōōn bōnōbōōs'. |

| Which bus/train do I take to get to …? | **¿Qué autobús/tren cojo para llegar a …?** |
| | ¿ke outōbōōs'/tren kō'hō pä'rä lyegär' ä …? |

| Do I have to change buses/trains to get to …? | **¿Tengo que cambiar de autobuses/trenes para llegar a …?** ¿teng'gō ke kämbyär' de outōbōō'ses/tre'nes pä'rä lyegär' ä …? |

| When is the next/last bus/train to …? | **¿Cuándo sale el próximo/último autobús/tren a …?** ¿kōō·än'dō sä'le el prō'gzēmō/ōōl'tēmō outōbōōs'/tren ä …? |

| Can you tell me when we reach …? | **¿Me puede avisar cuándo lleguemos a …?** |
| | ¿me pōō·e'de ävēsär' kōō·än'dō lyege'mōs ä …? |

| Do I get off here for …? | **¿Tengo que bajarme aquí para …?** |
| | ¿teng'gō ke bähär'me äkē' pä'rä …? |

| Please let me off here. | **Por favor, déjeme bajar aquí.** |
| | pōr fävōr', de'heme bähär' äkē'. |

TRAIN-STATION & AIRPORT SIGNS

| **Llegada** lyegä'dä | Arrival |

Resguardo de equipaje rezgōō·är'dō de ekēpä'*he*	Baggage Check
Recoger el equipaje rekō*her*' el ekēpä'*he*	Baggage Pick-up
Cambio käm'byō	Change
Aduana ädōō·ä'nä	Customs
Salidas de trenes/de aviones sälē'däs de tre'nes/de ävyō'nes	Departure
Entrada enträ'dä	Entrance
Salida sälē'dä	Exit
Información enförmäsyōn'	Information
Objetos perdidos ōb*he*'tōs perdē'dōs	Lost & Found
Consignas kōnsēg'näs	Luggage Lockers
No fumar nō fōōmär'	No Smoking
Reservas reser'väs	Reservations
Billetes bēlye'tes	Tickets
Baños bä'nyōs	Toilets
A los andenes/trenes ä lōs ände'nes/tre'nes	To the Platforms/ Trains
Sala de espera sä'lä de espe'rä	Waiting Room

SPANISH

TAKING THE TRAIN

English	Spanish
Could you tell me where the train station is?	**¿Me podría decir dónde está la estación del tren?** ¿me pōdrē'ä deser' dōn'de estä' lä estäsyōn' del tren?
Could I have a train schedule to …	**Quisiera un horario del tren a …** kēsye'rä ōōn ōrär'yō del tren ä …

175

TAKING THE TRAIN

| When is the next/last train to …? | ¿Cuándo sale el próximo/último tren a …? |
| | ¿kōō·än'dō sä'le el prō'gzēmō/ōōl'tēmō tren ä …? |

| I would like to reserve a seat/couchette in 1st/2nd class. | Quisiera reservar un asiento/una litera en primera/segunda clase. |
| | kēsye'rä reservar' ōōn äsyen'tō/ōō'nä lēte'rä en prēme'rä/segōōn'dä klä'se. |

| one-way/round trip | viaje sencillo/de ida y vuelta |
| | vyä'/he sensē'lyō/de e'dä ē vōō·el'tä |

| smoking/non-smoking | fumar/no fumar fōōmär/nō fōōmär |

| aisle/window seat | asiento de pasillo/de ventana |
| | äsyen'tō de päsē'lyō/de ventä'nä |

| At what time does the night train to … leave? | ¿A qué hora sale el tren nocturno a …? |
| | ¿ä ke ō'rä sä'le el tren nōktōōr'nō ä …? |

| At what time does it arrive? | ¿A qué hora llega? |
| | ¿ä ke ō'rä lye'gä? |

| Do I have to change trains? At what stop? | ¿Tengo que cambiar de tren? ¿En qué estación? ¿teng'gō ke kämbyär' de tren? ¿en ke estäsyōn'? |

| I have a rail pass. Must I pay a supplement to ride this train? | Tengo un rail pass. ¿Tengo que pagar suplemento para tomar este tren? |
| | teng'gō ōōn re·ēl' päs. ¿teng'gō ke pägär' sōōplemen'tō pä'rä tōmär' es'te tren? |

| Could you tell me where platform/track … is? | ¿Podría decirme dónde está el andén/la vía …? ¿pōdrē'ä desēr'me dōn'de estä' el änden'/lä vē'ä …? |

| Could you tell me where car number … is? | ¿Podría decirme dónde está el vagón número …? ¿pōdrē'ä desēr'me dōn'de estä' el vägōn' nōō'merō…? |

Could you help me find my seat/couchette, please?	**¿Podría ayudarme a buscar mi asiento/ litera, por favor?** ¿pōdrē'ä äyōōdär'me ä bōōskär' mē äsyen'tō/lēte'rä, pōr fävōr'?
Is this seat taken?	**¿Está ocupado este asiento?** ¿estä' ōkōōpä'dō es'te äsyen'tō?
Excuse me, I think this is my seat.	**Disculpe, creo que ése es mi asiento.** dēskōōl'pe, kre'ō ke e'se es mē äsyen'tō.
Could you save my seat, please?	**¿Podría guardar mi asiento, por favor?** ¿pōdrē'ä gōō·ärdär' mē äsyen'tō, pōr fävōr'?
Where is the dining car?	**¿Dónde está el vagón-restaurante?** ¿dōn'de estä' el vägōn' restourän'te?
Where are the toilets?	**¿Dónde están los baños?** ¿dōn'de estän' los bä'nyōs?

**For Europass and Flexipass users. With these passes you will only have access to certain countries. If your train goes through a country that is not on your pass, you will be required to pay an extra fare.

My rail pass only covers Spain/Portugal/ France/Italy/Switzer- land/Germany/ Austria.	**Mi rail pass sólo vale para España/ Portugal/Francia/Italia/Suiza/ Alemania/Austria.** mē re'ēl päs sō'lō vä'le pä'rä espä'nyä/pōrtōōgäl'/frän'syä/ētä'lyä/sōō·ē' sä/älemä'nyä/ous'trē·ä.
How much extra do I have to pay since my train goes through ...?	**¿Cuánto más tengo que pagar si mi tren pasa por ...?** ¿kōō·än'tō mäs teng'gō ke pägär' sē mē tren pä'sä pōr ...?
Is there another way to get to ... without having to go through ...?	**¿Hay otro camino para llegar a ... sin tener que pasar por ...?** ¿ī ō'trō kämē'nō pä'rä lyegär' ä ... sēn tener' ke päsär' pōr ...?

SPANISH

177

BY BOAT

Is there a boat that goes to …?	**¿Hay algún barco que vaya a …?** ¿ī älgōōn' bär'kō ke vä'yä ä …?
When does the next/last boat leave?	**¿Cuándo sale el próximo/último barco?** ¿kōō·än'do sä'le el prō'gzēmō/ōōl'tēmō bär'kō?
I have a rail pass. Do I get a discount? How much?	**Tengo un rail pass. ¿Me hacen descuento? ¿Cuánto?** teng'gō ōōn re'ēl päs. ¿me ä'sen deskōō·en'tō? ¿kōō·än'to?
At what time does the boat arrive?	**¿A qué hora llega el barco?** ¿ä ke ō'rä lye'gä el bär'kō?
How early must I get on board?	**¿Con cuánto tiempo de adelanto tengo que subir a bordo?** ¿kōn kōō·än'tō tyem'pō de ädelän'tō teng'gō ke sōōbēr' ä bōr·dō?
Can I buy seasickness pills nearby?	**¿Puedo comprar pastillas contra el mareo cerca de aquí?** ¿pōō·e'dō kōmprär' pästē'lyäs kōn'trä el märe'ō ser'kä de äkē'?

GETTING AROUND BY CAR

I'd like to rent a car…	**Quisiera alquilar un coche…** kēsye'rä älkēlär' ōōn kō'tshe …
for … days.	**por … días.** pōr … dē'äs.
for a week.	**por una semana.** pōr ōō'nä semä'nä.
What is your daily/weekly rate?	**¿Cuál es la tarifa diaria/semanal?** ¿kōō·äl' es lä tärē'fä dyä'rē·ä/semänäl'?
Do I need insurance?	**¿Necesito seguro?** ¿nesesē'tō segōō'rō?
Is mileage included?	**¿Está incluido el kilometraje?** ¿estä' ēnklōō·e'do el kēlōmeträ'he?
How much is it?	**¿Cuánto cuesta?** ¿kōō·än'tō kōō·es'tä?

ROAD SIGNS

Alto äl'tō	Stop
De un sólo sentido de ōōn sō'lō sentē'dō	One Way
Prohibido entrar prō·ēbē'dō enträr'	Do Not Enter
No tiene usted la preferencia no tye'ne ōōste' lä preferen'syä	Yield
Estacionamiento prohibido estäsyōnämyen'tō prō·ēbē'dō	No Parking

TAXI

I'd like to go to …	**Quisiera ir a …** kēsye'rä ēr ä …
What is the fare?	**¿Cuál es la tarifa?** ¿kōō·äl' es lä tärē'fä?
Please stop here.	**Por favor, pare aquí.** pōr fävōr', pä're äkē'.
Can you wait for me?	**¿Puede esperarme?** ¿pōō·e'de esperär'me?

GETTING AROUND ON FOOT

Excuse me, could you tell me how to get to …?	**Disculpe, ¿podría decirme cómo llegar a …?** dēskōōl'pe, ¿pōdrē'ä desēr'me kō'mō lyegär' ä …?
Is it nearby/far?	**¿Está cerca/lejos?** ¿estä' ser'kä/le'hōs?
Can I walk or should I take the bus/subway?	**¿Puedo caminar o es mejor coger el autobús/el metro?** ¿pōō·e'dō kämēnär' ō es mehōr' kō'her el outōbōōs'/el me'trō?
Could you direct me to the nearest bus/subway station/stop?	**¿Podría decirme cómo llegar a la estación/parada más cercana de autobús/metro?** ¿pōdrē'ä desēr'me kō'mō lyegär' ä lä estäsyōn'/pärä'dä mäs serkä'nä de outōbōōs'/me'trō?

SPANISH

179

EATING OUT

Straight ahead.	**Siga todo recto.** sē'gä tō'dō rek'tō.
Go right/left.	**Doble a la derecha/a la izquierda.** dō'ble ä lä dere'tshä/ä lä ēskyer'dä.
At the corner/traffic light.	**En la esquina/el semáforo.** en lä eskē'nä/el semä'fōrō.
I'm lost.	**Me he perdido.** me e perdē'dō.
Could you show me where we are on this map?	**¿Podría enseñarme en este plano en dónde estamos?** ¿pōdrē'ä ensenyär'me en es'te plä'nō en dōn'de estä'mōs?

EATING OUT

Could we have a table outside/inside?	**¿Podría darnos una mesa fuera/dentro?** ¿pōdrē'ä där'nōs ōō'nä me'sä fōō·e'rä/den'trō?
Do you have a fixed-price menu?	**¿Tiene un menú de precio fijo?** ¿tye'ne ōōn menōō' de pre'syō fē'hō?
Is service included?	**¿Está incluido el servicio?** ¿estä' ēnklōō·ē'dō el servē'syō?
Is there a cover charge?	**¿Se paga por los cubiertos?** ¿se pä'gä pōr lōs kōōbyer'tōs?
Separate checks, please.	**Cuentas separadas, por favor.** kōō·en'täs sepärä'däs, pōr fävōr'.
I'd like some apple/orange/grapefruit juice.	**Quisiera un zumo de manzana/naranja/pomelo.** kēsye'rä ōōn sōō'mō de mansä'nä/närän'hä/pōme'lō.
I'd like some coffee/tea with milk/lemon.	**Quisiera café/té con leche/limón.** kēsye'rä käfe'/te kōn le'tshe/lēmōn'.
I'd like a soda/beer/mineral water.	**Quisiera una soda/una cerveza/un agua mineral.** kēsye'rä ōō'nä sō'dä/ōō'nä servē'sä/ōō'n ä'gōō·ä mēneräl'.

180

I'd like a glass/bottle of red/white/rose wine.	**Quisiera una copa/una botella de vino tinto/blanco/rosado.** kēsye'rä ōō'nä kō'pä/ōō'nä bōte'lyä de vē'nō tēn'tō/bläng'kō/rōsä'dō.
dry/sweet	**seco/dulce** se'kō/dōōl'se
Cheers!	**¡Salud!** ¡sälōōd'!
What is the special of the day?	**¿Cuál es el plato del día?** ¿kōō·äl' es el plä'tō del dē'ä?
Do you have a tourist menu?	**¿Tiene un menú para turistas?** ¿tye'ne ōōn menōō' pä'rä tōōrēs'täs?
What is this? (pointing to item on menu)	**¿Qué es esto?** ¿ke es es'tō?
I'll have this.	**Tomaré esto.** tōmare' es'tō.
I'd like some salt/pepper/cheese/sugar/milk.	**Quisiera sal/pimienta/queso/azúcar/leche.** kēsye'rä säl/pēmyen'tä/ke'sō/äsōō'kär/le'tshe.
More juice/coffee/tea/cream/lemon/milk/beer/wine.	**Más zumo/café/té/crema(nata)/limón/cerveza/vino.** mäs sōō'mō/käfe'/te/kre'mä(nä'tä)/lēmōn'/serve'sä/vē'nō.
I cannot eat/drink sugar/salt/alcohol.	**No puedo tomar azúcar/sal/alcohol.** nō pōō·e'dō tōmär' äsōō'kär/säl/älkō·ōl'.
I am a diabetic.	**Soy diabético/diabética.** soi dyäbe'tēkō/dyäbe'tēkä.
I am a vegetarian.	**Soy vegetariano/vegetariana.** soi vehetäryä'nō/vehetäryä'nä.
May I have the check, please.	**Quisiera la cuenta, por favor.** kēsye'rä lä kōō·en'tä, pōr fävōr'.
Keep the change.	**Quédese con el cambio.** ke'dese kōn el käm'byō.

SPANISH

FOOD SHOPPING & PICNIC FOOD

Can you make me a sandwich.	**¿Podría hacerme un sandwich/bocadillo?** ¿pōdrē´ä äser´me ōōn sändōō·ētsh´/bōkädē´lyō?
To take out.	**Para llevar.** pä´rä lye´vär.
I'd like some ...	**Quisiera ...** kēsye´rä ...
I'll have a little more.	**Quisiera un poquito más.** kēsye´rä ōōn pōkē´tō mäs.
That's too much.	**Es demasiado.** es demäsyä´dō.
Do you have ...	**¿Tiene ...?** ¿tye´ne ...?
I'd like ...	**Quisiera ...** kēsye´rä ...
a box of	**una caja de** ōō´nä kä´hä de
a can of	**una lata de** ōō´nä lä´tä de
a jar of	**un tarro de** ōōn tä´rō de
a half kilo of	**medio kilo de** me´dyō kē´lō de
a kilo of	**un kilo de** ōōn kē´lō de
a half liter of	**medio litro de** medyō lē´trō de
a liter of	**un litro de** ōōn lē´trō de
a packet of	**un paquete de** ōōn päke´te de
a slice of	**una rebanada de** ōō´nä rebänä´dä de
a bottle opener	**un abridor** ōōn äbrēdōr´
a can opener	**un abrelatas** ōōn äbrelä´täs
a cork screw	**un sacacorchos** ōōn säkäkōr´tshōs
it sliced	**eso en rebanadas** e´sō en rebänä´däs
Do you have any plastic forks/spoons/knives and napkins?	**¿Tiene tenedores/cucharas/cuchillos de plástico y servilletas?** ¿tye´ne tenedō´res/ kōōtshä´räs/kōōtshē´lyōs de pläs´tēkō ē servēlye´täs?
May I have a bag?	**¿Podría darme una bolsa?** ¿pōdrē´ä där´me ōō´nä bōl´sä?

Is there a park nearby? **¿Hay un parque cerca de aquí?**
¿ī ōōn pär'ke ser'kä de äkē'?

May we picnic there? **¿Podemos hacer picnic allí?**
¿pōde'mōs äser' pēknēk' älyē'?

May we picnic here? **¿Podemos hacer picnic aquí?**
¿pōde'mōs äser' pēknēk' äkē'?

Fruits

apples	**manzanas** mänsä'näs
apricots	**albaricoques** älbärēkō'kes
bananas	**plátanos** plä'tänōs
blueberries	**arándanos** ärän'dänōs
cantaloupe	**melón** melōn'
cherries	**cerezas** sere'säs
dates	**dátiles** dä'tēles
figs	**higos** ē'gōs
grapefruit	**pomelos** pōme'lōs
grapes	**uvas** ōō'väs
lemons	**limones** lēmō'nes
nectarines	**nectarinas** nektärē'näs
oranges	**naranjas** närän'häs
peaches	**melocotones** melōkōtō'nes
pears	**peras** pe'räs
pineapple	**piña** pē'nyä
plums	**ciruelas** sērōō·e'läs
raisins	**pasas** pä'säs
raspberries	**frambuesas** främbōō·e'säs
strawberries	**fresas** fre'säs
tangerines	**mandarinas** mändärē'näs
watermelon	**sandía** sändē'ä

Vegetables

artichokes	**alcachofas** älkätshō'fäs

SPANISH

FOOD SHOPPING

asparagus	**espárragos** espä'rägōs
green/kidney beans	**judías verdes/moradas**
	hōōdē'äs ver'des/mōrä'däs
broccoli	**bróculi** brō'kōōlē
red cabbage	**lombarda/col** lōmbär'dä/kōl
carrots	**zanahorias** sänä-ōr'yäs
cauliflower	**coliflor** kōlēflōr'
celery	**apio** ä'pyō
corn	**maíz** mä·ēs'
cucumber	**pepino** pepē'nō
eggplant	**berenjena** beren*he*'nä
fennel	**hinojo** ēnō'*h*ō
french fries	**patatas fritas** pätä'täs frē'täs
garlic	**ajo** ä'*h*ō
leeks	**puerro** pōō·e'rō
lentils	**lentejas** lente'*h*äs
lettuce	**lechuga** letshōō'gä
mushrooms	**setas** se'täs
black/green olives	**aceitunas negras/verdes**
	äse·ētōō'näs ne'gräs/ver'des
onions	**cebollas** sebō'lyäs
peas	**guisantes** gēsän'tes
hot/sweet peppers	**pimiento picante/dulce**
	pēmyen'tō pēkän'te/dōōl'se
pickles	**pepinillos en vinagre** pepēnē'lyōs en vēnä'gre
potatoes	**patatas** pätä'täs
radishes	**rábanos** rä'bänōs
rice	**arroz** ärōs'
spinach	**espinacas** espēnä'käs
tomatoes	**tomates** tōmä'tes
zucchini	**calabacines** käläbäsē'nes

Meats/Cold Cuts

beef	**carne de vaca** kär'ne de vä'kä
bologna	**mortadela** mōrtäde'lä

chicken	**pollo** pō′lyō
fish	**pescado** peskä′dō
ham	**jamón** *h*ämōn′
hamburger/ground	**hamburguesa/carne picada**
beef	ämbōōrge′sä/kär′ne pēkä′dä
hot dogs/frankfurters	**hot dog/perrito caliente/salchicha de**
	Frankfurt *h*ōt dōg/perē′tō kälyen′te/
	sältshē′tshä de frängk′fōort
lamb	**cordero** kōrde′rō
pork	**cerdo** ser′dō
roast beef	**roast beef/asado de vaca**
	rōst bēf/äsä′dō de vä′kä
salami	**salami** sälä′mē
sausage	**salchicha** sältshē′tshä
turkey	**pavo** pä′vō
veal	**ternera** terne′rä

Nuts

almonds	**almendras** älmen′dräs
brazil nuts	**nueces de Brasil** nōō·e′ses de bräsēl′
chestnuts	**castañas** kästä′nyäs
hazelnuts	**avellanas** ävelyä′näs
peanuts	**cacahuetes** käkä-ōō·e′tes
walnuts	**nueces** nōō·e′ses

Condiments

butter	**mantequilla** mäntekē′lyä
honey	**miel** myel′
horseradish	**rábano picante** rä′bänō pēkän′te
jam/jelly	**jalea** *h*äle′ä
ketchup	**ketchup** ketshäp′
margarine	**margarina** märgärē′nä
mayonnaise	**mayonesa** mäyōne′sä
mustard	**mostaza** mōstä′sä

FOOD SHOPPING

vegetable/olive oil	**aceite vegetal/de oliva**
	äse'ēte ve*h*etäl'/de ōlē'vä
pepper	**pimienta** pēmyen'tä
mild/hot salsa	**salsa suave/picante** säl'sä sōō·ä've/pēkän'te
salt	**sal** säl
sugar	**azúcar** äsōō'kär
tabasco/hot sauce	**salsa tabasco/picante**
	säl'sä täbäs'kō/pēkän'te
vinegar	**vinagre** vēnäg'gre

Miscellaneous

bread	**pan** pän
cake	**pastel** pästel'
candy	**dulce** dōōl'se
cereal	**cereal** sere·äl'
cheese	**queso** ke'sō
chocolate	**chocolate** tshōkōlä'te
cookies	**galletas** gälye'täs
crackers	**galletas saladas** gälye'täs sälä'däs
eggs	**huevos** ōō·e'vōs
ice cream	**helado** elä'dō
popcorn	**palomitas** pälōmē'täs
potato chips	**patatas fritas** pätä'täs frē'täs
rolls	**panecillos salados** pänesē'lyōs sälä'dōs
spaghetti	**espaguetis** espäge'tēs
yogurt	**yogur** yōgōōr'

Drinks

beer	**cerveza** serve'sä
coffee	**café** käfe'
hot chocolate	**chocolate caliente** tshōkōlä'te kälyen'te
apple juice	**zumo de manzana** sōō'mō de mänsä'nä
cranberry juice	**zumo de arándano encarnado**
	sōō'mō de ärän'dänō enkärnä'dō

grapefruit juice	**zumo de pomelo** sōō'mō de pōme'lō
orange juice	**zumo de naranja** sōō'mō de närän'hä
tomato juice	**zumo de tomate** sōō'mō de tōmä'te
milk	**leche** le'tshe
soft drinks	**refrescos** refres'kōs
tea	**té** te
sparkling/mineral water	**agua con gas/mineral** ä'gōō·ä kōn gäs/mēnerä!'
red/white/rose wine	**vino tinto/blanco/rosado** vē'nō tēn'tō/bläng'kō/rōsä'dō
dry/sweet	**seco/dulce** se'kō/dōōl'se

USING THE TELEPHONE

Can I use local currency to make a local/long-distance call or do I need to buy a phone card?	**¿Puedo usar monedas para hacer una llamada local/de larga distancia o tengo que comprar una tarjeta telefónica?** ¿pōō·e'dō ōōsär' mōne'däs pä'rä äser' ōō'nä lyä'mä lōkäl'/de lär'gä dēstän'syä ō teng'gō ke kōmprär' ōō'nä tärhe'tä telefō'nēkä?
Do I need to buy tokens?	**¿Tengo que comprar fichas?** ¿teng'gō ke kōmprär' fē'tshäs?
Where can I buy tokens/a phone card?	**¿Dónde puedo comprar fichas/una tarjeta telefónica?** ¿dōn'de pōō·e'dō kōmprär' fē'tshäs/ōō'nä tärhe'tä telefō'nēkä?
… tokens, please. How much?	**… fichas, por favor. ¿Cuánto es?** … fē'tshäs, pōr fävōr'. ¿kōō·än'tō es?
I'd like to buy phone card. How much does it cost?	**Quisiera comprar una tarjeta telefónica. ¿Cuánto cuesta?** kēsye'rä kōmprär' ōō'nä tärhe'tä telefō'nēkä. ¿kōō·än'tō kōō·es'tä?
How do you use the phone card?	**¿Cómo se usa la tarjeta telefónica?** ¿kō'mō se ōō'sä lä tärhe'tä telefō'nēkä?

SPANISH

187

POST OFFICE

Excuse me, where is the nearest phone?	**Disculpe, ¿dónde está el teléfono más cercano?** dēskōōl'pe, ¿dōn'de estä' el tele'fōnō mäs serkä'nō?
I'd like to make a collect call.	**Quisiera hacer una llamada por cobrar.** kēsye'rä äser' ōō'nä lyämä'dä pōr kōbrär'.
The number is …	**El número es …** el nōō'merō es …
Hello. This is …	**Hola. Soy …** ō'lä. soi …
May I speak to …	**¿Podría hablar con …?** ¿pōdrē'ä äblär' kōn …?

POST OFFICE

| Can you direct me to the nearest post office? | **¿Podría decirme cómo llegar a la oficina postal más cercana?** ¿pōdrē'ä deser'me kō'mō lyegär' ä lä ōfēsē'nä pōstäl' mäs serkä'nä? |
| Which window is for … | **¿Qué ventanilla es para …** ¿ke ventänē'lyä es pä'rä … |

	stamps?	**sellos?** se'lyōs
	sending/cashing a money order?	**enviar/cobrar giros postales?** envyär'/kōbrär' *he*'rōs pōstä'les?
	airmail writing paper?	**papel para correo aéreo?** päpel' pä'rä kōre'ō ä·e're·ō

I'd like … stamps for postcards/letters to America.	**Quisiera … sellos para postales/cartas a los Estados Unidos.** kēsye'rä … se'lyōs pä'rä pōstä'les/kär'täs ä lōs estä'dōs ōōnē'dōs.
I'd like to send this airmail.	**Quisiera enviar esto por correo aéreo.** kēsye'rä envyär' es'tō pōr kōre'ō ä·e're·ō.
How much does it cost?	**¿Cuánto cuesta?** ¿kōō·än'tō kōō·es'tä?

188

PHARMACY & DRUGSTORE

Can you direct me to the nearest pharmacy?	**¿Podría decirme cómo voy a la farmacia más cercana?** ¿pōdrē'ä desēr'me kō'mō voi ä lä färmä'syä mäs serkä'nä?
I'd like a/an/some ...	**Quisiera un/una/algunos/algunas ...** kēsye'rä ōōn/ōō'nä/älgōō'nōs/älgōō'näs ...
aspirin	**aspirina** äspērēnä
Band-Aids	**esparadrapo** espärädrä'pō
cough medicine	**medicina para la tos** medēsē'nä pä'rä lä tōs
contraceptives	**anticonceptivos** äntēkōnseptē'vōs
eye drops	**gotas para los ojos** gō'täs pä'rä lōs ō'hōs
insect repellant	**repelente de insectos** repelen'te de ēnsek'tōs
sanitary napkins	**compresas** kōmpre'säs
Could you give me something for ...?	**¿Podría darme algo para ...?** ¿pōdrē'ä där'me äl'gō pä'rä ...?
constipation	**el estreñimiento** el estrenyēmyen'tō
diarrhea	**la diarrea** lä dyäre'ä
a headache	**el dolor de cabeza** el dōlōr' de käbe'sä
hay fever	**la fiebre de heno** lä fye'bre de e'nō
indigestion	**la indigestión** lä ēndēhestyōn'
itching	**los picores** lōs pēkō'res
nausea/travel sick- ness	**el mareo** el märe'ō
a rash	**una erupción de la piel** ōō'nä erōōpsyōn' de lä pyel'
sore throat	**el dolor de garganta** el dōlōr' de gärgän'tä
sunburn	**una quemadura de sol** ōō'nä kemädōō'rä de sōl
May I have a/an/ some ...?	**¿Podría darme ...?** ¿pōdrē'ä där'me ...?

deodorant	**un desodorante** ōōn desōdōrän'te
razor	**una maquinilla de afeitar** ōō'na mäkēnē'lyä de äfe·ētär'
razor blades	**hojas de afeitar** ō'häs de äfe·ētär'
shampoo/conditioner	**un champú/acondicionador** ōōn tshämpōō'/äkōndēsyōnädōr'
soap	**un jabón** ōōn häbōn'
suntan oil/cream/lotion	**aceite/crema/loción para el sol** äse'ēte/krē'mä/lōsyōn' pä'rä el sōl
tissues	**pañuelos** pänyōō·e'lōs
toilet paper	**papel de baño** päpel' de bä'nyō
toothbrush	**un cepillo de dientes** ōōn sepē'lyō de dyen'tes
toothpaste	**una pasta de dientes** ōō'nä päs'tä de dyen'tes
cleaning/soaking solution for contact lenses	**una solución limpiadora y humedecedora para lentes de contacto** ōō'nä sōlōōsyōn' lēmpyädō'rä ē ōōmedesedō'rä pä'rä len'tes de kōntäk'tō
How much does it cost?	**¿Cuánto cuesta?** ¿kōō·än'tō kōō·es'tä?

I'd like to buy …	**Quisiera comprar …** kēsye'rä kōmprär' …
a pack/carton of cigarettes.	**una cajetilla/un paquete de cigarillos.** ōō'nä kä*h*etē'lyä/ōōn päke'te de sēgärē'lyōs.
a cigarette lighter.	**un encendedor.** ōōn ensendedōr'.
a cigar.	**un puro.** ōōn pōō'rō.
May I have some matches?	**¿Podría darme unas cerillas?** ¿pōdrē'ä där'me ōō'näs serē'lyäs?

PHOTOGRAPHY

I'd like to buy a roll of film.	**Quisiera comprar un carrete.** kēsye'rä kōmprär' ōōn käre'te.
Black and white/Color.	**Blanco-negro/Color.** bläng'kō-ne'grō/kōlōr'.
How much are they?	**¿Cuánto cuestan?** ¿kōō·än'tō kōō·es'tän?
I'd like to buy batteries for this camera.	**Quisiera comprar baterías para esta cámara.** kēsye'rä kōmprär' bäterē'äs pä'rä es'tä kä'märä.

HEALTH

The Doctor

I don't feel well.	**No me siento bien.** nō me syen'tō byen'.
Could you direct me to a doctor that speaks English.	**¿Podría decirme dónde hay un médico que hable inglés?** ¿pōdrē'ä desēr'me dōn'de ī ōōn me'dēkō ke ä'ble ēng·gles'?
I have (a) …	**Tengo …** teng'gō …
burn.	**una quemadura.** ōō'nä kemädōō'rä
chest pains.	**dolor en el pecho.** dōlōr' en el pe'tshō
cold.	**un resfriado.** ōōn resfrē·ä'dō
cough.	**tos.** tōs
cramps.	**convulsiones.** kōnvōōlsyō'nes
cut.	**un corte.** ōōn kōr'te
diarrhea.	**diarrea.** dyäre'ä
fever.	**fiebre.** fye'bre
flu.	**gripe.** grē'pe
infection.	**una infección.** ōō'nä ēnfeksyōn'
nausea.	**náuseas.** nou'se·äs
rash.	**una erupción de la piel.** ōō'nä erōōpsyōn' de lä pyel'
sore throat.	**dolor de garganta.** dōlōr' de gärgän'tä
sprained ankle.	**un tobillo torcido.** ōōn tōbē'lyō tōrse'dō

191

SPANISH

stomach ache.	**dolor de estómago.** dōlōr' de estō'mägō
It hurts here.	**Me duele aquí.** me dōō·e'le äkē'.
I've been vomiting.	**He vomitado.** e vōmētä'dō.
I'm having difficulty breathing.	**Tengo dificultades para respirar.** teng'gō dēfēkōōltä'des pä'rä respērär'.
I'm allergic to penicillin.	**Soy alérgico/alérgica a la penicilina.** soi äler'hēkō/äler'hēkä ä lä penēsēlē'nä.
I'm diabetic.	**Soy diabético/diabética.** soi dyäbe'tēkō/dyäbe'tēkä.
I don't smoke/drink.	**No fumo/bebo alcohol.** nō fōō'mō/be'bō älkō·ōl'.

The Dentist

Could you direct me to a dentist that speaks English?	**¿Podría decirme dónde hay un dentista que hable inglés?** ¿pōdrē'ä desēr'me dōn'de ī ōōn dentēs'tä ke ä'ble ēng·gles'?
I have a toothache. This tooth.	**Tengo dolor de muelas. Este diente.** teng'gō dōlōr' de mōō·e'läs. es'te dyen'te.
My tooth is loose.	**Este diente está flojo.** es'te dyen'te estä' flōhō.
My tooth is broken.	**Este diente está partido.** es'te dyen'te estä' pärtē'dō.
I've broken/lost a filling.	**Se me rompió/Se me cayó un empaste.** se me rōmpyō/se me käyō ōōn empäs'te.

Paying

How much does this cost?	**¿Cuánto cuesta?** ¿kōō·än'tō kōō·es'tä?

192

I have health insurance.	**Tengo un seguro médico.** teng'gō ōōn segōō'rō me'dēkō.
I'm supposed to call this number.	**Tengo que llamar a este número.** teng'gō ke lyämär' ä es'te nōō'merō.
How much do I owe you?	**¿Cuánto le debo?** ¿kōō·än'tō le de'bō?

SIGHTSEEING

Can you recommend ...?	**¿Puede recomendarme ...?** ¿pōō·e'de rekōmendär'me ...?
a good, inexpensive restaurant	**un restaurante bueno y económico** ōōn restourän'te bōō·e'nō ē ekōnō'mēkō
a fun nightclub	**un club nocturno divertido** ōōn klōōb nōktōōr'nō dēverte'dō
a good place to dance	**un buen lugar para bailar** ōōn bōō·en' lōōgär' pä'rä bīlär'
Can you tell me where the tourist office is?	**¿Podría decirme dónde está la oficina de turismo?** ¿pōdrē'ä desēr'me dōn'de estä' lä ōfēsē'nä de tōōrēs'mō?
What are the main points of interest here?	**¿Cuáles son los lugares de mayor interés aquí?** ¿kōō·ä'les sōn lōs lōōgä'res de mäyōr' ēnteres' äkē'?
What time does it open/close?	**¿A qué hora abre/cierra?** ¿ä ke ō'rä ä'bre/sye'rä?
What time is the last entry?	**¿A qué hora es la última entrada?** ¿ä ke ō'rä es lä ōōl'tēmä enträ'dä?
How much is the admission? Free.	**¿Cuánto cuesta la entrada? Libre.** ¿kōō·än'tō kōō·es'tä lä enträ'dä? lē'bre.

193

SIGHTSEEING

Is there a discount for students/children/teachers/senior citizens?	**¿Hay descuento para estudiantes/niños/profesores/personas de la tercera edad?** ¿ī deskōō·en'tō pä'rä estōōdyän'tes/nē'nyōs/prōfesō'res/persō'näs de lä terse'rä edäd'?
Is the ticket good all day?	**¿El billete vale todo el día?** ¿el bēlye'te vä'le tō'dō el dē'ä?
Is there a sightseeing tour?	**¿Hay una visita guiada?** ¿ī ōō'nä vēsē'tä gē·ä'dä?
What time does it start?	**¿A qué hora empieza?** ¿ä ke ō'rä empye'sä?
How much does it cost?	**¿Cuánto cuesta?** ¿kōō·än'tō kōō·es'tä?
How long is it?	**¿Cuánto tiempo dura?** ¿kōō·än'tō tyem'pō dōō'rä?
Does the guide speak English?	**¿Habla inglés el guía?** ¿ä'blä eng·gles' el gē'ä?
Am I allowed to take pictures/a video?	**¿Puedo hacer fotos/un vídeo?** ¿pōō·e'dō äser' fō'tōs/ōōn vē'de·ō?
Can you direct me to the …?	**¿Podría decirme cómo voy …?** ¿pōdrē'ä desēr'me kōmō voi …?

art gallery	**a la galería de arte** ä lä gälerē'ä de är'te
beach	**a la playa** ä lä plä'yä
castle	**al castillo** äl kästē'lyō
cathedral	**a la catedral** ä lä kätedräl'
cemetery	**al cementerio** äl sementer'yō
church	**a la iglesia** ä lä ēgle'syä
fountain	**a la fuente** ä lä fōō·en'te
gardens	**a los jardines** ä lōs härdē'nes
harbor	**al puerto** äl pōō·er'tō
lake	**al lago** äl lä'gō
monastery	**al monasterio** äl mōnäster'yō

mountains	**a las montañas** ä läs mōntä′nyäs
movies	**al cine** äl sē′ne
museum	**al museo** äl mōōse′ō
old city	**al casco antiguo** äl käs′kō äntē′gōō·ō
palace	**al palacio** äl pälä′syō
ruins	**a las ruinas** ä läs rōō·ē′näs
shops/bazaar	**a las tiendas/al bazar**
	ä läs tyen′däs/äl bäsär′
statue	**a la estatua** ä lä estä′tōō·ä
tomb	**a la tumba** ä lä tōōm′bä
trails (for hiking)	**camino (para pasear a pie)**
	kämē′nō (pä′rä päse·är′ ä pye′)
university	**a la universidad** ä lä ōōnēversēdäd′
zoo	**al zoológico** äl sō·ōlō′hēkō

Is it far from here?	**¿Está lejos de aquí?** ¿estä′ le′hōs de äkē′?
Can we walk there?	**¿Podemos caminar hasta allí?**
	¿pōde′mōs kämēnär′ äs′tä älyē′?
Straight ahead.	**Siga todo recto.** sē′gä tō′dō rek′tō.
Go right/left.	**Doble a la derecha/izquierda.**
	dō′ble ä lä dere′tshä/ēskyer′dä.
At the corner/traffic light.	**En la esquina/el semáforo.**
	en lä eskē′nä/el semä′fōrō.

DISCOUNT INFORMATION

Do I get a discount with my student/teacher's/senior citizens card?	**¿Me dan descuento con mi carnet de estudiante/profesor/persona de la tercera edad?** ¿me dän deskōō·en′tō kōn mē kärnet′ de estōōdyan′te/prōfesōr′/persō′nä de lä terse′rä edäd′?
Do I get a discount with my Eurailpass/Europass/Flexipass?	**¿Me dan descuento con mi Eurailpass/Europass/Flexipass?** ¿me dän deskōō·en′tō kōn mē e·ōōre′ēlpäs′/e·ōō′rōpäs′/flek′sēpäs`?

SPANISH

195

LOSS & THEFT

| How much of a discount? | **¿Qué descuento hacen?** ¿ke deskōō·en'tō ä'sen? |
| How much do I owe? | **¿Cuánto le debo?** ¿kōō·än'tō le de'bō? |

EMERGENCIES & ACCIDENTS

Please call the police.	**Por favor, ¡llame a la policía!** pōr fävōr', ¡lyä'me ä lä pōlēsē'ä!
Please call a doctor/an ambulance, quickly.	**Por favor, llame a un médico/una ambulancia, rápido.** pōr fävōr', lyä'me ä ōōn me'dēkō/ōō'nä ämbōōlän'syä, rä'pēdo.
Hurry!	**¡De prisa!** ¡de prē'sä!
Danger!	**¡Cuidado!** ¡kōō·ēdä'dō!
Someone has been hurt/robbed.	**Han herido/robado a alguien.** än erē'dō/rōbä'dō ä älgyen'.
I'm hurt.	**Estoy herido/herida.** estoi' erē'dō/erē'dä.
Where is the hospital?	**¿Dónde está el hospital?** ¿dōn'de estä' el ōspētäl'?
There's a fire.	**Hay un fuego.** ī ōōn fōō·e'gō.
Help!/Thief!/Pickpocket!	**¡Auxilio!/¡Ladrón!/¡Carterista!** ¡ougzē'lyō!/¡lädrōn'!/¡kärterēs'tä!
Police!	**¡Policía!** ¡pōlēsē'ä!
Stop that man/woman!	**¡Detenga a ese hombre/esa mujer!** ¡deteng'gä ä e'se ōm'bre/e'sä mōō/her'!

LOSS & THEFT

| Can you help me, please? | **¿Me puede ayudar, por favor?** ¿me pōō·e'de äyōōdär', pōr fävōr'? |

Where is the police station?	**¿Dónde está el puesto de policía?** ¿dōn'de está' el pōō·es'tō de pōlēsē'ä?
Where is the American consulate/embassy?	**¿Dónde está el consulado norteamericano/la embajada norteamericana?** ¿dōn'de está' el kōnsōōlä'dō nōrte·ämerēkä'nō/ lä embä*h*ä'dä nōrte·ämerēkä'nä?
Can you tell me where the lost and found is?	**¿Puede decirme dónde se recuperan las cosas perdidas?** ¿pōō·e'de desēr'me dōn'de se rekōōpe'rän läs kō'säs perdē'däs?
Someone has stolen my …	**Me han robado mi …** me än rōbä'dō mē …
I have lost my …	**He perdido mi …** e perdē'dō mē …
I left my … on the bus/train.	**He dejado mi … en el autobús/en el tren.** e de*h*ä'dō mē … en el outōbōōs'/en el tren.

backpack	**mochila** mōtshē'lä
camera	**cámara** kä'märä
credit cards	**tarjetas de crédito** tär*h*e'täs de kre'dētō
glasses	**gafas** gä'fäs
luggage	**equipaje** ekēpä'*h*e
money	**dinero** dēne'rō
passport	**pasaporte** päsäpōr'te
railpass	**railpass** re'elpäs
traveler's checks	**cheques de viaje** tshe'kes de vyä'*h*e
wallet	**cartera/billetera** kärte'rä/bēlyete'rä

DEALING WITH PROBLEM PEOPLE

Leave me alone or I'll call the police.	**¡Déjeme en paz o llamaré a la policía!** de'*h*eme en päs ō lyämäre' ä lä pōlēsē'ä.
Stop following me.	**¡Deje de seguirme!** de'*h*e de segēr'me.
I'm not interested.	**No me interesa.** nō me ēntere'sä.

197

SPANISH

NUMBERS

I'm married.	**Estoy casado/casada.** estoi̇ käsä'dō/käsä'dä.
I'm waiting for my boyfriend/husband.	**Estoy esperando a mi novio/mi marido.** estoi̇ esperän'dō ä mē nō'vyō/mē mare'dō.
Enough!	**¡Basta!** ¡bäs'tä!
Go away!	**¡Váyase!** ¡vä'yäse!

NUMBERS

zero	**cero** se'rō
one	**uno, una** ōo'nō, ōo'nä
two	**dos** dōs
three	**tres** tres
four	**cuatro** kōo·ä'trō
five	**cinco** sēng'kō
six	**seis** se'ēs
seven	**siete** sye'te
eight	**ocho** ō'tshō
nine	**nueve** nōo·e've
ten	**diez** dyes'
eleven	**once** ōn'se
twelve	**doce** dō'se
thirteen	**trece** tre'se
fourteen	**catorce** kätōr'se
fifteen	**quince** kēn'se
sixteen	**dieciséis** dyesēse'ēs
seventeen	**diecisiete** dyesēsye'te
eighteen	**dieciocho** dyesē·ō'tshō
nineteen	**diecinueve** dyesēnōo·e've
twenty	**veinte** ve'ēnte
twenty-one	**veintiuno** ve·ēntē·ōo'nō
twenty-two	**veintidós** ve·ēntēdōs'
twenty-three	**veintitrés** ve·ēntētres'
twenty-four	**veinticuatro** ve·ēntēkōo·ä'trō
thirty	**treinta** tre'ēntä

forty	**cuarenta** kōō·ären'tä
fifty	**cincuenta** sēng·kōō·en'tä
sixty	**sesenta** sesen'tä
seventy	**setenta** seten'tä
eighty	**ochenta** ōtshen'tä
ninety	**noventa** nōven'tä
one hundred	**cien** syen'
one thousand	**mil** mēl
one million	**un millón** ōōn mēlyōn'

DAYS

What day is today?	**¿Qué día es hoy?** ¿ke dē'ä es oi?
It's Monday.	**Es lunes.** es lōō'nes.
… Tuesday.	**… martes.** … mär'tes.
… Wednesday.	**… miércoles.** … myer'kōles.
… Thursday.	**… jueves.** … hōō·e'ves.
… Friday.	**… viernes.** … vyer'nes.
… Saturday.	**… sábado.** … sä'bädō.
… Sunday.	**… domingo.** … dōmēng'gō.

TIME

Time is told by the 24-hour clock. You can also reference the numbers section.

Excuse me. Can you tell me the time?	**Disculpe, ¿podría decirme qué hora es?** dēskōōl'pe, ¿pōdrē'ä deser'me ke ō'rä es?
I'll meet you in …	**Lo/La veré en …** lō/lä vere' en …
ten minutes.	**diez minutos.** dyes' mēnōō'tōs
a quarter of an hour.	**un cuarto de hora.** ōōn kōō·är'tō de ō'rä
a half hour.	**media hora.** me'dyä ō'rä

TIME

three quarters of an hour.	**tres cuartos de hora.** tres kōō·är'tōs de ō'rä
It is five past one.	**Es la una y cinco.** es lä ōō'nä ē sēng'kō.
It is ten past two.	**Son las dos y diez.** sōn läs dōs ē dyes.
It is a quarter past three.	**Son las tres y cuarto.** sōn läs tres ē kōō·är'to.
It is twenty past four.	**Son las cuatro y veinte.** sōn läs kōō·ä'trō ē ve'ēnte.
It is twenty-five past five.	**Son las cinco y veinticinco.** sōn läs sēng'kō ē ve·ēntēsēng'kō.
It is half past six.	**Son las seis y media.** sōn läs se'ēs ē me'dyä.
It is twenty-five to seven.	**Son las siete menos veinticinco.** sōn läs sye'te me'nōs ve·ēntēsēng'kō.
It is twenty to eight.	**Son las ocho menos veinte.** sōn läs ō'tshō me'nōs ve'ēnte.
It is a quarter to nine.	**Son las nueve menos cuarto.** sōn läs nōō·e've me'nōs kōō·är'to.
It is ten to ten.	**Son las diez menos diez.** sōn läs dyes' me'nōs dyes'.
It is five to eleven.	**Son las once menos cinco.** sōn läs ōn'se me'nōs sēng'kō.
It is noon.	**Es mediodía.** es medyōdē'ä.
It is midnight.	**Es medianoche.** es medyänō'tshe.
yesterday	**ayer** äyer'
last night	**anoche** änō'tshe
today	**hoy** oi
tonight	**esta noche** es'tä nō'tshe
tomorrow	**mañana** mänyä'nä
morning	**la mañana** lä mänyä'nä

200

afternoon	**la tarde** lä tär'de
evening	**la tarde/noche** lä tär'de/nō'tshe
night	**la noche** lä nō'tshe
day before yesterday	**anteayer** änte·äyer'
in two/three days	**en dos/tres días** en dōs/tres dē'äs

MONTHS

January	**enero** ene'rō
February	**febrero** febre'rō
March	**marzo** mär'sō
April	**abril** äbrēl'
May	**mayo** mä'yō
June	**junio** hoō'nyō
July	**julio** hoō'lyō
August	**agosto** ägōs'tō
September	**septiembre** septyem'bre
October	**octubre** ōktoō'bre
November	**noviembre** nōvyem'bre
December	**diciembre** dēsyem'bre

Merry Christmas!	**¡Feliz Navidad!** ¡felēs' nävēdäd'!
Happy Easter!	**¡Felices Pascuas!** ¡felē'ses päs'koō·äs!
Happy New Year!	**¡Feliz Año Nuevo!** ¡felēs' ä'nyō noō·e'vō!
Happy Birthday!	**¡Feliz cumpleaños!** ¡felēs' koōmple·ä'nyōs!

COLORS

beige	**beige** be'he
black	**negro** ne'grō
blue	**azul** äsoōl'
brown	**marrón** märōn'
gold	**oro** ō'rō
green	**verde** ver'de
gray	**gris** grēs
yellow	**amarillo** ämärē'lyō

COLORS

orange	**naranja** närän'*h*ä
pink	**rosa** rō'sä
purple	**púrpura** pōōr'pōōrä
red	**rojo** rō'hō
silver	**plata** plä'tä
white	**blanco** bläng'kō

All words and phrases are accompanied by simplified pronunciation. The sound symbols are the ones you are familiar with from your high-school or college dictionaries of the *English* language, but applied here to foreign languages – a unique feature of **Langenscheidt's European Phrasebook**.

PORTUGUESE

Symbol	Approximate Sound	Examples
	VOWELS	
ä	The *a* of *father*.	*nada* nä'dä
e	The *e* of *met* (but tending toward the *a* of *fate*).	*entrada* eNnträ'dä
ō	The *o* of *nose* (but without the "upglide").	*favor* fävōr'
ōō	The *u* of *rule* (but without the "upglide").	*por* pōōr
ə	The neutral sound (unstressed): the *a* of *ago* or the *u* of *focus*.	
N	This symbol does not stand for a sound but shows that the preceding vowel is nasal – is pronounced through nose and mouth at the same time. Nasal sounds have to be learned by listening. (See also below.)	*câmbio* käNm'byōō *tempo* teNm'pōō *vinte* viNn'tə *compreende* kôNmpre-eNndə
	CONSONANTS	
b	The *b* of *bed*.	*barato* bä'rätōō
d	The *d* of *do*.	*direita* dire'itä
f	The *f* of *far*.	*fechado* feshä'dōō

203

Symbol	Approximate Sound	Examples
g	The g of go.	pegar pegär'
k	The k of key, the c of can.	que ke
l	The l of love.	modula mōōshi'lä
m	The m of me.	men me'ōō
n	The n of no.	canada känädä'
ng	The ng of sing.	banco bäng'kōō
p	The p of pin.	posso pō'sōō
r	The r of run, but with a stronger "trill" in many words, especially words with rr.	carro kä'rōō
s	The s of sun.	cidada sidä'də
sh	The sh in wish.	isto ish'tōō
t	The t of toy.	preto pre'tōō
v	The v of vat.	verde ver'də
y	The y of year.	Maio mä'yōō
z	The z of zeal.	Dezembro dezeNm'rōō
zh	The s of measure or the si of vision.	cevejas sere'zhäsh

A special situation in Portuguese is nazalization. The tourist may need most of the following explanation.

N   This symbol **does not stand for a sound** but indicates nazalization. It is used in three situations:

1. N is preceded by a vowel and followed by **m** or **n**: The combination is nazalized, but only slightly, and the **m** or **n** is clearly heard (unlike in French nasals).

an, am	câmbio käNm'byōō, refrigerantes refrizheräNn'tesh
em, en	tempo teNm'pōō, homens ō'meNnsh
im, in	vinte viNn'tə, incluído iNnklōō·i'dōō
om, on	compreende kôNmpre·eNn'də, contra kôNn'trä

In final position, this **m** or **n** may be barely audible.

> bem beNm, bagagem bägä'zheNm
> sim siNm, mim miNm
> bom bôNm, marron märrôNn'
> um ōōNm, algum äl'gōōNm

2. N is preceded by a vowel in the final syllable, but no **m** or **n** follows: The vowel is nazalized.

> irmã irmäN', irmãs irmäNsh', amanhã ämänyäN',
> avõ ävôN'

3. N is shown between two vowels: The first vowel is nazalized and glides into the second (unaccented) vowel.

> não näN'ōō
> alemães älemäN'esh
> cãibra käN'ibrä
> limões limôN'esh

Words of more than one syllable are given with a stress mark.

A raised dot separates two neighboring vowel symbols, and occasionally two consonant symbols. This dot is merely a convenience to the eye; it does not indicate a break in pronunciation.

EVERYDAY EXPRESSIONS

Yes. **Sim.** siNm.

No. **Não.** näN'ōō.

Please. **Por favor.** pōōr fävōr'.

Thank you. **Obrigado/Obrigada.** ōōbrigä'dōō/ōōbrigä'dä.

You're welcome. **De nada.** də nä'dä.

Excuse me. **Com licença.** kôNm lisen'sä.

I beg your pardon. **Desculpe-me/perdão.** dəshkōōl'pem/perdäN'ōō.

Sorry. **Desculpe/sinto muito.** dəshkōōl'pə/siNn'tōō mōō·iNn'tōō.

How much is this/that? **Quanto custa isto/aquele?** kväNn'tōō kōōsh'tä ish'tōō/äke'lə?

What time is it? **Que horas são?** ke ō'räsh säN'ōō?

At what time does the ... open/close? **A que horas o/a ... abre/fecha?** ä ke ō'räsh ōō/ä ... ä'brə/fe'shä?

Where can I find the/a restroom? **Onde eu posso encontrar o/um banheiro?** ôNn'də e'ōō pō'sōō eNnkôNnträr'ōō/ōōNm bänye'irōō?

Is the water safe to drink? **A água é saudável para beber?** ä ä'gōō·ä e sä·ōōdä'vel pä'rä beber'?

Is this free? (city map, museum, etc.) **Isto é gratuito?** ish'tōō e grätōō·i'tōō?

NOTEWORTHY SIGNS

Cautela. kä·ōōte'lä. Caution

GREETINGS

Fechado para reforma.
feshä'dōō pä'rä refôr'mä.

Closed for Restoration

Não tocar. näN'o tōōkär'.

Do Not Touch

Saída de emergência.
sä·ï'dä də emerzheNn'tsyä.

Emergency Exit

Não entrar. näN'ōō eNnträr'.

Do Not Enter

Entrada gratuita. eNnträ'dä grätōō·ï'tä.

Free Admission

Mantenha distância.
mäNnte'nyä dishtäNn'syä

Keep Out

Entrada proibida. eNnträ'dä.

No Entry

Proibido fumar. prō·ibï'dōō fōōmär'.

No Smoking

Aberto de ... à ... äber'tōō də ... ä ...

Open from ... to ...

Água não potável. ä'gōō·ä näN'ōō pōōtä'vel.

Undrinkable Water

Homens. ō'meNnsh.

Men

Mulheres. mōōlye'resh.

Women

GREETINGS

Good morning.	**Bom dia.** bôNm dï'ä.
Good afternoon.	**Boa tarde.** bō'ä tär'də.
Good night.	**Boa noite.** bō'ä nō'itə.
Hello/Hi.	**Olá/Oi.** ōlä'/ō'i.
What's your name?	**Qual é o seu nome?** kväl e ōō se'ōō nō'mə?
My name is ...	**Meu nome é ...** me'ōō nō'mə e ...
How are you?	**Como está você?** kōmeshtä' vōse'?
Fine thanks. And you?	**Bem obrigado/obrigada. E você?** beNm ōōbrigä'dōō/ōōbrigä'dä. e vōse'?

PORTUGUESE

Where are you from?	**De onde você é?** də ôNn'də vōse' e?
I'm from …	**Eu sou de …** e'ōō sō'ōō də …
It was nice meeting you.	**Foi um prazer conhecer você.** fō'i ōōNm präser' kōnyeser' vōse'.
Good-bye.	**Adeus.** äde'ōōsh.
Have a good trip.	**Faça uma boa viagem.** fä'sä ōō'mä bō'ä vi·ä'zheNm.
Miss	**Senhora** senyō'rä
Mrs./Madam	**Senhora/Madame** senyō'rä/mädäm'ə
Mr./Sir	**Senhor.** senyōr'

CONVERSING & GETTING TO KNOW PEOPLE

Do you speak English/French/Italian/German/Spanish?	**Você fala Inglês/Francês/Italiano/Alemão/Espanhol?** vōse' fä'lä inglesh'/fränsesh'/itälyä'nōō/äləmäN'ōō/eshpänyōl?
I don't understand.	**Eu não compreendo.** e'ōō näN'ōō kôNmpre·eNn'dōō.
Could you speak more slowly please?	**Você poderia falar mais devagar, por favor?** vōse' pōōderi'ä fälär' mä'ish devägär, pōōr fävôr'?
Could you repeat that please?	**Você poderia repetir isto, por favor?** vōse' pōōderi'ä repetir' ish'tōō, pōōr fävôr'?
I don't speak French/Italian/German/Spanish.	**Eu não falo Francês/Italiano/Alemão/Espanhol.** e'ōō näN'ōō fä'lōō fränsesh'/itälyä'nōō/äləmäN'ōō/eshpänyōl'.
Is there someone here who speaks English?	**Tem alguém aqui que fala Inglês?** teNm älgeNm' äki'ke fä'lä inglesh'?
Do you understand?	**Você compreende?** vōse' kôNmpre·eNn'də?

209

Just a moment. I'll see if I can find it in my phrasebook.

Um momento. Eu verei se posso encontrá-lo/la no meu manual de expressões. ōōNm mōōneNn'tōō. e'ōō vere'i se pō'sōō eNnkôNnträ'-lōō/lä nōō me'ōō mänōō-äl' də eshpresôN'esh.

Please point to your question/answer in the book.

Por favor, indique a sua pergunta/resposta no livro. pōōr fävôr, iNndi'ke ä sōō'ä pergōōNn'tä/resh'pôshtä nōō liv'rōō.

My name is ... What's yours?

Meu nome é ... Qual é o seu? me'ōō nô'mə e ... kväl e ōō se'ōō?

It's nice to meet you.

É um prazer conhecer você. e ōōNm präzer' kōnyeser' vōse'.

This is my friend (female)/sister/wife/daughter.

Esta é minha amiga/irmã/esposa/filha. esh'tä e mi'nyä ämi'gä/irmäN'/eshpō'sä/fil'yä.

This is my friend (male)/brother/husband/son.

Este é meu amigo/irmão/esposo /filho. esh'tə e me'ōō ämi'gōō/irmäN'ōō/eshpō'sōō/fil'yōō.

Where are you from?

De onde você é ? də ôNn'də vōse'e?

What city?

Que cidade? ke sidä'də?

I'm from the United States/Canada/Australia/England.

Eu sou dos Estados Unidos/Canadá/Australia/Inglaterra. e'ōō sō'ōō dōsh eshtä'dōōsh ōōni'dōōsh/känädä'/ä-ōōshträ'lyä/ingläte'rä.

Are you here on vacation?

Você está aqui em férias? vōse' eshtä' aki' eNm fe'ri·äsh?

Do you like it here?

Você gosta daqui? vōse' gōōsh'tä däki'?

How long have you been here?

A quanto tempo você está aqui? ä kräNn'tōō teNm'pōō vōse' eshtä' aki'?

I just got here.	**Eu terminei de chegar.** e'o͞o termine'i də shegär' …
I've been here for … days.	**Eu estou aqui à … dias.** e'o͞o eshto'o͞o äki' ä … di'äsh.
I love it.	**Eu adoro.** e'o͞o ädo'ro͞o.
It's okay.	**Está bem.** eshtä' beNm.
I don't like it.	**Eu não gosto.** e'o͞o näN'o͞o gösh'to͞o.
It's too noisy/crowded/ dirty/boring.	**Está muito barulhento/cheio/sujo/chato.** estä' mo͞o·iNn'to͞o bäro͞olyeNn'to͞o/she'i·o͞o/ so͞o'zho͞o/shä'to͞o.
Where are you staying?	**Onde você está hospedado?** ôNn'də vōse' eshtä'o͞oshpedä'do͞o?
I'm staying at the … youth hostel/camp-ground.	**Eu estou hospedado no albergue da juventude/acampamento …** e'o͞o eshto'o͞o o͞oshpedä'do͞o no͞o älber'gə dä zho͞oveNntoo'də/ äkäNmpämeNn'to͞o …
Where were you before you came here?	**Onde você estava antes de vir para cá?** ôNn'də vōse' eshtä'vä äNn'tesh də vir pä'rä kä?
Did you stay at a youth hostel/campground there?	**Você ficou hospedado em um albergue da juventude/acampamento lá?** vōse' fiko'o͞o o͞oshpedä'do͞o eNm o͞oNm älber'gə dä zho͞oveNntoo'də/äkäNmpämeNn'to͞o lä?
Did you like that city/ country/youth hos-tel/campground?	**Você gostou desta/e cidade/país/ albergue da juventude/acampamento?** vōse' go͞oshto'o͞o desh'tä/e sidä'də/pä·ish'/ älber'gə dä zho͞oveNntoo'də/äkäNmpämeNn'to͞o?
Why not?	**Por que não?** po͞or ke näN'o͞o?
Where are you going from here?	**Para onde você vai daqui?** pä'rä ôNn'də vōse' vä'i däki'?

USEFUL WORDS & EXPRESSIONS

Did you ever stay at the youth hostel in …?
Você já se hospedou no albergue da juventude em …? vōse' zhä se ōōshpedō'ōō nō älber'gə dä zhōōveNntōō'də eNm …?

I'm going there next.
Eu estou indo para lá depois. e'ōō eshtō'ōō iNn'dōō pä'rä lä depō'ish.

It was nice meeting you.
Foi um prazer conhecer você. fō'i ōōNm präzer' kōnyeser' vōse'.

Here is my address. Write to me sometime.
Aqui está o meu endereço. Escreva para mim algum dia. äki' eshtä' ōō me'ōō eNndere'sōō. eshkre'vä pä'rä miNm äl'gōōNm di'ä.

May I have your address? I'll write to you.
Eu posso ter o seu endereço? Eu escreverei para você. e'ōō pō'sōō ter ōō se'ōō eNndere'sōō? e'ōō eshkrevere'i pä'rä vōse'.

USEFUL WORDS & EXPRESSIONS

Is it …?
É …/está …? e …/eshtä' …?

Is it … or …?
É …/está …ou …? e …/eshtä' … ō'ōō …?

It is …
É …/está … e …/eshtä' …

cheap/expensive	**barato/caro** bärä'tōō/kä'rōō
early/late	**cedo/tarde** se'dōō/tär'də
near/far	**perto/longe** per'tōō/lôN'zhə
open/closed	**aberto/fechado** äber'tōō/feshä'dōō
right/left	**direita/esquerda** dire'itä/eshker'dä
vacant/occupied	**desocupado/ocupado** dezōkōōpä'dōō/ōkōōpä'dōō

entrance/exit
entrada/saída enträ'dä/sä·i'dä

with/without
com/sem kôNm/seNm

ARRIVAL & DEPARTURE

Your passport please. **Seu passaporte, por favor.**
se'oo päsäpōr'tə, pōōr fävōr'.

I'm here on vacation/ **Eu estou aqui em férias/negócios.**
business. e'oo eshtō'oo aki' eNm fe'ri·äsh/negō'syoōsh.

I have nothing to **Eu não tenho nada a declarar.**
declare. e'oo näN'oo te'nyoo nä'dä ä deklärär'.

I'll be staying … **Eu ficarei …** e'oo fikäre'i …

  a week   **uma semana** oo'mä semä'nä
  two/three weeks **duas/três semanas**
       doo'äsh/tresh semä'nyäsh

  a month   **um mês** oomesh'
  two/three months **dois/três meses** dō'ish/tresh me'zesh

That's my backpack. **Esta é a minha mochila.**
esh'tä e ä mi'nyä mōōshi'lä.

Where can I catch a **Onde eu posso pegar um autocarro/**
bus/the subway into **metro para a cidade?** ôNn'də e'oo pō'soo
town? pegär' oōNm ä-oōtōkä'rōō/me'trōō pä'rä ä
       sidä'də?

Which number do I **Que número eu pego?**
take? ke noō'merōō e'oo pe'gōō?

Which stop do I get off **Em que paragem de carro eu desço para**
for the center of town? **o centro da cidade?** eNm ke pärä'zheNm də
       kä'rōō e'oo de'shōō pä'rä oo seNn'trōō dä sidä'də?

Can you let me know **Você pode me avisar quando nós**
when we get to that **chegarmos nesta paragem de carro?**
stop? vōse' pō'də me ävizär' kväNn'dōō nōsh
       shegär'mōōsh nesh'tä pärä'zheNm də kä'rōō?

Where is gate num- **Onde está o portão de número …?**
ber …? ôNn'də eshtä' oo pōōrtäN'oo də noō'merōō …?

CHANGING MONEY

CHANGING MONEY

Excuse me, can you tell me where the nearest bank is?	**Com licença, você pode me dizer onde fica o banco mais próximo?** kôNm lisen'sä, vōse' pō'də mə dizer' ôNn'də fi'kä ōō bäN'kōō mä'ish prō'simōō?
… money exchange is?	**… casa de câmbio?** … kä'zä də käNm'byōō?
… cash machine is?	**… caixa automático?** … kä'shä ä·ōōtōmä'tikōō?
I would like to exchange this currency.	**Eu gostaria de trocar este dinheiro.** e'ōō gōōshtäri'ä də trōōkär' esh'tə dinye'irōō.
I would like to exchange these traveler's checks.	**Eu gostaria de trocar este traveller's cheque/cheque de viagem.** e'ōō gōōshtäri'ä də trōōkär' esh'tə tre'vəlers she'kə/she'kə də vi·ä'zheNm.
What is your exchange rate for U.S. dollars/traveler's checks?	**Qual é a sua taxa de câmbio para o dólar Americano/traveller's cheque/cheque de viagem?** kväl e ä sōō'ä tä'shä də käNm'byōō pä'rä ōō dō'lär ämerikä'nōō/tre'vəlers she'kə/she'kə də vi·ä'zheNm?
What is your commission rate?	**Qual é a sua taxa de comissão?** kväl e ä sōō'ä tä'shä də kōōmisäN'ōō?
Is there a service charge?	**Tem taxa de serviço?** teNm tä'shä də servi'sōō?
I would like a cash advance on my credit card.	**Eu gostaria de um dinheiro adiantado no meu cartão de crédito.** e'ōō gōōshtäri'ä də ōōNm dinye'irōō ädyäNntä'dōō nōō me'ōō kärtäN'ōō də kre'ditōō.
I would like small/large bills.	**Eu gostaria de notas pequenas/grandes.** e'ōō gōōstäri'ä də nō'täsh peke'näsh/grän'desh.

214

I think you made a mistake.	**Eu acho que você se enganou.** e'ōō ä'shōō ke vōse' se eng·gäno'ōō.

YOUTH HOSTELS

Excuse me, can you direct me to the youth hostel?	**Com licença, você pode me direcionar para o albergue da juventude?** kôNm lisen'sä, vōse' po'də me direksyōōnär' pä'rä ōō älber'gə dä zhōōveNntōō'də?
Do you have any beds available?	**Você tem camas disponíveis?** vōse' teNm kä'mäsh dispōōni've·ish?
For one man/two men.	**Para um homem/dois homens.** pärä ōōNm ō'meNn/dō'ish ō'meNnsh.
For one woman/two women.	**Para uma mulher/duas mulheres.** pära ōōmä mōōlyer'/dōō'äsh mōōlye'resh.
We'd like to be in the same room.	**Nós gostaríamos de ficar no mesmo quarto.** nōsh gōōshtäri'ämōōsh də fikär nōō mezh'mōō kvär'tōō.
How much is it per night?	**Quanto custa por noite?** kväNn'tōō kōōsh'tä pōōr nō'itə?
Is there a limit on how many nights I/we can stay?	**Tem um limite na quantidade de noites em que eu posso/nós podemos ficar?** teNm ōōNm limi'tə nä kväNntidä'də də nō'itesh eNmke e'ōō pōsōō/nōsh pōōde'mōōsh fikär'?
I'll/We'll be staying …	**Eu ficarei/nós ficaremos …** e'ōō fikäre·i/ nōsh fikäre'mōōsh …
tonight only	**apenas hoje à noite** äpe'näsh ō'zhə ä nō'itə
two/three nights	**duas/três noites** dōō'äsh/tresh nō'itesh
four/five nights	**quatro/cinco noites** kvä'trōō/sing'kōō nō'itesh
a week	**uma semana** ōō'mä semä'nä

YOUTH HOSTELS

Does it include breakfast?

Isto inclue pequeno almoço?
ish'tōō in'klōō·e peke'nōō älmō'sōō?

Do you serve lunch and dinner?

Vocês servem almoço e jantar?
vōsesh' ser'veNm älmō'sōō e zhäNntär'?

What are the hours for breakfast/lunch/dinner?

Quais são os horários para o pequeno almoço/almoço/jantar? kväish säN'ōō ōsh ōrär'yōsh pä'rä ōō peke'nōō älmō'sōō/älmō'sōō/zhäNntär'?

What are the lockout hours?

A que horas a portaria fecha?
ä ke ō'räsh ä pōōrtäri'ä fe'shä?

Can I leave my bags here during lockout?

Eu posso deixar as minhas malas aqui durante o fechamento da portaria?
e'ōō pō'sōō deshär' äsh mi'nyäsh mä'läsh äki' dōōräNn'tə ōō feshämeNn'tōō dä pōōrtäri'ä?

Do I take my key with me or leave it with you when I go out?

Eu levo a minha chave comigo ou a - deixo com vocês quando sair?
e'ōō le'vōō ä mi'nyä shä've kōōmi'gōō ō'ōō ä de'ishōō kôNm vōsesh' kväNndōō sä'ir?

Do you have lockers?

Vocês tem guarda-volumes?
vōsesh' teNm gōō·är'dä-vōlōō'mesh?

What time is the curfew?

A que horas é o toque de recolher?
ä ke ō'räsh e ōō tō'kə də rekōlyer'?

What time is checkout?

A que horas encerra a diária?
ä ke ō'räsh ense'rä ä di·är'yä?

Are there cooking/laundry facilities?

Tem instalações para cozinhar/lavar roupa? teNm iNnstäläsôN'esh pä'rä kōōzinyär/lävär' rō'ōōpä?

Is there a reduction for children?

Tem redução/desconto para crianças?
teNm redōōsäN'ōō/deshkôNn'tōō pä'rä kri·äN'säsh?

HOTEL OR OTHER ACCOMMODATIONS

Vagas/não temos vagas.　　　　　　vacancy/no vacancy
väˈgäsh/näNˈoo teˈmoosh väˈgäsh.

Quartos para alugar.　　　　　　　rooms for rent
kvärˈtoosh päˈrä äloogärˈ.

Fechado para férias. feshäˈdoo päˈrä feˈri-äsh.　Closed for Vacation

I'm looking for …	**Eu estou procurando …** eˈoo eshtoˈoo prökooräNnˈdoo …
an inexpensive hotel	**um hotel barato** oomöteľ bäräˈtoo
a pension	**uma pensão** ooˈmä peNnsäNˈoo
a room	**um quarto** ooNm kvärˈtoo
I have a reservation.	**Eu tenho uma reserva.** eˈoo teˈnyoo ooˈmä reserˈvä.
Do you have a room for tonight?	**Você tem um quarto para hoje à noite?** vöseˈ teNm ooNm kvärˈtoo päˈrä oˈzhə ä nöˈitə?
I'd like your cheapest room.	**Eu gostaria de ficar com o seu quarto mais barato.** eˈoo göoshtäriˈä də fikärˈ kôNm oo seˈoo krärˈtoo mäˈish bäräˈtoo.
I'd like a single/double room …	**Eu gostaria de um quarto individual/casal …** eˈoo göoshtäriˈä də ooNm kvärˈtoo iNndividoo-äľ/käzäľ …
with a private bath.	**com um banheiro privado.** kôNm ooNm bänyeˈiroo priväˈdoo
with a shared bath.	**com um banheiro coletivo.** kôNm ooNm bänyeˈiroo kölektiˈvoo
for … days/a week.	**por … dias/uma semana.** poor … diˈäsh/ooˈmä semäˈnä
How much is the room?	**Quanto custa o quarto?** kväNnˈtoo kooshˈtä oo kvärˈtoo?

217

CAMPING ACCOMMODATIONS

May I see the room?	**Eu posso ver o quarto?** e'oo pō'soo ver oo kvär'too?
Does it include break-fast?	**Inclue pequeno almoço?** iNn'klōō·e peke'nōō älmō'sōō?
I'll take it.	**Eu ficarei com ele.** e'oo fikäre'i kôNm el'ə.
Do you have anything cheaper?	**Você tem alguma coisa mais barata?** vōse' teNm älgōō'mä kō'izä mä'ish bärä'tä?
What time is check-out?	**A que horas encerra a diária?** ä ke ō'räsh ense'rä ä di·är'yä?

CAMPING ACCOMMODATIONS

Can you direct me to the nearest camp-ground?	**Você pode me direcionar para o acampamento mais próximo?** vōse' pō'də me direksyōōnär' pä'rä ōō äkôNmpämeNn'tōō mä'ish prō'simōō?
How much is it per night/per person/per tent?	**Quanto custa por noite/por pessoa/por barraca?** KväNn'tōō kōōsh'tä pōōr nō'itə/pōōr pesō'ä/pōōr bärä'kä?
Are showers included?	**Duchas estão incluídas?** dōō'shäsh eshtäN'ōō iNnklōō'däsh?
Where can I buy a shower token?	**Onde eu posso comprar uma ficha para a ducha?** ôNn'də e'ōō pō'sōō kôNmprär' ōō'mä fi'shä pä'rä ä dōō'shä?
How much are they?	**Quanto custam?** kväNn'tōō kōōsh'täNm?
How many do I need?	**Quantas eu preciso?** kväNn'täsh e'ōō presi'zōō?
Are there cooking/laundry facilities?	**Tem instalações para cozinhar/lavar roupa?** teNm instäläsôN'esh pä'rä kōōzinyär/lävär' rō'ōōpä?

SIGNS

Can we rent a bed/mattress/tent?	**Nós podemos alugar uma cama/colchão/barraca?** nōsh pōōde'mōōsh älōōgär' ōō'mä kä'mä/kōlshäN'ōō/bärä'kä?
May we light a fire?	**Nós podemos acender um fogo?** nōsh pōōde'mōōsh äseNnder' ōōNm fō'gōō?
Where can I find …	**Onde eu posso encontrar …** ôNn'də e'ōō pō'sōō eNnkôNnträr' …

the drinking water?
água potável? ä'gōō·ä pōōtä'vel?

a camping equipment store?
uma loja com equipamentos para acampamento? ōō'mä lō'zhä kôNm ekipameNn'tōōsh pä'rä äkäNmpämeNn'tōō?

a grocery store?
uma mercearia? ōō'mä merse·äri'ä?

a bank?
um banco? ōōNm bäng'kōō?

the laundry facilities?
uma lavanderia? ōō'mä läväNnderi'ä?

a telephone?
um telefone? ōōNm telefō'nə?

a restaurant?
um restaurante? ōōNm reshtä·ōōräNnt'?

electric hook-ups?
extensão eléctrica? eshtensäN'ōō elek'trikä?

Is there a swimming pool?	**Tem piscina?** teNm pishi'nä?
How much does it cost?	**Quanto custa isto?** kväNn'tōō kōōsh'tä ish'tōō?
May we camp here/over there?	**Nós podemos acampar aqui/lá?** nōsh pōōde' mōōsh äkäNmpär' äki'/lä?

SIGNS

Proibido acampar prō·ibi'dōō äkäNmpär'	No Camping
Proibido ultrapassar prō·ibi'dōō ōōlträpäsär'	No Trespassing
Propriedade privada prōpri·edä'də privä'dä	Private Property

219

CAMPING EQUIPMENT

I'd like to buy a/an/ some …	**Eu gostaria de comprar um/uma/algum/ alguma …** e'ōō gōōshtäri'ä də kôNmprär' ōōNm/ōō'mä/al'gōōNm/älgōō'mä …
I'd like to rent a/an/ some …	**Eu gostaria de alugar um/uma/algum/ alguma …** e'ōō gōōshtäri'ä də älōōgär' ōōNm/ ōō'mä/äl'gōōNm/älgōōmä …

air mattress/air mattresses.	**colchão de ar/colchões de ar.** kōlshäN'ōō də är/kōlshôN'esh də är
butane gas.	**gás butano.** gäsh bōōtä'nōō
charcoal.	**carvão.** kärväN'ōō
compass.	**bússola.** bōō'sōlä
eating utensils.	**utensílios para comida.** ōōtensi'lyōōsh pä'rä kōōmi'dä
flashlight.	**lâmpada/holofote.** läNm'pädä/ōōlōōfō'tə
folding chairs/ table.	**cadeiras/mesas dobráveis.** käde'iräsh/ me'zäsh dōōbrä've·ish
ground sheet.	**toalha de piquenique.** tō·ä'lyä də pikeni'kə
ice pack.	**pacote de gelo.** päkō'tə də zhe'lōō
insect spray.	**spray contra insectos.** sprä'i kôNn'trä insek'tōs
kerosene.	**querosene.** kerōōse'nə
lantern.	**lanterna.** läNnter'nä
matches.	**fósforos.** fōsh'fōōrōōsh
rope.	**corda.** kōr'dä
sleeping bag.	**saco de dormir.** sä'kōō də dōōrmir'
soap.	**sabonete.** säbōōne'tə
tent.	**barraca.** bärä'kä
towel/towels.	**toalha/toalhas.** tō·ä'lyä/tō·ä'lyäsh

PORTUGUESE

CHECKING OUT

I'd like to check out. May I have my bill please?	**Eu gostaria de encerrar a minha estadia. Eu posso ter a minha conta, por favor?** e'ōō gōōshtäri'ä də enserär' ä mi'nyä eshtädi'ä. e'ōō pō'sōō ter ä mi'nyä kôNn'tä, pōōr fävōr?
Could you give me a receipt.	**Você poderia me dar um recibo?** vōse' pōōderi'ä me där ōōNm resi'bōō?
Could you explain this item/charge?	**Você poderia me explicar este item/ esta conta?** vōse' pōōderi'ä me eshplikär' esh'tə i'teNm/esh'täk kôNn'tä?
Thank you.	**Obrigado/Obrigada.** ōōbrigä'dōō/ōōbrigä'dä.
I enjoyed my stay.	**Eu gostei da minha estadia.** e'ōō gōōshte'i dä mi'nyä eshtädi'ä.
We enjoyed our stay.	**Nós gostamos da nossa estadia.** nōsh gōōshtä'mōōsh dä nō'sä eshtädi'ä.

TRANSPORTATION BY AIR

Is there a bus/train to the airport?	**Tem um autocarro/comboio para o aeroporto?** teNm ōōNm ä-ōōtōkä'rōō/ kôNmbō'yōō pä'rä ōō ä-erōpōr'tōō?
At what time does it leave?	**A que horas ele parte?** ä ke ō'räsh el'ə pär'tə?
How long does it take to get there?	**Quanto tempo ele leva para chegar até lá?** kväNn'tōō teNm'pōō el'ə le'vä pä'rä shegär' äte' lä?
Is there an earlier/later bus/train?	**Tem um autocarro/comboio mais cedo/ mais tarde?** teNm ōōNm ä-ōōtōkä'rōō/ kôNmbō'yōō mä'ish se'dōō/mä'ish tär'də?

221

RIDING THE BUS & SUBWAY

How much does it cost?	**Quanto custa isto?** kväNn'tōō kōōsh'tä ish'tōō?
I'd like a flight to …	**Eu gostaria de um vôo para …** e'ōō gōōshtäri'ä də ōōNm vō'ōō pä'rä …
a one-way/round trip ticket	**um bilhete de uma só mão/ida e volta** ōōNm bilye'te də ōō'mä sō mäNōō/ī'dä e vōl'tä.
your cheapest fare	**sua tarifa mais barata** sōō'ä täri'fä mä'ish bärä'tä
an aisle/window seat	**um assento no corredor/na janela** ōōNm äseNn'tōō nōō kōredōr'/nä zhäne'lä
Is there a bus/train to the center of town?	**Tem um autocarro/comboio para o centro da cidade?** teNm ōōNm ä-ōōtōkä'rōō/ kôNmbō'yōō pä'rä ōō seNn'trōō dä sidä'də?

RIDING THE BUS & SUBWAY

Could you tell me where the nearest bus/subway station is?	**Você poderia me dizer onde fica a estação de autocarro/metro mais próxima?** vōse' pōōderi'ä me dizer' ôNn'də fi'kä ä eshtäsäN'ōō də ä-ōōtōkä'rōō/me'trōō mä'ish prō'simä?
Could you tell me where the nearest bus/subway stop is?	**Você poderia me dizer onde fica a paragem de autocarro/a estação de metro mais próxima?** vōse' pōōderi'ä me dizer' ôNn'də fi'kä ä pärä'zheNm də ä-ōōtōkä'rōō/ ä eshtäsäN'ōō də me'trōō mä'ish prō'simä?
Where can I buy a ticket?	**Onde eu posso comprar um bilhete?** ôNn'də e'ōō pō'sōō kôNmprär' ōōNm bilye'tə?
How much does it cost?	**Quanto custa isto?** kväNn'tōō kōōsh'tä ish'tōō?

222

PORTUGUESE

Can I use this ticket for the subway and the bus?	**Eu posso usar este bilhete para o metro e o autocarro?** e'ōō pô'sōō ōōzär' esh'tə bilye'tə pä'rä ōō me'trōō e ōō ä-ōōtōkä'rōō?
I'd like to buy … tickets.	**Eu gostaria de comprar … bilhetes.** e'ōō gōōshtäri'ä de kôNmprär' … bilye'tesh.
I'd like to buy a book of tickets/weekly pass.	**Eu gostaria de comprar uma caderneta de módulos/um bilhete semanal.** e'ōō gōōshtäri'ä de kôNmprär' ōō'mä käderne'tä də mō'dōōlōōsh/ōōNm bilye'tə semänäl'.
Which bus/train do I take to get to …?	**Qual é o autocarro/comboio que eu pego para ir para …?** kväl e ōō ä-ōōtōkä'rōō/kôNmbō'yōō ke e'ōō pe'gōō pä'rä ir pä'rä …?
Do I have to change buses/trains to get to …?	**Eu tenho que trocar de autocarro/comboio para ir para …?** e'ōō te'nyōō ke trōōkär' də ä-ōōtōkä'rōō/kôNmbō'yōō pä'rä ir pä'rä …?
When is the next/last bus/train to …?	**Quando é o próximo/último autocarro/comboio para …?** kväNn'dōō e ōō prô'simōō/ōōl'timōō ä-ōōtōkä'rōō/kôNmbō'yōō pä'rä …?
Can you tell me when we reach …?	**Você pode me dizer quando nós chegarmos …?** vōse' pô'də me dizer' kväNn'dōō nōsh shegär'mōōsh …?
Do I get off here for …?	**Eu desço aqui para …?** e'ōō de'shōō äki' pä'rä …?
Please let me off here.	**Por favor, me deixe aqui.** pōōr fävōr', me de'ishə äki'.

TRAIN-STATION & AIRPORT SIGNS

Chegada shegä'dä	Arrival
Guiché de bagagem gishe' də bägä'zheNm	Baggage Check
Coleta de bagagem kōōle'tä də bägä'zheNm	Baggage Pick-up

223

TAKING THE TRAIN

Mudar/Trocar mōōdär′/trōōkär′	Change
Alfândega älfäNn′degä	Customs
Partida pärti′dä	Departure
Entrada enträ′dä	Entrance
Saída sä·ĭ′dä	Exit
Informação infôrmäsäN′ōō	Information
Achados & Perdidos äshä′dōōsh e perdi′dōōsh	Lost & Found
Cacife käsi′fə	Luggage Lockers
Proibido Fumar prō·ibi′dōō fōōmär′	No Smoking
Reservas rezer′väsh	Reservations
Bilhetes bilye′tesh	Tickets
Banheiros bänye′irōōsh	Toilets
Para as Plataformas/os Comboios pä′rä äsh plätäfôr′mäsh/ōōsh kôNmbô′yōōsh	To the Platforms/ Trains
Sala de Espera sä′lä də eshpe′rä	Waiting Room

TAKING THE TRAIN

Could you tell me where the train station is?	**Você poderia me dizer onde fica a estação de comboio?** vōse′ pōōderi′ä me dizer′ ôNn′də fi′kä ä eshtasäN′ōō də kôNmbô′yōō?
Could I have a train schedule to …	**Eu poderia ter um horário de comboio para …?** e′ōō pōōderi′ä ter ōōNm ōrär′yō də kôNmbô′yōō pä′rä …?

I would like to reserve a seat/couchette in 1st/2nd class.	**Eu gostaria de reservar um assento/ carruagem/beliche na primeira/segunda classe.** e'ōō gōōshtäri'ä də rezervär' ōōNm äseNn'tōō/kärōō-ä'zhəNm/beli'shə nä prime'irä/ segōōn'dä klä'sə.
one-way/round trip	**bilhete de uma só mão/bilhete de ida e volta** bilye'tə də ōō'mä sō mäN'ōō/bilye'tə də i'dä e vōl'tä
smoking/non-smoking	**fumante/não fumante** fōōmäNn'tə/näN'ōō fōōmäNn'tə
aisle/window seat	**assento no corredor/na janela** äseNn'tōō nōō kōredōr'/nä zhäne'lä
At what time does the night train to … leave?	**A que horas o comboio noturno para … parte?** ä ke ō'räsh ōō kôNmbō'yōō nōōtōōr'nōō pä'rä … pär'tə?
At what time does it arrive?	**A que horas ele chega?** ä ke ō'räsh el'ə she'gä?
Do I have to change trains? At what stop?	**Eu tenho que trocar de comboios? Em que estação?** e'ōō te'nyōō ke trōōkär' də kôNmbō'yōōsh? eNm ke eshtäsäNōō?
I have a rail pass. Must I pay a supplement to ride this train?	**Eu tenho rail pass . Eu preciso pagar um complemento para andar neste comboio?** e'ōō te'nyōō rel pes. e'ōō presi'zōō pä'gär ōōNm kôNmplemeNn'tōō pä'rä äNndär' nesh'tə koNmbō'yōō?
Could you tell me where platform/ track … is?	**Você poderia me dizer onde a plataforma/via …está?** vōse' pōōderi'ä me dizer' ôNn'də ä plätäfōr'mä/vi'ä … eshtä'?
Could you tell me where car number … is?	**Você poderia me dizer onde o vagão de número … está?** vōse' pōōderi'ä me dizer' ôNn'də ōō vägäN'ōō də nōō'merōō … eshtä'?

TAKING THE TRAIN

Could you help me find my seat/couchette, please?

Você poderia me ajudar a encontrar meu assento/carruagem, por favor? vōse' pōō' deri'ä me äzhōōdär' ä eNnkôNnträr me'ōō äseNn'tōō/kärōō·ä'zheNm, pōōr fävōr?

Is this seat taken?

Este assento está ocupado? esh'tə äseNn'tōō eshtä' ōkōōpä'dōō?

Excuse me, I think this is my seat.

Com licença, eu acho que este é o meu assento. kôNm lisen'sä, e'ōō ä'shōō ke esh'tə e ō me'ōō äseNn'tōō.

Could you save my seat, please?

Você poderia guardar meu assento, por favor? vōse' pōōderi'ä gōō·ärdär' me'ōō äseNn'tōō, pōōr fävōr?

Where is the dining car?

Onde está o vagão - restaurante? ôNn'də eshtä' ōō vägäN'ōō-restä·ōōräN'tə?

Where are the toilets?

Onde estão os banheiros? ôNn'də eshtäN'ōō ōsh bänye'irōōsh?

**For Europass and Flexipass users. With these passes you will only have access to certain countries. If your train goes through a country that is not on your pass, you will be required to pay an extra fare.

My rail pass only covers Spain/Portugal/France/Italy/Switzerland/Germany/Austria.

Meu rail pass apenas cobre Espanha/Portugal/França/Itália/Suíça/Alemanha/Austria. me'ōō rel pes äpe'näsh kō'brə espä'nyä/pōrtōōgäl'/frän'sä/itä'lyä/sōō·i'sä/älemä'nyä/ä'ōōshtri·ä.

How much extra do I have to pay since my train goes through …?

Quanto eu tenho que pagar uma vez que meu comboio passa por …? kväNn'tōō e'ōō te'nyōō ke pägär' ōō'mä vez ke me'ōō kôNmbō'yōō pä'sä pōōr …?

Is there another way to get to … without having to go through …?	**Tem outro caminho para ir para … sem ter que passar por …?** teNm ō'ōōtrō kämi'nyōō pä'rä ir pä'rä … seNm ter päsär' pōōr …?

BY BOAT

Is there a boat that goes to …?	**Tem um barco que vai para …?** teNm ōōNm bär'kōō ke vä'i pä'rä …?
When does the next/last boat leave?	**Quando o próximo/último barco parte?** kväNn'dōō ōō prō'simō/ōōl'timōō bär'kōō pär'te?
I have a rail pass. Do I get a discount?	**Eu tenho um rail pass. Eu tenho um desconto?** e'ōō tenyōō ōōNm rel pes. e'ōō te'nyōō ōōNm deshkôNn'tōō?
How much?	**Quanto custa?** kväNn'tōō kōōsh'tä?
At what time does the boat arrive?	**A que horas o barco chega?** ä ke ō'räsh ōō bär'kōō she'gä?
How early must I get on board?	**A que horas eu preciso estar no embarque?** ä ke ō'räsh e'ōō presi'zōō eshtär' nōō eNmbär'ke?
Can I buy seasickness pills nearby?	**Posso comprar um remédio contra enjôo/maresia aqui perto?** pō'sōō kôNmprär' ōōNm reme'di·ōō kôNn'trä enzho'ōō/märezi'ä äki' per'tōō?

GETTING AROUND BY CAR

I'd like to rent a car …	**Eu gostaria de alugar um carro …** e'ōō gōōshtäri'ä de älōōgär' ōōNm kä'rōō …
for … days.	**por … dias.** pōōr … di'äsh
for a week.	**por uma semana.** pōōr ōō'mä semä'nä

What is your daily/ weekly rate?	**Qual é sua tarifa diária/semanal?** kväl e sōō'ä täri'fä di·är'yä/semänäl'?
Do I need insurance?	**Eu preciso de um seguro?** e'ōō presi'zōō də ōōNm segōō'rōō?
Is mileage included?	**A quilometragem está incluída?** ä kilōōmeträ'zheNm eshtä' iNnklōō·i'dä?
How much is it?	**Quanto custa?** kväNn'tōō kōōsh'tä?

ROAD SIGNS

Pare. pä'rə	Stop
Sentido único seNnti'dōō ōō'nikōō	One Way
Proibido a entrada prō·ibi'dōō ä eNnträ'dä	Do Not Enter
Prioridade pri·ōridä'də	Yield
Estacionamento proibido eshtäsyönämeNn'tōō pro·ibi'dōō	No Parking

TAXI

I'd like to go to …	**Eu gostaria de ir para …** e'ōō gōōshtäri'ä də ir pä'rä …
What is the fare?	**Qual é a tarifa?** kväl e ä täri'fä?
Please stop here.	**Por favor, pare aqui.** pōōr fävōr', pä'rə aki'.
Can you wait for me?	**Você pode me esperar?** vōse' pō'də me eshperär'?

GETTING AROUND ON FOOT

Excuse me, could you tell me how to get to …?	**Com licença, você poderia me dizer como ir para …?** kôNm lisen'sä, vōse' pōōderi'ä me dizer' kō'mōō ir pä'rä …?

228

Is it nearby/far? **É aqui perto/longe?** e äui' per'tōō/lôN'zhə?

Can I walk or should I take the bus/subway? **Eu posso ir a pé ou eu deveria pegar um autocarro/metro?** e'ōō pô'soo ir ä pe ō'ōō e'ōō deveri'ä pegär' ōōNm ä-ōōtōkä'rōō/me'trōō?

Could you direct me to the nearest bus/subway station/stop? **Você poderia me direcionar para a paragem de autocarro/estação de metro mais próxima?** vōse' pōōderi'ä me direk-syōōnär' pä'rä ä pärä'zhəNm de ä-ōōtōkä'rōō/eshtäsäN'ōō də me'trōō mä'ish prō'simä?

Straight ahead. **Siga em frente.** si'gä eNm freNn'tə.

Go right/left. **Vá à direita/esquerda.** vä ä dire'itä/eshker'dä.

At the corner/traffic light. **Na esquina/no semáforo.** nä eshki'nä/nōō semä'fōōrōō.

I'm lost. **Eu estou perdido/perdida.** e'ōō eshtō'ōō perdi'dōō/perdi'dä.

Could you show me where we are on this map? **Você poderia me mostrar onde nós estamos neste mapa?** vōse' pōōderi'ä me mōōshträr' ôNndə nōsh eshtä'mōōsh nesh'tə mä'pä?

EATING OUT

Could we have a table outside/inside? **Nós poderíamos ter uma mesa fora/dentro?** nōsh pōōderi'ämōōsh ter ōō'mä me'zä fō'rä/deNn'trōō?

Do you have a fixed-price menu? **Você tem um menu/cardápio com um preço fixo?** vōse' teNm ōōNm menōō'/kärdä'pyōō kôNm ōōNm pre'sōō fik'sōō?

Is service included? **O serviço está incluído?** ōō servi'sōō eshtä' iNnklōō·i'dōō?

229

EATING OUT

Is there a cover charge?	**Tem uma taxa de serviço?** teNm ōō'mä tä'shä də servi'sōō?
Separate checks, please.	**Contas separadas, por favor.** kôNn'täsh sepärä'däsh, pōōr fävōr.
I'd like some apple/orange/grapefruit juice.	**Eu gostaria de um sumo de maçã/laranja/toranja.** e'ōō gōōshtäri'ä də ōōNm sōō'mōō də mäsä'/lärän'zhä/tōōrän'zhä.
I'd like some coffee/tea with cream/lemon.	**Eu gostaria de um café/chá com creme/limão.** e'ōō gōōshtäri'ä də ōōNm käfe'/shä kôNm kre'mə/limäN'ōō.
I'd like a soda/beer/mineral water.	**Eu gostaria de uma soda/cerveja/água mineral.** e'ōō gōōshtäri'ä də ōō'mä sō'dä/serve'zhä/ä'gōō-ä mineräl'.
I'd like a glass/bottle of red/white/rose wine.	**Eu gostaria de uma taça/garrafa de vinho tinto/branco/rosé.** e'ōō gōōshtäri'ä də ōō'mä tä'sä/gärä'fä də vi'nyōō tiNn'tōō/bräN'kōō/rōze'.
dry/sweet	**seco/doce** se'kōō/dō'sə
Cheers!	**à sua!** ä sōō'ä!
What is the special of the day?	**Qual é o prato do dia?** kväl e ōō prä'tōō dōō di'ä?
Do you have a tourist menu?	**Você tem um menu/cardápio para turista?** vōse' teNm ōōNm menōō'/kärdä'pyōō pä'rä tōōrish'tä?
What is this? (pointing to item on menu)	**O que é isto?** ōō ke e ish'tōō?
I'll have this.	**Eu irei pedir este.** e'ōō ire'i pedir' esh'tə?

I'd like some salt/pepper/cheese/sugar/milk.	**Eu gostaria de um pouco de sal/pimenta/queijo/açucar/leite.** e'ōō gōōshtäri'ä də ōōNm pō'ōōkōō də säl/pimeNn'tä/ke'izhōō/äsōō'kär/le'itə.
More juice/coffee/tea/cream/lemon/milk/beer/wine.	**Mais sumo/café/chá/creme/limão/leite/cerveja/vinho.** mä'ish sōō'mōō/käfe'/shä/kre'mə/limäN'ōō/le'itə/serve'zhä/vi'nyōō.
I cannot eat sugar/salt/drink alcohol.	**Eu não posso comer açucar/sal/tomar álcool** e'ōō näN'ōō pō'sōō kōōmer' äsōō'kär/säl/tōōmär äl'kō·öl.
I am a diabetic.	**Eu sou diabético/diabética.** e'ōō sō'ōō di·äbe'tikōō/di·äbe'tikä.
I am a vegetarian.	**Eu sou vegetariano/vegetariana.** e'ōō sō'ōō vezhetäryä'nōō/vezhetäryä'nä.
May I have the check, please.	**Eu posso ter a conta, por favor?** e'ōō pō'sōō ter ä kôNn'tä, pōōr fävōr?
Keep the change.	**Fique com o troco.** fi'kə kôNm ōō trō'kōō.

FOOD SHOPPING & PICNIC FOOD

Can you make me a sandwich.	**Você pode me fazer um sanduíche?** vōse' pō'də me fäzer' ōōNm säNndōō·i'shə?
To take out.	**Para levar.** pä'rä levär'.
I'd like some …	**Eu gostaria de algum/alguma …** e'ōō gōōshtäri'ä də äl'gōōNm/älgōō'mä …
I'll have a little more.	**Eu quero um pouco mais.** e'ōō ke'rōō ōōNm pō'ōōkōō mä'ish.
That's too much.	**Isto é demais.** ish'tōō e demä'ish.
Do you have …	**Você tem …** vōse' teNm …
I'd like …	**Eu gostaria de …** e'ōō gōōshtäri'ä də …

FOOD SHOPPING

a box of	**uma caixa de** o͞o'mä kä'ishä də
a can of	**uma lata de** o͞o'mä lä'tä də
a jar of	**um pote de** o͞oNm pō'tə də
a half kilo of	**meio quilo de** me'i·o͞o ki'lo͞o də
a kilo of	**um quilo de** o͞oNm ki'lo͞o də
a half liter of	**meio litro** me'i·o͞o li'tro͞o
a liter	**um litro** o͞oNm li'tro͞o
a packet of	**um pacote de** o͞oNm päko'tə də
a slice of	**uma fatia de** o͞o'mä fäti'ä də
a bottle opener	**um abridor de garrafa** o͞oNm äbridōr' də gärä'fä
a can opener	**um abridor de lata** o͞oNm äbridōr' də lä'tä
a cork screw	**um saca - rolha** o͞oNm sä'kä-rō'lyä
it sliced	**fatiado** fätyä'do͞o

Do you have any plastic forks and napkins?
Você tem alguns garfos de plástico e guardanapos? vōse' teNm älgo͞onsh' gär'fo͞osh də pläshtiko͞o e go͞o·ärdänä'po͞osh?

Do you have any plastic spoons and knives?
Você tem algumas colheres e facas de plástico? vōse' teNm älgo͞o'mäsh kōlye'resh e fä'käsh də pläsh'tiko͞o?

May I have a bag?
Eu posso ter um saco? e'o͞o pō'so͞o ter o͞oNm säko͞o?

Is there a park nearby?
Tem um parque por perto? teNm o͞oNm pär'kə po͞or per'to͞o?

May we picnic there?
Nós podemos fazer um piquenique lá? nōsh po͞ode'mo͞osh fäzer' o͞oNm pikəni'kə lä?

May we picnic here?
Nós podemos fazer um piquenique aqui? nosh po͞ode'mo͞osh fäzer' o͞oNm pikəni'kə aki'?

Fruits

apples	**maçãs** mäsäsh'
apricots	**damascos** dämäsh'ko͞osh

232

bananas	**bananas** bänä'näsh
blueberries	**mirtilos** mirti'lōōsh
cantaloupe	**melão** meläN'ōō
cherries	**cerejas** sere'zhäsh
dates	**tâmaras** tä'märäsh
figs	**figos** fi'gōōsh
grapefruit	**toranja** tōōrän'zhä
grapes	**uvas** ōō'väsh
lemons	**limões** limôN'esh
nectarines	**nactarinas** näktäri'näsh
oranges	**laranjas** lärän'zhäsh
peach	**pêssego** pe'segōō
pear	**pêra** pe'rä
pineapple	**ananas** ä'nänäsh
plums	**ameixas** äme'ishäsh
raisins	**passas de uva** pä'säsh də ōō'vä
raspberries	**framboesas** fräNmbōō-e'zäsh
strawberries	**morangos** mōōräN'gōōsh
tangerines	**tangerinas** täNnzheri'näsh
watermelon	**melancia** melänsi'ä

Vegetables

artichokes	**alcachofra** älkäshō'frä
asparagus	**espargo** eshpär'gōō
green/kidney beans	**feijão verde/feijão** fe-izhäN'ōō ver'də/ fe-izhäN'ōō
broccoli	**brócolos** brō'kōōlōōsh
red/cabbage	**repolho vermelho/repolho** repō'lyōō verme'lyōō/repō'lyōō
carrots	**cenouras** senō'ōōräsh
cauliflower	**couve - flor** kō'ōōvə-flōr'
celery	**aipo** ä'ipōō
corn	**milho** mi'lyōō
cucumber	**pepino** pepi'nōō
eggplant	**berinjela** berinzhe'lä

FOOD SHOPPING

fennel	**funcho** fōōn'shōō
french fries	**batatas fritas** bätä'täsh fri'täsh
garlic	**alho** a'lyōō
leeks	**alho poró** ä'lyōō pō'rōō
lentils	**lentilhas** lenti'lyäsh
lettuce	**alface** älfä'sə
mushrooms	**fungos/cogumelos** fōōN'gōōsh, kōōgōōme'lōōsh
black/green olives	**azeitonas pretas/verdes** äze-itō'näsh pre'täsh/ver'desh
onions	**cebolas** sebō'läsh
peas	**ervilhas** ervi'lyäsh
hot/sweet peppers	**pimentões picantes/doces** pimeNntôN'esh pikäNn'tesh/dō'sesh
pickles	**picles/pickles** pik'lesh/pik'əlsh
potatoes	**batatas** bätä'täsh
radishes	**rabanetes** räbäne'tesh
rice	**arroz** ärōzh'
sauerkraut	**choucroute** shōōkrōōt'
spinach	**espinafre** eshpinä'frə
tomatoes	**tomates** tōōmä'tesh
zucchini	**courgettte** kō·ōōrzhet'

Meats/Cold Cuts

beef	**carne de vaca** kär'nə də vä'kä
bologna	**mortadela** mōōrtäde'lä
chicken	**galinha** gali'nyä
fish	**peixe** pe'ishə
ham	**presunto, fiambre (cooked)** prezōōn'tōō, fyaNm'brə
hamburger/ground beef	**hamburguer/carne de hamburguer** äNm'bōōrger/kär'nə də äNm'bōōrger
hot dog/frankfurters	**cachorro quente/salsichas** käshō'rōō keNn'tə/sälshi'shäsh
lamb	**carneiro** kärne'irōō

pork	**porco** pōr'kōō
roast beef	**rosbife** rōōshbi'fə
salami	**salami** sälä'mi
sausage	**salsicha/chouriço/lingüiça** sälshi'shä/shō-ōōri'sōō/lingōō-i'sä
turkey	**peru** perōō'
veal	**vitela** vite'lä

Nuts

almonds	**amêndoas** ämeNn'dōō-äsh
brazil nuts	**castanha do Pará** käshtä'nyä dōō pärä'
cashews	**castanhas de cajú** käshtä'nyäsh də käzhōō'
chestnuts	**castanhas** käshtä'nyäsh
hazelnuts	**avelãs** äveläsh'
peanuts	**amendoins** ämeNn'dōō-insh
walnuts	**nozes** nō'zesh

Condiments

butter	**manteiga** mäNnte'igä
honey	**mel** mel
horseradish	**rábano** rä'bänōō
jam/jelly	**geléia** zhele'i-ä
ketchup	**ketchup/molho de tomate** ke'tshəp/mō'lyōō də tōōmä'tə
margarine	**margarina** märgäri'nä
mayonnaise	**maionese** mäyōōne'zə
mustard	**mostarda** mōōshtär'dä
vegetable/olive oil	**óleo vegetal/azeite (de oliva)** ō'le-ōō vezhetäl'/äze'itə (də ōli'vä)
pepper	**pimenta** pimeNn'tä
mild/hot salsa	**salsa branda/picante** säl'sä bräNn'dä/pikäNn'tə
salt	**sal** säl
sugar	**açucar** äsōō'kär

FOOD SHOPPING

tabasco/hot sauce	**molho de pimenta picante** mōlyōōdə pimeNn'tä pikäNn'tə
vinegar	**vinagre** vinä'grə

Miscellaneous

bread	**pão** päN'ōō
cake	**bolo/torta** bō'lōō/tōr'tä
candy	**bombom/bala** bôNmbôNm'/bä'lä
cereal	**cereal** sere-äl'
cheese	**queijo** ke'izhōō
chocolate	**chocolate** shōōkōōlä'tə
cookies	**biscoito** bishkō'itōō
crackers	**bolacha de água e sal** bōōlä'shä də ä'gōō-ä e säl
eggs	**ovos** ō'vōōsh
ice cream	**sorvete** sōōrve'tə
popcorn	**pipoca** pipō'kä
potato chips	**batata frita** bätä'tä fri'tä
rolls	**enrolados** enrōōlä'dōōsh
spaghetti	**espaguete** eshpäge'tə
yogurt	**iogurte** i·ōgōōr'tə

Drinks

beer	**cerveja** serve'zhä
coffee	**café** käfe'
hot chocolate	**chocolate quente** shōōkōōlä'tə keNn'tə
apple juice	**sumo de maçã** sōō'mōō də mäsä'
cranberry juice	**sumo de murtinho** sōō'mōō də mōōrti'nyōō
grapefruit juice	**sumo de toranja** sōō'mōō də tōōrän'zhä
orange juice	**sumo de laranja** sōō'mōō də lärän'zhä
tomato juice	**sumo de tomate** sōō'mōō də tōōmä'tə
milk	**leite** le'itə
soft drinks	**refrigerantes** refrizheräNn'tesh
tea	**chá** shä

236

TELEPHONE

sparkling/mineral water	**água mineral com gás/sem gás**
	ä'gōō·ä mineräl' kôNm gäsh/seNm gäsh
red/white/rose wine	**vinho tinto/branco/rosé**
	vi'nyō tiNn'tōō/bräng'kōō/rōze'
dry/sweet	**seco/doce** se'kōō/dō'sə

USING THE TELEPHONE

Can I use local currency to make a local/long-distance call or do I need to buy a phone card?	**Eu posso usar a moeda local para fazer uma ligação local/interurbana ou eu preciso comprar um cartão telefônico?** e'ōō pō'sōō ōōzär' mōō·e'dä lōōkäl' pä'rä fäzer' ōō'mä ligäsäN'ōō lōōkäl'/iNnterōōrbä'nä ō'ōō e'ōō presi'zōō kôNmprär' ōōNm kärtäN'ōō telefo'nikōō?
Do I need to buy tokens?	**Eu preciso comprar fichas?** e'ōō presi'sōō kôNmprär' fi'shäsh?
Where can I buy tokens/a phone card?	**Onde eu posso comprar fichas/um cartão telefônico?** ôNn'də e'ōō pō'sōō kôNmprär' fi'shäsh/ōōNm kärtäN'ōō telefo'nikōō?
… tokens, please. How much?	**… fichas, por favor. Quanto custa?** … fi'shäsh, pōōr fävōr'. kväNn'tōō kōōsh'tä?
I'd like to buy phone card.	**Eu gostaria de comprar cartão telefônico.** e'ōō gōōshtäri'ä də kôNmprär' kärtäN'ōō telefo'nikōō.
How much does it cost?	**Quanto custa isto?** kväNn'tōō kōōsh'tä ish'tōō?
How do you use the phone card?	**Como se usa o cartão telefônico?** kō'mōō se ōō'zä ō kärtäN'ōō telefo'nikōō?
Excuse me, where is the nearest phone?	**Com licença, onde fica o telefone mais próximo?** kôNm lisen'sä, ôNn'də fi'kä ō telefo'nə mä'ish prō'simōō?

I'd like to make a collect call.

Eu gostaria de fazer uma ligação a cobrar. e'ōō gōōshtäri'ä də fäzer' ōō'mä ligäsäN'ōō ä kōōbrär'.

The number is …

O número é … ōō nōō'merōō e …

Hello. This is …

Alô. Aqui é … älō'. äki' e …

May I speak to …

Eu posso falar com … e'ōō pō'sōō fälär' kôNm …

POST OFFICE

Can you direct me to the nearest post office?

Você pode me direcionar para a estação dos correios mais próxima? vōse' pō'də me direksyōōnär' pä'rä ä eshtäsäN'ōō dōsh kōōre'i·ōōsh mä'ish prō'simä?

Which window is for …?

Qual é o guichê para …? kväl e ōō gishe' pä'rä …?

    stamps
    sending/cashing a
    money order
    airmail writing
    paper

    selos se'lōōsh
    enviar/receber dinheiro
    envi·är'/reseber' dinye'irōō
    papel de cartas via aéreo
    papel' də kär'täsh vi'ä ä·e're·ōō

I'd like … stamps for postcards/letters to America.

Eu gostaria … selos para cartões postais/cartas para América. e'ōō gōōshtäri'ä … se'lōōsh pä'rä kärtôN'esh pōōstä'ish/kär'täsh pä'rä äme'rikä.

I'd like to send this airmail.

Eu gostaria de enviar esta correspondência via aérea. e'ōō gōōshtäri'ä də envi·är' esh'tä kōōreshpôNdeN'syä vi'ä ä·e're·ä.

How much does it cost?

Quanto custa isto? kväNn'tōō kōōsh'tä ish'tōō?

238

PHARMACY & DRUGSTORE

| Can you direct me to the nearest pharmacy? | **Você poderia me direcionar para a farmácia mais próxima?** vōse′ pōōderi′ä me direksōōnär′ pä′rä ä färmä′syä mä′ish prō′simä? |

| I'd like a/an/some … | **Eu gostaria de um/uma/algum/alguma …** e′ōō gōōshtäri′ä də ōōNm/ōō′mä/ äl′gōōNm/älgōō′mä … |

aspirin	**aspirina** äshpiri′nä
Band-Aids	**Band-Aids** ben′de·id
cough medicine	**remédio para tosse** reme′dyōō pä′rä tō′sə
contraceptives	**contraceptivos** kôNnträsepti′vōōsh
eye drops	**colírio** kōōli′ri·ōō
insect repellant	**repelente contra insetos** repeleNn′tə kôNn′trä inse′tōōsh
sanitary napkins	**penso higiénico** peNn′sōō izhi·e′nikōō

| Could you give me something for … | **Você poderia me dar alguma coisa para …** vōse′ pōōderi′ä me där älgōō′mä kō′izä pä′rä … |

constipation	**prisão de ventre** prizäN′ōō də veNn′trə
diarrhea	**diarréia** di·äre′i·ä
hay fever	**febre dos fenos** fe′brə dōsh fe′nōōsh
a headache	**dor de cabeça** dōr də käbe′sä
indigestion	**indigestão** iNndizheshtäN′ōō
itching	**coceira** kōōse′irä
nausea/travel sickness	**náusea/maresia/enjôo em viagem** nä′ōōse·ä/märezi′ä/enzhō′ōō eNm vi·ä′zhəNm
a rash	**irritação na pele** iritäsäN′ōō nä pe′lə
sore throat	**dor de garganta** dōr də gärgäNn′tä
sunburn	**queimadura de sol** ke·imädōō′rä də sōl

239

TOBACCO SHOP

May I have a/an/ some …?	**Eu posso ter um/uma/algum/alguma …?** e'ōō pō'sōō ter ōōNm/ōō'mä/äl'gōōNm/ älgōō'mä …

deodorant	**desodorizante** dezōdōōrizaNn'tə
razor	**barbeador** bärbe·ädōr'
razor blades	**lâminas para barbear** lä'minäsh pä'rä bärbe·är'
shampoo/condi- tioner	**champô/condicionador** shäNmpō'/kôNndisyōnädōr'
soap	**sabonete** säbōōne'tə
suntan oil/cream/ lotion	**óleo/creme/loção bronzeador** ō'le·ōō/kre'mə/lōōsäN'ōō brōNnze·ädōr'
tissues	**lenços de papel** len'sōōsh də päpel'
toilet paper	**papel higiénico** päpel' izhi·e'nikōō
toothbrush	**escova de dente** eshkō'vä də deNn'tə
toothpaste	**pasta dentífrica** päsh'ta deNnti'frika
cleaning/soaking solution for con- tact lenses	**solução para limpar/embeber lentes de contacto** sōōlōōsäN'ōō pä'rä liNmpär'/ eNmbeber' leNn'tesh de kôNntäk'tōō

How much does it cost?	**Quanto custa isto?** kväNn'tōō kōōsh'tä ish'tōō?

TOBACCO SHOP

I'd like to buy …	**Eu gostaria de comprar …** e'ōō gōōshtäri'ä də kôNmprär' …

a pack/carton of cigarettes.	**um maço/uma carteira de cigarros.** ōōNm mä'sōō/ōō'mä kärte'irä də sigä'rōōsh.
a cigarette lighter.	**um isqueiro para cigarros.** ōōNm ishke'irōō pä'rä sigä'rōōsh
a cigar.	**um charuto.** ōōNm shärōō'tōō

May I have some matches?	**Eu posso ter um fósforo?** e'ōō pō'sōō ter ōōNm fōsh'fōōrōō?

PORTUGUESE

PHOTOGRAPHY

I'd like to buy a roll of film.
Eu gostaria de comprar um filme.
e'ōo gōoshtäri'ä də kôNmprär' ōoNm fil'mə.

Black and white/Color.
Preto e branco/Colorido
pre'tōo e bräng'kōo/kōolōori'dōo

How much are they?
Quanto custam? kväNn'tōo kōosh'täNm?

I'd like to buy batteries for this camera.
Eu gostaria de comprar baterias para esta câmera. e'ōo gōoshtäri'ä də kôNmprär' bäteri'äsh pä'rä esh'tä kä'merä.

HEALTH

The Doctor

I don't feel well.
Eu não me sinto bem.
e'ōo näN'ōo me siNn'tōo beNm.

Could you direct me to a doctor that speaks English.
Você poderia me direcionar para um médico que fala Inglês? vōse' pōoderi'ä me direksyōonär' pä'rä ōoNm me'dikōo ke fä'lä inglesh'?

I have (a) …
Eu tenho (um/uma) …
e'ōo te'nyōo (ōoNm/ōo'mä) …

burn	**queimadura** ke·imädōo'rä
chest pains	**dor no peito** dōr nōo pe'itōo
cold	**frio/gripe** fri'ōo/gri'pə
cough	**tosse** tō'sə
cramps	**cãibra** käN'ibrä
cut	**corte/ferimento** kōr'tə/ferimeNn'tōo
diarrhea	**diarréia** di·äre'i·ä
fever	**febre** fe'brə
flu	**gripe** gri'pə
infection	**infecção** infesäN'ōo
nausea	**náusea** nä'ōoze·ä

241

rash	**irritação na pele** iritäsäN'ōō nä pe'lə
sore throat	**dor de garganta** dōr də gärgäNn'tä
sprained ankle	**tornozelo torcido**
	tōōrnōōze'lōō tōōrsi'dōō
stomach ache	**dor de estômago** dōr də eshtō'mägōō

It hurts here.   **Dói aqui.** dō'i äki'.

I've been vomiting.   **Eu estive vomitando.**
e'ōō eshti'və vōōmitäNn'dōō.

I'm having difficulty breathing.   **Eu estou tendo dificuldades para respirar.** e'ōō eshtō'ōō teNn'dōō difikōōldä'desh pä'rä reshpirär'.

I'm allergic to penicillin.   **Eu sou alérgico à penicilina.** e'ōō sō'ōō äler'zhikōō a penisili'nä.

I'm diabetic.   **Eu sou diabético/diabética.** e'ōō sō'ōō di·äbe'tikōō/di·äbe'tikä.

I don't smoke/drink.   **Eu não fumo/bebo.** e'ōō näN'ōō fōō'mōō/be'bōō.

The Dentist

Could you direct me to a dentist that speaks English?   **Você poderia me direcionar para um dentista que fala Inglês?** vōse' pōōderi'ä me direksōōnär' pä'rä ōōNm deNntish'tä ke fä'lä inglesh'?

I have a toothache. This tooth.   **Eu tenho dor de dente. Este dente.** e'ōō te'nyōō dōr də deNn'tə. esh'tə deNn'tə.

My tooth is loose.   **Meu dente está solto.** me'ōō deNn'tə eshtä' sōl'tōō.

My tooth is broken.   **Meu dente está quebrado.** me'ōō deNn'tə eshtä' kebrä'dōō.

I've broken/lost a fill-ing. | **Eu quebrei/perdi uma obturação.**
e'ōō kebre'i/perdi' ōō'mä ōbtōōräsäN'ōō.

Paying

How much does this cost? | **Quanto custa isto?**
kväNn'tōō kōōsh'tä ish'tōō?

I have health insur-ance. | **Eu tenho seguro contra a enfermidade.**
e'ōō te'nyōō segōō'rōō kôNn'trä ä eNnfermidä'də.

I'm supposed to call this number. | **Eu preciso ligar para este número.**
e'ōō presi'zōō ligär' pä'rä esh'tə nōō'merōō.

How much do I owe you? | **Quanto eu lhe devo?**
kväNn'tōō e'ōō lye de'vōō?

SIGHTSEEING

Can you recom-mend …? | **Você pode recomendar …?**
vōse' pōdə rekōmeNndär' …?

   a good, inexpen-sive restaurant?
a fun nightclub? | **um restaurante bom e barato?**
ōōNm reshtä·ōōräNn'tə bôNm e bärä'tōō?
Uma boate animada/divertida?
ōō'mä bōō·ä'tə änimä'dä/diverti'dä?

   a good place to dance? | **Um bom local para dançar?**
ōōNm bôNm lōōkäl' pä'rä dänsär'?

Can you tell me where the tourist office is? | **Você pode me dizer onde fica a agência de turismo?** vōse' pō'də me dizer' ôNn'də fi'kä ä äzhen'syä də tōōriz'mōō?

What are the main points of interest here? | **Quais são os pontos mais interessantes aqui?** kvä'ish säN'ōō ōsh pôNn'tōōsh mä'ish iNnteresäNn'tesh äki'?

What time does it open/close? | **A que horas isto abre/fecha?**
ä ke ō'räsh ish'tōō ä'brə/fe'shä?

243

SIGHTSEEING

What time is the last entry?

Qual é o último horário para visitas?
kväl e o͞o o͞ol'timo͞o o͝rär'yo͝ pä'rä vizi'täsh?

How much is the admission? Free?

Quanto custa a entrada? Gratuita?
kväNn'to͞o ko͞osh'tä ä eNnträ'dä? gräto͞o-i'tä?

Is there a discount for students/children/teachers/senior citizens?

Tem um desconto para estudantes/crianças/professores/idosos? teNm o͞oNm deshkôNn'to͞o pä'rä eshto͞odäNn'tesh/kri-än'säsh/pro͞ofeso͝'resh/ido'zo͞osh?

Is the ticket good all day?

O bilhete serve para todo o dia?
o͞o bilye'tə ser'və pä'rä to͝'do͞o o͞o di'ä?

Is there a sightseeing tour?

Tem passeios turísticos?
teNm päse'i-o͞osh to͞orish'tiko͞osh?

What time does it start?

Que horas começa?
ke o͝'räsh ko͞ome'sä?

How much does it cost?

Quanto custa isto?
kväNn'to͞o ko͞osh'tä ish'to͞o?

How long is it?

Qual é a duração? kväl e ä do͞oräsäN'o͞o?

Does the guide speak English?

O/A guia fala Inglês?
o͞o/ä gi'ä fä'lä inglesh'?

Am I allowed to take pictures/a video?

É permitido fotografar/filmar?
e permiti'do͞o fo͞oto͞ográfär'/filmär'?

Can you direct me to the …?

Você pode me direcionar para a/o …?
vo͞ose' po͝'də me direksyo͞onär' pä'rä ä/o͞o …?

art gallery	**galeria de arte** gäleri'ä də är'tə
beach	**praia** prä'yä
castle	**castelo** käshte'lo͞o
cathedral	**catedral** kätedräl'
cemetery	**cemitério** semiter'yo͞o
church	**igreja** igre'zhä
fountain	**fonte** fôNn'tə

244

PORTUGUESE

gardens	**jardins** zhärdiNsh'
harbor	**porto** pōr'tōō
lake	**lago** lä'gōō
monastery	**mosteiro/convento** mōōshte'irōō/ kôNveNn'tōō
mountains	**montanhas** môNntä'nyäsh
movies	**cinemas** sine'mäsh
museum	**museu** mōōze'ōō
old city	**cidade antiga** sitä'də äNnti'gä
palace	**palácio** pälä'syōō
ruins	**ruínas** rōō·i'näsh
shops/bazaar	**lojas/bazar** lō'zhäsh/bäzär'
statue	**estátua** eshtä'tōō·ä
tomb	**túmulo** tōō'mōōlōō
trails (for hiking)	**trilhas** tri'lyäsh
university	**universidade** ōōniversidä'də
zoo	**zoológico** zō·ōōlō'zhikōō

Is it far from here?	**Ele/Ela é longe daqui?** el'ə/el'ä e lôN'zhə däki'?
Can we walk there?	**Nós podemos caminhar até lá?** nōsh pōōde'mōōsh käminyär' äte' lä?
Straight ahead.	**Siga em frente.** si'gä eNm freNn'tə.
Go right/left.	**Vá à direita/esquerda.** vä ä dire'itä/eshker'dä.
At the corner/traffic light.	**Na esquina/no semáforo.** nä eshki'nä/nōō semä'fōōrōō

DISCOUNT INFORMATION

Do I get a discount with my student/ teacher's/senior citizens card?	**Eu tenho desconto com a minha carteira de estudante/professor/idoso?** e'ōō te'nyōō deshkôNn'tōō koNm ä mi'nyä kärte'irä də eshtōōdäNn'tə/prōōfesōr'/idō'zōō?

245

EMERGENCIES

Do I get a discount with my Eurailpass/Europass/Flexipass?	**Eu tenho desconto com o meu Eurail-pass/Europass/Flexipass?** e'ōō te'nyōō deshkôNn'tōō kôNm ōō me'ōō yōōrel'pes/ yōō'rōpes/fle'ksipes?
How much of a discount?	**Quanto é o desconto?** kväNn'tōō e ōō deshkôNn'tōō?
How much do I owe?	**Quanto eu lhe devo?** kväNn'tōō e'ōō lye de'vōō?

EMERGENCIES & ACCIDENTS

Please call the police.	**Por favor, chame a polícia.** pōōr fävōr, shä'mə ä pōōli'si·ä.
Please call a doctor/an ambulance, quickly.	**Por favor, chame um médico/uma ambulância, rapidamente.** pōōr fävōr, shä'mə ōōNm me'dikōō/ōō'mä äNmbōōläNn'si·ä, räpidämeNn'tə.
Hurry!	**Se apresse!** se äpre'se!
Danger!	**Perigo!** peri'gōō!
Someone has been hurt/robbed.	**Alguém foi ferido/roubado.** älgeNm' fō'i feri'dōō/rō·ōōbä'dōō.
I'm hurt.	**Eu estou ferido/ferida.** e'ōō eshtō'ōō feri'dōō/feri'dä.
Where is the hospital?	**Onde fica o hospital?** ôNn'də fi'kä ōō ōshpitäl'?
There's a fire.	**Tem incêndio.** teNm i'seNndyōō.
Help!/Thief!/Pick-pocket!	**Socorro!/Ladrão!/Batedor de carteira!** sōōkō'rōō! lädräN'ōō!/bätädōr' də kärte'irä!
Police!	**Polícia!** pōōli'si·ä!

246

Stop that man/woman!	**Pare este homem/esta mulher!** pä'rə esh'tə ō'meNm/esh'tä mōōlyer'!

LOSS & THEFT

Can you help me, please?	**Você pode me ajudar, por favor?** vōse' pō'də me äzhōōdär', pōōr fävōr?
Where is the police station?	**Onde fica o posto policial?** ôNn'də fi'kä ōō pōsh'tōō pōōlisyäl'?
Where is the American consulate/embassy?	**Onde fica o consulado Americano?/a embaixada Americana?** ôNn'də fi'kä ōō kônsōōlä'dōō ämerikä'nōō/ä eNmbä·ishä'dä ämerikä'nä?
Can you tell me where the lost and found is?	**Você pode me dizer onde fica os achados e perdidos?** vōse' pō'də me dizer' ôNn'də fi'kä ōsh äshä'dōōsh e perdi'dōōsh?
Someone has stolen my ...	**Alguém roubou meu/minha ...** älgeNm' rō·ōōbō'ōō me'ōō/mi'nyä ...
I have lost my ...	**Eu perdi meu/minha ...** e'ōō perdi' me'ōō/mi'nyä ...
I left my ... on the bus/train.	**Eu deixei meu/minha ... no autocarro/comboio.** e'ōō deshe·i' me'ōō/mi'nyä ... nōō ä·ōōtōkä'rōō/kôNmbō'yōō.

backpack	**mochila** mōōshi'lä
camera	**câmera** kä'merä
credit cards	**cartões de crédito** kärtôN'esh də kre'ditōō
glasses	**óculos** ō'kōōlōōsh
luggage	**bagagem** bägä'zheNm
money	**dinheiro** dinye'irōō
passport	**passaporte** päsäpōr'tə
rail pass	**rail pass** rel'pes

247

NUMBERS

traveler's checks	**traveller's cheque/cheque de viagem**
	tre'vələrsshe'kə/she'kə də vi·ä'zheNm
wallet	**carteira (de bolso)** kärte'irä (də bōl'sōō)

DEALING WITH PROBLEM PEOPLE

Leave me alone or I'll call the police.	**Me deixe só ou eu chamarei a polícia.** me de'ishə sō ō'ōō e'ōō shämäre'i ä pōōli'si·ä.
Stop following me.	**Pare de me seguir.** pä'rə də me segir'.
I'm not interested.	**Eu não estou interessado/interessada.** e'ōō näN'ōō eshtō'ōō iNnteresä'dō/iNnteresä'dä.
I'm married.	**Eu sou casado/casada.** e'ōō sō'ōō käzä'dō/käzä'dä.
I'm waiting for my boyfriend/husband.	**Eu estou esperando por meu namorado/esposo.** e'ōō estō'ōō eshperäNn'dō pōōr me'ōō nämōōrä'dō/eshpō'zōō.
Enough!	**Chega!** she'gä!
Go away!	**Vá embora!** vä eNmbō'rä!

NUMBERS

zero	**zero** ze'rōō
one	**um** ōōNm
two	**dois** dō'ish
three	**três** tresh
four	**quatro** kvä'trōō
five	**cinco** sing'kōō
six	**seis** se'ish
seven	**sete** se'tə
eight	**oito** ō'itōō
nine	**nove** nō'və
ten	**dez** desh
eleven	**onze** ôNn'zə

248

twelve	**doze** dōˈzə
thirteen	**treze** treˈzə
fourteen	**catorze/quatorze** kätōrˈzə/kvätōrˈzə
fifteen	**quinze** kiNnˈzə
sixteen	**dezasseis** dezäseˈish
seventeen	**dezassete** dezäseˈtə
eighteen	**dezoito** dezōˈitōō
nineteen	**dezanove** dezänōˈvə
twenty	**vinte** viNnˈtə
twenty-one	**vinte e um** viNnˈtə e ōōNm
twenty-two	**vinte e dois** viNnˈtə e dōˈish
twenty-three	**vinte e três** viNnˈtə e tresh
twenty-four	**vinte e quatro** viNnˈtə e kväˈtrōō
thirty	**trinta** triNnˈtä
forty	**quarenta** kväreNnˈtä
fifty	**cinquenta** singkveNnˈtä
sixty	**sessenta** seseNnˈtä
seventy	**setenta** seteNnˈtä
eighty	**oitenta** ō·iteNnˈtä
ninety	**noventa** nōveNnˈtä
one hundred	**cem** seNm
one thousand	**mil** mil
one million	**um milhão** ōōNm milyäNˈōō

DAYS

What day is today?	**Que dia é hoje?** ke diˈä e ōˈzhə?
It's Monday.	**Hoje é segunda–feira.** ōˈzhə e segōōNnˈdä-feˈirä.
… Tuesday.	**… terça-feira.** … terˈsä-feˈirä.
… Wednesday.	**… quarta-feira.** … kvärˈtä-feˈirä.
… Thursday.	**… quinta-feira.** … kviNnˈtä-feˈirä.
… Friday.	**… sexta-feira.** … seshˈtä-feˈirä.
… Saturday.	**… sábado.** … säˈbädōō.
… Sunday.	**… domingo.** … dōōmingˈgōō.

249

TIME

Time is told by the 24 hour clock. You can also reference the numbers section.

Excuse me. Can you tell me the time?
Com licença. Você pode me dizer que horas são? kôNm lisen'sä. vōse' pö'də me dizer' ke ō'räsh säN'ōō?

I'll meet you in …
Eu encontrarei você em … e'ōō eNnkôNntträre'i vōse' eNm …

    ten minutes
    dez minutos desh minōō'tōōsh

    a quarter of an hour
    um quarto de hora ōōNm kvär'tōō də ō'rä

    a half hour
    meia hora me'i·ä ō'rä

    three quarters of an hour
    três quartos de hora tresh kvär'tōōsh də ō'rä

It is …
São … säN'ōō …

    five past one.
    uma e cinco ōō'mä e sing'kōō

    ten past two.
    duas e dez dōō'äsh e desh

    a quarter past three.
    três e quinze tresh e kiNn'zə

    twenty past four.
    quatro e vinte kvä'trōō e viNn'tə

    twenty-five past five.
    cinco e vinte e cinco sing'kōō e viNn'tə e sing'kōō

    half past six.
    seis e meia se'ish e me'i·ä

    twenty-five to seven.
    vinte e cinco para as sete viNn'tə e sing'kōō pä'rä äsh se'tə

    twenty to eight.
    vinte para as oito viNn'tə pä'rä äsh ō'itōō

    a quarter to nine.
    quinze para as nove kiNn'zə pä'rä äsh nō've

    ten to ten.
    dez para as dez desh pä'rä äsh desh

    five to eleven.
    cinco para as onze sing'kōō pä'rä äsh ôNn'zə

    noon.
    meio-dia me'i·ō di'ä

midnight.	**meia-noite** meïˑa-nōˈitə
yesterday	**ontem** ôNnˈteNm
last night	**ontem à noite** ôNnˈteNm ä nōˈitə
today	**hoje** ōˈzhə
tonight	**hoje à noite** ōˈzhə ä nōˈitə
tomorrow	**amanhã** ämänyäNˈ
morning	**manhã** mänyäNˈ
afternoon	**tarde** tärˈdə
evening	**final de tarde** finälˈ ˈdə tärˈdə
night	**noite** nōˈitə
day before yesterday	**antes de ontem** äNnˈtesh də ôNnˈteNm
in two/three days	**em dois/três dias** eNm dōˈish/tresh dïˈäsh

MONTHS

January	**Janeiro** zhäneˈirōō
February	**Fevereiro** fevəreˈirōō
March	**Março** märˈsōō
April	**Abril** äbrilˈ
May	**Maio** mäˈyōō
June	**Junho** zhōōˈnyōō
July	**Julho** zhōōˈlyōō
August	**Agosto** ägōshˈtōō
September	**Setembro** seteNmˈbrōō
October	**Outubro** ō·ōōtōōˈbrōō
November	**Novembro** nōveNmˈbrōō
December	**Dezembro** dezeNmˈbrōō

Merry Christmas!	**Feliz Natal!** felishˈ nätälˈ!
Happy Easter!	**Feliz Páscoa!** felishˈ päshˈkōō·ä
Happy New Year!	**Feliz Ano Novo!** felishˈ äˈnōō nōˈvōō!
Happy Birthday!	**Feliz aniversário!** felishˈ äniversärˈyōō!

COLORS

beige	**beige** beˈzhə

COLORS

black	**preto** pre'tōō
blue	**azul** äzōōl'
brown	**castanho** käsh'tänyōō
gold	**dourado** dō·ōōrä'dōō
green	**verde** ver'də
gray	**cinza** siNn'zä
yellow	**amarelo** ämäre'lōō
orange	**laranja** lärän'zhä
pink	**cor-de-rosa** kōr də rō'zä
purple	**roxo** rō'shōō
red	**vermelho** verme'lyōō
silver	**prata** prä'tä
white	**branco** bräng'kōō

HOW DO YOU PRONOUNCE IT?

All words and phrases are accompanied by simplified pronunciation. The sound symbols you find in **Langenscheidt's European Phrasebook** are the symbols you are familiar with from your high-school or college dictionaries of the *English* language.

For Dutch, these basic symbols are supplemented by six symbols that have no equivalents in English. These six are in italics – with the understanding that you may use the sound of the familiar symbol (the preceding symbol in the table below) until you have learned the specific Dutch sound.

Symbol	Approximate Sound	Examples
VOWELS		
ä	The *a* of *father*.	*vader* vä′dər
ä	A sound that has to be learned by listening. (Pronounce the preceding vowel ä but much shorter.) *Until you have learned this sound, use the* u *of* up *or the* o *of* mother, *which will be understood.*	*kan* kän
ā	The *a* of *fate* (but without the "upglide").	*meer* mār
ā	A sound that has to be learned by listening. *Until you have learned this sound, use the* a *of* fate, *which will be understood.*	*deur* dār
e	The *e* of *met*.	*met* met
e	A sound that has to be learned by listening. *Until you have learned this sound, use the* e *of* met, *which will be understood.*	*Duits* dets

DUTCH

253

Symbol	Approximate Sound	Examples
ē	The *e* of *he*.	*bier* bēr
ē̄	A sound that has to be learned by listening. ***Until you have learned this sound, use the e of*** he, ***which will be understood.***	*buur* bē̄r *student* stē̄dentʼ
i	The *i* of *fit*.	*ik* ik
í	A sound that has to be learned by listening. ***Until you have learned this sound, use the i of*** fit, ***which will be understood.***	*nummer* níʼmər
ī	The *i* of *time*.	*pijn* pīn
ō	The *o* of *nose* (but without the "upglide").	*boot* bōt
ô	The *o* of *often*.	*pot* pôt
oi	The *oi* of *voice*.	*toilet* toiletʼ
ōō	The *u* of *rule*.	*boer* bōōr
ŏŏ	The *u* of *book*.	*zoet* zŏŏt
ou	The *ou* of *house*.	*zout* zouʼt
ə	The neutral sound (unstressed): the *a* of *ago* or the *u* of *focus*.	*beter* beʼtər
N	This symbol does not stand for a sound but shows that the preceding vowel is nasal – is pronounced through nose and mouth at the same time. Nasal sounds have to be learned by listening. (Try not to use the *ng* of *sing* in their place.)	(in words of French origin:) *restaurant* restôräNtʼ *pardon* pärdôNʼ *terrain* tereNʼ

Symbol	Approximate Sound	Examples
	CONSONANTS	
b	The *b* of *boy*.	*ben* ben
d	The *d* of *do*.	*dank* dängk
f	The *f* of *fat*.	*feest* fāst
g	The *g* of *go*.	*Engels* eng'əls
h	The *h* of *hot*.	*het* het
h	A sound that has to be learned by listening. This "guttural" sound resembles the *ch* of Scottish *loch*.	*goed* *h*ōōd
k	The *k* of *key*.	*kan* kän
l	The *l* of *love* (not of *fall*).	*land* länt
m	The *m* of *me*.	*miju* mīu
n	The *n* of *no*.	*niet* nit
ng	The *ng* of *sing*.	*dank* dängk
p	The *p* of *pin*.	*paspoort* päs'pōōrt
r	The *r* has to be learned by listening. ***Until you have learned this sound, use the*** r ***of*** run ***or*** fairy.	*vrij* vrī
s	The *s* of *sun* (not of *praise*).	*suede* suä'də
sh	The *sh* of *shine*.	*champignons* shämpingyôNs'
sh	A sound that has to be learned listening.	*school* s*h*ōl
t	The *t* of *toy*.	*toegang* tōō*h*äng

Symbol	Approximate Sound	Examples
v	The *v* of English *vat*.	*vader* vä'dər
		warm värm
y	The *y* of *year*.	*ja* yä
z	The *z* of *zeal* or the *s* of *praise*.	*zon* zōn
zh	The *s* of *measure* or the *si* of *vision*.	*bagage* bähä'zhə

Words of more than one syllable are given with a heavy stress mark ('): **toegang** tōō'häng.

EVERYDAY EXPRESSIONS

Yes.	**Ja.** yä.
No.	**Nee.** nā.
Please.	**Alstublieft/Alsjeblief.** äst*ē*blift'/ästy*ə*blif'.
Thank you.	**Dank u/je.** dängk *ē*/ye.
You're welcome.	**Graag gedaan.** häh*ə*dän'.
Excuse me.	**Pardon.** pärdôN'.
I beg your pardon.	**Pardon.** pärdôN'.
Sorry.	**Sorry.** sô'rē.
How much is this/that?	**Hoeveel kost dit/kost dat?** hōō'vāl kô'stit/kô'stät?
What time is it?	**Hoe laat is het?** hōō lät is het?
At what time does the … open/close?	**Hoe laat gaat … open/dicht?** hōō lät *h*ät … ō'p*ə*/di*h*t?
Where can I find the/a restroom?	**Waar kan ik het/een toilet vinden?** vär k*ä*n ik het/ān toilet' vin'd*ə*?
Is the water safe to drink?	**Is het veilig om het water te drinken?** is het vī'/i*h* ôm het vä't*ə*r te dring'k*ə*?
Is this free? (city map, museum, etc.)	**Is dit gratis?** is dit *h*ä'tis?

DUTCH

NOTEWORTHY SIGNS

Let op let ôp	Caution
Gesloten wegens restauratie h*ə*slō't*ə* vä'h*ə*ns restôrä'tsē	Closed for Restoration
Niet aanraken nit änrä'k*ə*	Do Not Touch

GREETINGS

Nooduitgang nōdˈetˈhäng	Emergency Exit
Geen toegang hān tōōˈhäng	Do Not Enter
Vrije toegang vriˈə tōōˈhäng	Free Admission
Niet betreden nit bətrāˈdə	Keep Out
Geen ingang hān inˈhäng	No Entry
Niet roken nit rōˈkə	No Smoking
Open van … tot … ōˈpə vän … tôt …	Open from … to …
Geen drinkwater hān dringkˈvätər	Undrinkable Water
Heren häˈrən	Men
Dames däˈməs	Women

GREETINGS

Good morning.	**Goedemorgen.** hōōdəmôrˈhə.
Good afternoon.	**Goedemiddag.** hōōdəmiˈdäh.
Good night.	**Goedenavond.** hōōdənäˈvônt.
Hello/Hi.	**Hallo.** hälōˈ.
What's your name?	**Hoe heet u/jij?** hōō hät ē/yī?
My name is …	**Ik heet …** ik hät …
How are you?	**Hoe gaat het?** hōō hät het?
Fine thanks. And you?	**Goed, dank u/je wel. En met u/jou?** hōōt, dängk ē/ye väl. en met ē/you?
Where are you from?	**Waar komt u/kom je vandaan?** vär kômt ē/kôm ye vändänˈ?
I'm from …	**Ik kom uit …** ik kôm et …

It was nice meeting you.	**Leuk u/je ontmoet te hebben.** lāk ē̆/ye ôntmōōt' te heb'ə.
Good-bye.	**Tot ziens.** tôt zēns.
Have a good trip.	**Goede reis.** hōō'də rīs.
Miss	**Mevrouw** mevrou'
Mrs./Madam	**Mevrouw** mevrou'
Mr./Sir	**Meneer** menār'

CONVERSING & GETTING TO KNOW PEOPLE

Do you speak English/ French/Italian/ German/Spanish?	**Spreekt u/Spreek je Engels/Frans/ Italiaans/Duits/Spaans?** sprākt ē̆/sprāk ye eng'əls/fräns/itǎlyäns'/dets/späns?
I don't understand.	**Ik versta het niet.** ik vərstǎ' het nit.
Could you speak more slowly please?	**Kunt u/Kun je wat langzamer spreken, alstublieft/alsjeblief?** kint ē̆/kin ye vät lǎng'zämər sprā'kə, ǎstēblift'/ǎstyəblif'?
Could you repeat that please?	**Kunt u/Kun je dat alstublieft/alsjeblief herhalen?** kint ē̆/kin ye dǎt ǎstēblift'/ǎstyəblif' herhǎ'lə?
I don't speak French/ Italian/German/ Dutch.	**Ik spreek geen Frans/Italiaans/Duits/ Nederlands.** ik sprāk hān fräns/itǎlyäns'/dets/ nǎ'dərlǎnts.
Is there someone here who speaks English?	**Is hier iemand die Engels spreekt?** is hēr ē'mǎnt dē eng'əls sprākt?
Do you understand?	**Begrijpt u/Begrijp je?** bəhīpt' ē̆/bəhīp' ye?
Just a moment. I'll see if I can find it in my phrasebook.	**Een ogenblikje. Ik zal eens kijken of het in mijn taalgids staat.** ān ō̆hənblik'yə. ik zǎl āns kī'kə ôf het in min tǎl'hits stät.

259

Please point to your question/answer in the book.	**Kunt u/Kun je uw/je vraag/antwoord in het boek aanwijzen?** kint ē/kin ye yōō/ ye vräk/äntvôrt in het bōōk änvī'zə?
My name is … What's yours?	**Ik heet … Hoe heet u/jij?** ik hāt … hōō hāt ē/yī?
It's nice to meet you.	**Goedendag.** hōōdəndäh'.
This is my friend/sister/brother/wife/husband/daughter/son …	**Dit is mijn vriend/zus/broer/vrouw/man/dochter/zoon …** dit is mīn vrēnt/zis/brōōr/vrou/män/dôh'tər/zōn …
Where are you from?	**Waar komt u/kom je vandaan?** vär kômt ē/kôm ye vändän'?
What city?	**Welke stad?** vel'ke stät?
I'm from the United States/Canada/Australia/England.	**Ik kom uit de Verenigde Staten/Canada/Australië/Engeland.** ik kôm et də verä'ni/hdə stä'tən/kä'nädä/ousträl'yə/eng'əlänt.
Are you here on vacation?	**Bent u/Ben je hier met vakantie?** bent ē/ben ye hēr met väkän'sē?
Do you like it here?	**Bevalt het u/je hier?** bəvält' het ē/ye hēr?
How long have you been here?	**Hoe lang bent u/ben je al hier?** hōō läng bent ē/ben ye äl hēr?
I just got here.	**Ik ben net aangekomen.** ik ben net än'həkômə.
I've been here for … days.	**Ik ben hier al … dagen.** ik ben hēr äl … dä'hə.
I love it.	**Het bevalt me.** het bəvält me.
It's okay.	**Dat is oké.** dät is ōkā'.
I don't like it.	**Daar houd ik niet van.** där hout ik nit vän.

It's too noisy/crowded/dirty/boring. | **Het is te lawaaierig/druk/vuil/saai.** het is te lävä yərih/drēk/vel/sī.

Where are you staying? | **Waar verblijft u/verblijf je?** vär vərblīft′ ē/vərblīf′ ye?

I'm staying at the … youth hostel/campground. | **Ik verblijf in de … jeugdherberg/op de … camping.** ik vərblīf′ in də yāh′derberh/ôp de … kem′ping.

Where were you before you came here? | **Waar bent u/ben je geweest voor u/je naar hier kwam?** vär bent ē/ben ye həvāst′ vôr ē/ye när hēr kväm?

Did you stay at a youth hostel/campground there? | **Bent u/Ben je daar in een jeugdherberg/op een camping geweest?** bent ē/ben ye där in ān yāh′derberh/ôp ān kem′ping həvāst′?

Did you like that city/country/youth hostel/campground? | **Vond u/je die stad/dat land/die jeugdherberg/die camping leuk?** vônt ē/ye dē stät/dät länt/dē yāh′derberh/dē kem′ping lāk?

Why not? | **Waarom niet?** värôm′ nit?

Where are you going from here? | **Waar gaat u/ga je van hier uit naar toe?** vär hät ē/hä ye vän hēr et när tŏŏ?

Did you ever stay at the youth hostel in …? | **Bent u/Ben je ooit in de jeugdherberg in … geweest?** bent ē/ben ye oit in de yāh′derberh in … həvāst?

I'm going there next. | **Ik ga daar binnenkort heen.** ik hä där binənkôrt′ hān.

It was nice meeting you. | **Leuk u/je ontmoet te hebben.** lāk ē/ye ôntmŏŏt′ te he′bə.

Here is my address. Write to me sometime. | **Hier is mijn adres. Schrijf me eens een keer.** hēr is mīn ädres′. shīf me äns ān kār.

DUTCH

261

ARRIVAL & DEPARTURE

May I have your address? I'll write to you.

Mag ik uw/je adres hebben? Ik zal u/je schrijven. mäh ik yōō/ye ädres' he'bə? ik zäl ē/ye shī'və.

USEFUL WORDS & EXPRESSIONS

Is it …?

Is het …? is het …?

Is it … or …?

Is het … of …? is het … ôf …?

It is …

Het is … het is …

cheap/expensive
goedkoop/duur hōōtkōp'/dēr

early/late
vroeg/laat vrōōh/lät

near/far
dichtbij/ver weg dihtbī'/ver väk

open/closed
open/gesloten ō'pən/həslō'tə.

right/left
rechts/links rehts/lingks

vacant/occupied
vrij/bezet vrī/bəzet'

entrance/exit

ingang/uitgang in'häng/et·häng

with/without

met/zonder met/zôn'dər

ARRIVAL & DEPARTURE

Your passport please.

Uw paspoort, alstublieft. yōō päs'pōōrt, ästəblift'.

I'm here on vacation/business.

Ik ben hier op vakantie/voor zaken. ik ben hēr ôp väkän'tsē/vôr zä'kə.

I have nothing to declare.

Ik heb niets aan te geven. ik heb nits än te he'və.

I'll be staying …

Ik wil … blijven ik vil … blī'və.

a week
een week än väk

two/three weeks
twee/drie weken tvä/drē vä'kə

a month
een maand än mänt

two/three months
twee/drie maanden trä/drē män'də

That's my backpack.	**Dat is mijn rugzak.** dăt is mīn rih'zăk
Where can I catch a bus/the subway into town?	**Waar kan ik een bus/de metro naar de stad nemen?** văr kăn ik ăn bēs/də mā'trō năr də stăt nā'mə?
Which number do I take?	**Welke lijn moet ik nemen?** vel'kə līn mōōt ik nā'mə?
Which stop do I get off for the center of town?	**Bij welke halte moet ik uitstappen voor het centrum van de stad?** bī vel'kə hăl'tə mōōt ik et'stăpə vôr het sen'trōōm văn de stăt?
Can you let me know when we get to that stop?	**Kunt u me waarschuwen als we bij die halte zijn?** kint ē me văr'shivə ăls vā bī dē hăl'tə zīn?
Where is gate number ...?	**Waar is gate nummer ...?** văr is hăt nĭ'mər ...?

CHANGING MONEY

Excuse me, can you tell me where the nearest bank is?	**Pardon, kunt u me zeggen waar de dichtstbijzijnde bank is?** părdôN, kint ē me ze'gə văr de dihtst'bīzin'də băngk is?
... money exchange is?	**... het dichtstbijzijnde wisselkantoor is?** ... het dihtst'bīzin'də vi'səlkăntōōr' is?
... cash machine is?	**... de dichtstbijzijnde geldautomaat is?** ... də dihtst'bīzin'də helt'outōmăt' is?
I would like to exchange this currency.	**Ik wou dit geld wisselen.** ik vou dit helt vis'ələ.
I would like to exchange these traveler's checks.	**Ik wou deze travellercheques verzilveren.** ik vou dā'zə tre'vələrsheks' vərzil'vərə.

263

YOUTH HOSTELS

What is your exchange rate for U.S. dollars/traveler's checks?	**Hoe is de wisselkoers voor Amerikaanse dollars/travellercheques?** hōō is də vi'səl-kōōrs vôr ämerikän'sə dô'lärs/tre'vələrsheks'?
What is your commission rate?	**Hoe hoog is uw provisie?** hōō hōh is yōō prōvē'sē?
Is there a service charge?	**Zijn er administratiekosten aan verbonden?** zin er ädministrä'tsēkô'stən än vərbôn'də?
I would like a cash advance on my credit card.	**Ik had graag een contante uitbetaling op basis van mijn creditcard.** ik hät *häh* ān kôntän'tə *et'*bətäling ôp bä'sis vän mīn kre'ditkärt.
I would like small/large bills.	**Ik had graag biljetten in het klein/groot.** ik hät *häh* bilye'tə in het klīn/hōt.
I think you made a mistake.	**Ik denk dat u zich vergist heeft.** ik dengk dät *ē zih* vərhist' häft.

YOUTH HOSTELS

YOUTH HOSTELS

Excuse me, can you direct me to the youth hostel?	**Pardon, kunt u mij de weg wijzen naar de jeugdherberg?** pärdôN', k*i*nt *ē* mī de veh vī'zə när də yāh'derber*h*?
Do you have any beds available?	**Heeft u bedden vrij?** häft *ē* be'də vrī?
For one/two.	**Voor één persoon/twee personen.** vôr än persōn'/tvā persō'nə.
… women	**… vrouwen** … vrou'ən
… men	**… mannen** … mä'nən
We'd like to be in the same room.	**We zouden het liefst in één kamer slapen.** vā zou'dən het lēfst in ān kä'mər slä'pən.
How much is it per night?	**Wat is de prijs per nacht?** vät is de prīs per nä*h*t?

Is there a limit on how many nights I/we can stay? **Is er een maximum aantal nachten dat ik kan/we kunnen blijven?** is er än mäk'simõŏm än'täl näh'tə dät ik kän/vä k*i*nə blī'və?

I'll/We'll be staying … **Ik wil/We willen … blijven.** ik vil/vā vi'lə … blī'və.

tonight only **alleen vannacht** älān' vänäht'

two/three nights **twee/drie nachten** tvā/drē näh'tə

four/five nights **vier/vijf nachten** vēr/vīf näh'tə

a week **een week** ān vāk

Does it include breakfast? **Is het ontbijt inbegrepen?** is het ôntbīt' in'bəhāpə?

Do you serve lunch and dinner? **Serveert u ook een middag- en avondmaaltijd?** servärt' ē ôk än mi'däh- en ä'vôntmäl'tīt?

What are the hours for breakfast/lunch/dinner? **Wat zijn de tijden voor het ontbijt/de lunch/de avondmaaltijd?** vät zīn də tī'də vôr het ôntbīt'/de länsh/də ä'vôntmäl'tīt?

What are the lockout hours? **Tot hoe laat kunnen we binnenkomen?** tôt hōō lät k*i*nə vä bi'nəkô'mə?

Can I leave my bags here during lockout? **Kan ik mijn tassen hier laten tijdens sluitingstijd?** kän ik mīn tä'sə hēr lä'tə tī'dəns sle'tingstīt?

Do I take my key with me or leave it with you when I go out? **Kan ik mijn sleutels meenemen of moet ik ze bij u achterlaten als ik uitga?** kän ik mīn slä'təls mā'nämə ôf mōōt ik ze bī ē äh'tərlätən äls ik et'gä?

Do you have lockers? **Heeft u kluisjes?** häft ē kles'yes?

What time is the curfew? **Hoe laat gaat de avondklok in?** hōō lät hät də ä'vôntklôk in?

DUTCH

265

What time is check-out?	**Hoe laat moet ik/moeten we het hotel verlaten?** hōō lät mōōt ik/mōō'tə vä het hôtel' vərlä'tə?
Are there cooking/laundry facilities?	**Kan ik/Kunnen we hier ook zelf koken/wassen?** kän ik/kı'nə vä hēr ōk zelf kō'kə/vä'sə?
Is there a reduction for children?	**Is er korting voor kinderen?** is er kôr'ting vôr kin'dəre?

HOTEL OR OTHER ACCOMMODATIONS

kamers vrij/vol kä'mərs vrī/vôl	vacancy/no vacancy
Kamers te huur kä'mərs te hēr	Rooms for Rent
Gesloten in verband met vakantie həslō'tə in vərbänt' met väkän'sē	Closed for Vacation

I'm looking for …	**Ik zoek …** ik zōōk …
an inexpensive hotel.	**een niet te duur hotel.** ān nit te dēr hôtel'.
a pension.	**een pension.** ān pensyôN'.
a room.	**een kamer.** ān kä'mər.
I have a reservation.	**Ik had gereserveerd.** ik hät həresevērt'.
Do you have a room for tonight?	**Heeft u een kamer voor vannacht?** häft ē ān kä'mər vôr vänäht'?
I'd like your cheapest room.	**Ik had graag uw goedkoopste kamer.** ik hät häh yōō hōōtkōōp'stə kä'mər.
I'd like a single/double room …	**Ik had graag een eenpersoonskamer/tweepersoonskamer …** ik hät häh ān ān'persōnskä'mər/tvä'persōnskä'mər.
with a private bath.	**met eigen bad.** met ī'hə bät
with a shared bath.	**met een gemeenschappelijke badkamer.** met ān həmänshä'pəlī'kə bät'kämər

for … days/a week.	**voor … dagen/een week.**
	vôr … dä′hə, ān vāk
How much is the room?	**Hoeveel kost de kamer?**
	hōō′vāl kôst də kä′mər?
May I see the room?	**Kan ik de kamer eens zien?**
	kän ik də kä′mər āns zēn?
Does it include breakfast?	**Is het ontbijt inbegrepen?**
	is het ôntbīt′ in′bəhāpə?
I'll take it.	**Ja, ik neem de kamer.** yä, ik nām də kä′mər.
Do you have anything cheaper?	**Heeft u iets goedkopers?**
	häft ē ēts hōōtkō′pərs?
What time is checkout?	**Hoe laat moet ik/moeten we het hotel verlaten?** hōō lät mōōt ik/mōō′tə vā het hôtel′ vərlä′tə?

DUTCH

CAMPING ACCOMMODATIONS

Can you direct me to the nearest campground?	**Kunt u mij de weg wijzen naar de dichtstbijzijnde camping?** kint ē mī də vāh vī′zə när də di*h*tst′bīzin′də kem′ping?
How much is it per night?/per person?/per tent?	**Hoeveel kost het per nacht?/per persoon?/per tent?** hōō′vāl kôst het per nä*h*t?/per persōn′?/per tent?
Are showers included?	**Is het gebruik van de douches inbegrepen?** is het həbrek′ vän də dōō′shəs in′bəhāpə?
Where can I buy a shower token?	**Waar kan ik een douchemunt kopen?** vär kän ik ān dōō′shəmənt kô′pə?
How much are they?	**Hoe duur zijn ze?** hōō dēr zin zə?
How many do I need?	**Hoeveel heb ik er nodig?** hōō′vāl hep ik er nō′di*h*?

SIGNS

Are there cooking/ laundry facilities?	**Kunnen we hier ergens koken/wassen?** kı̆'nə vā hēr er'hens kō'kə/vä'sə?
Can we rent a bed/mat- tress/tent?	**Kunnen we een bed/matras/tent huren?** kı̆'nə vā ān bet/mäträs'/tent hē'rə?
May we light a fire?	**Mogen we een vuur aansteken?** mō'hə vā ān vēr än'stäkə?
Where can I find ...	**Waar kan ik ... vinden?** vär kän ik ... vin'də?

the drinking water?	**drinkbaar water** dringk'bär vä'tər
a camping equip- ment store?	**een campingwinkel** ān kem'pingving'kəl
a grocery store?	**een kruidenier** ān krədənēr'
a bank?	**een bank** ān bängk
laundry facilities?	**de wasserette** də väsəre'tə
a telephone?	**een telefoon** ān tä'lefōn
a restaurant?	**een restaurant** ān restôräNt'
electric hook-ups?	**elektrische aansluitingen** elek'trisə än'sletingə

Is there a swimming pool?	**Is er een zwembad aanwezig?** is er ān zvem'bät än'väzih?
How much does it cost?	**Hoeveel kost dat?** hōō'väl kô'stät?
May we camp here?/ over there?	**Mogen we hier kamperen?/daar ginds?** mō'hə vā hēr kämpā'rə? där hints?

SIGNS

Verboden te kamperen vərbō'də te kämpā'rə	No Camping
Geen doorgang hān dôr'häng	No Trespassing
Privé-terrein privä'-tereN'	Private Property

CAMPING EQUIPMENT

I'd like to buy a/an/ some …	**Ik wou een/enkele … kopen.** ik vou ān/eng'kələ … kö'pə.
I'd like to rent a/an/ some …	**Ik wou een/enkele … huren …** ik vou ān/eng'kələ … hē'rə.

air mattress/air mattresses.	**luchtbed/luchtbedden.** li*h*t'bet/li*h*t'bedə
butane gas.	**butagas.** bē'tä*h*äs
charcoal.	**houtskool.** houts'kōl
compass.	**kompas.** kômpäs'
eating utensils.	**eetgerei.** āt'*h*erī
flashlight.	**zaklantaarn.** zäk'läntärn
folding chairs/ table.	**klapstoelen/klaptafel.** klä*p*'stōōlə/klä*p*'täfəl
ground sheet.	**grondzeil.** *h*ôn'tsīl
ice pack.	**ijszak.** īs'zäk
insect spray.	**insectenspray.** insek'tənsprā
kerosene.	**petroleum.** petrō'lā·ŏŏm
lantern.	**lantaarn.** läntärn'
matches.	**lucifers.** li'sifers
rope.	**touw.** tou
sleeping bag.	**slaapzak.** släp'säk
soap.	**zeep.** zāp
tent.	**tent.** tent
towel/towels.	**handdoek/handdoeken.** hän'dōōk/hän'dōōkə

CHECKING OUT

I'd like to check out. May I have my bill please?	**Ik ga vertrekken. Kan ik de rekening krijgen, alstublieft?** ik *h*ä vərtre'kə. kän ik də re'kəning krī'*h*ə, ästəblift'?
Could you give me a receipt.	**Kunt u mij een kwitantie geven?** k*i*nt ē mī än kvitän'sē *h*ā'və?

DUTCH

269

TRANSPORTATION BY AIR

Could you explain this item/charge?	**Kunt u mij deze kosten/rekening even toelichten?** k*i*nt ē mī dā'zə kô'stə/re'kəning ā'və tōō'li*h*tə?
Thank you. I enjoyed my stay.	**Dank u. Ik vond het fijn om hier te zijn.** dángk ē. ik vônt het fīn ôm hēr te zīn.
We enjoyed our stay.	**We vonden het fijn om hier te zijn.** vā vôn'də het fīn ôm hēr te zīn.

TRANSPORTATION BY AIR

Is there a bus/train to the airport?	**Gaat er een bus/trein naar de luchthaven?** hät er ān bēs/trīn när də li*h*t'hävə?
At what time does it leave?	**Wanneer vertrekt hij?** vänār' vərtrekt' hī?
How long does it take to get there?	**Hoe lang doet hij erover?** hōō läng dōōt hī erō'vər?
Is there an earlier/later bus/train?	**Is er ook een vroegere/latere bus/trein?** is er ōk ān vrōō'hərə/lä'tərə bēs/trīn?
How much does it cost?	**Hoeveel kost het?** hōō'vāl kôst het?
I'd like a flight to …	**Ik had graag een vlucht naar …** ik hät *h*ä*h* ān vl*i*ht när …
a one-way/round trip ticket	**een enkel ticket/een rondreisticket** ān eng'kəl ti'kət/ān rônt'rīsti'kət
your cheapest fare	**uw goedkoopste ticket** yōō *h*ōōtkōp'stə ti'kət
an aisle/window seat	**een plaats aan het middenpad/raam** ān pläts än het mi'dənpät/räm
Is there a bus/train to the center of town?	**Gaat er een bus/trein naar het centrum van de stad?** hät er ān bēs/trīn när het sen'trōōm vän də stät?

270

RIDING THE BUS & SUBWAY

Could you tell me where the nearest bus/subway station is?

Kunt u mij zeggen waar het dichtstbij-zijnde bus-/metrostation is? k/nt ē mī ze'hə vär het di/htst'bīzin'də bēs-/mā'tröstătsyön' is?

Could you tell me where the nearest bus/subway stop is?

Kunt u mij zeggen waar de dichtstbijzijn-de bus-/metrohalte is? k/nt ē mī ze'hə vär də di/htst'bīzin'də bēs-/mā'tröhältə' is?

Where can I buy a ticket?

Waar kan ik een ticket kopen? vär kän ik ān ti'kət kö'pə?

How much does it cost?

Hoeveel kost het? hōō'väl kôst het?

Can I use this ticket for the subway and the bus?

Kan ik het ticket voor de metro en voor de bus gebruiken? kän ik het ti'kət vôr də mā'trö en vôr də bēs həbre'kə?

I'd like to buy ... tick-ets.

Ik had graag ... tickets. ik hät /häh ... ti'kəts.

I'd like to buy a book of tickets/weekly pass.

Ik had graag een strippenkaart/weekabonnement. ik hät /häh ān stri'pənkärt/väk'äbônəmənt.

Which bus/train do I take to get to ...?

Welke bus/trein moet ik nemen naar ...? vel'kə bēs/trīn mōōt ik nä'mə när ...?

Do I have to change buses/trains to get to ...?

Moet ik overstappen om bij ... te komen? mōōt ik ö'vərstäpən ôm bī ... te kô'mə?

When is the next/last bus/train to ...?

Wanneer gaat de volgende/laatste bus/trein naar ...? vänär' /hät də vôl'/hendə/läts'tə bēs/trīn när ...?

Can you tell me when we reach ...?

Kunt u mij waarschuwen als we bij ... komen? k/nt ē mī vär'shivə äls vā bī ... kô'mə?

271

TRAIN-STATION & AIRPORT SIGNS

Do I get off here for …?	**Moet ik hier uitstappen voor …?** mōōt ik hēr *et*'stäpə vôr …?
Please let me off here.	**Kunt u mij hier laten uitstappen, als-tublieft?** kint ē mī hēr lä'tə *et*'stäpə, ästēblift'?

TRAIN-STATION & AIRPORT SIGNS

Aankomst än'kômst	Arrival
Bagagecontrole bähä'zhəkôntrō'lə	Baggage Check
Ophalen van bagage ôp·hä'lə vän bähä'zhə	Baggage Pick-up
Wissel vi'səl	Change
Douane dōō·ä'ne	Customs
Vertrek vərtrek'	Departure
Ingang in'*h*äng	Entrance
Uitgang *et*'*h*äng	Exit
Inlichtingen in'li*h*tingə	Information
Gevonden voorwerpen *h*əvôn'də vôr'verpə	Lost & Found
Bagagekluizen bähä'zhəkleze	Luggage Lockers
Niet roken nit rō'kə	No Smoking
Reserveringen reservä'ringə	Reservations
Tickets ti'kəts	Tickets
Toiletten toile'tən	Toilets
Naar de perrons/treinen när də perôNs'/tri'nə	To the Platforms/Trains
Wachtruimte vä*h*t'remtə	Waiting Room

TAKING THE TRAIN

Could you tell me where the train station is?	**Kunt u mij zeggen waar het treinstation is?** kĭnt ē mī ze′hə vär het trīn′stätsôN′ is?
Could I have a train schedule to …	**Kunt u mij een reisschema van de trein naar … geven?** kĭnt ē mī ān rīs′hämä vän də trīn när … he′və?
When is the next/last train to …?	**Wanneer gaat de volgende/laatste trein naar …?** vänär hät də vôl′həndə/lät′stə trīn när …?
I would like to reserve a seat/couchette in 1st/2nd class.	**Ik wou een plaats/couchette eerste/ tweede klas reserveren.** ik vou ān pläts/ kōōshet′ är′stə/tvā′də kläs reservā′rə.
one-way/round trip	**enkele reis/rondreis** eng′kələ rīs/rônt′rīs
smoking/non-smoking	**rookcoupé/coupé niet-roken** rō′kōōpā′/kōōpā′ nit-rō′kə
aisle/window seat	**plaats aan het middenpad/raam** pläts än het mĭ′dənpät/räm
At what time does the night train to … leave?	**Hoe laat vertrekt de nachttrein naar …?** hōō lät vərtrekt′ də näh′trīn när …?
At what time does it arrive?	**Hoe laat komt hij aan?** hōō lät kômt hī än?
Do I have to change trains? At what stop?	**Moet ik overstappen? Bij welk station?** mōōt ik ō′vərstäpə? bī velk stätsyôN′?
I have a rail pass. Must I pay a supplement to ride this train?	**Ik heb een railpas. Moet ik een toeslag betalen om met deze trein mee te gaan?** ik hep ān räl′päs. mōōt ik ān tōō′släh bətä′lə ôm met dā′zə trīn te gän?

DUTCH

273

TAKING THE TRAIN

Could you tell me where platform/track … is?	**Kunt u mij zeggen waar perron/spoor … is?** kint ē mī ze'hə vär perôN'/spôr … is?
Could you tell me where car number … is?	**Kunt u mij zeggen waar wagon nummer … staat?** kint ē mī ze'hə vär vähôN' nī'mər … stät?
Could you help me find my seat/couchette, please?	**Kunt u mij alstublieft helpen bij het zoeken van mijn plaats/couchette?** kint ē mī ästēblift' hel'pə bī het zōō'kə vän mīn pläts/kōōshet'?
Is this seat taken?	**Is deze plaats bezet?** is dā'zə pläts bəzet'?
Excuse me, I think this is my seat.	**Pardon, ik geloof dat dit mijn plaats is.** pärdôN', ik həlôf' dät dit mīn pläts is.
Could you save my seat, please?	**Kunt u/Kun je mijn plaats vrijhouden, alstublieft/alsjeblief?** kint ē/kin ye mīn pläts vrī'houdə, ästēblift'/ästyəblif'?
Where is the dining car?	**Waar is de restauratiewagen?** vär is də restôrä'tsēvä'hə?
Where are the toilets?	**Waar is het toilet?** vär is het toilet'?

**For Europass and Flexipass users. With these passes you will only have access to certain countries. If your train goes through a country that is not on your pass, you will be required to pay an extra fare.

My rail pass only covers the Netherlands/ Belgium/France/Italy/ Switzerland/Germany/ Austria.	**Mijn railpas geldt alleen voor Nederland/België/Frankrijk/Italië/ Zwitserland/Duitsland/Oostenrijk.** mīn rāl'päs helt älän' vôr nä'dərlänt/bel'hē·e/ frängk'rīk/itäl'yə/zvit'sərlänt/dœts'länt/ō'stərīk.

How much extra do I have to pay since my train goes through …?	**Hoeveel moet ik extra betalen voor de treinreis door …?** hōō'vāl mōōt ik ek'strä bətä'lə vôr də trīn'rīs dôr …?
Is there another way to get to … without having to go through …?	**Is er een mogelijkheid om naar … te komen zonder door … te reizen?** is er ān mō'həlikīt' ôm när … te kô'mə zôn'də dôr … te rī'zə?

BY BOAT

Is there a boat that goes to …?	**Is er een boot die naar … gaat?** is er ān bōt dē när … hät?
When does the next/last boat leave?	**Wanneer vertrekt de volgende/laatste boot?** vänār' vərtrekt' də vôl'həndə/lät'stə bōt?
I have a rail pass. Do I get a discount? How much?	**Ik heb een railpas. Krijg ik korting? Hoeveel?** ik hep ān rāl'päs. krīh ik kôr'ting? hōō'vāl?
At what time does the boat arrive?	**Hoe laat komt de boot aan?** hōō lät kômt də bōt än?
How early must I get on board?	**Wanneer moet ik aan boord zijn?** vänār' mōōt ik än bôrt zīn?
Can I buy seasickness pills nearby?	**Kan ik hier in de buurt pillen tegen zeeziekte kopen?** kän ik hēr in də bērt pi'lə tā'hə zā'zēktə kō'pə?

GETTING AROUND BY CAR

I'd like to rent a car…	**Ik wou graag een auto huren …** ik vou häh än ou'tō hē'rə …
for … days.	**voor … dagen.** vôr … dä'hə
for a week.	**voor een week.** vôr ān vāk

DUTCH

275

GETTING AROUND ON FOOT

What is your daily/ weekly rate?	**Wat is het tarief per dag/week?** vät is het tärēf per däh/väk?
Do I need insurance?	**Heb ik een verzekering nodig?** hep ik än vərzā'kəring nō'dih?
Is mileage included?	**Is het aantal kilometers inbegrepen?** is het än'täl kē'lōmā'tərs in'bəhāpə?
How much is it?	**Hoeveel kost het?** hōō'väl kôst het?

ROAD SIGNS

Stop stôp	Stop
Eenrichtingsverkeer ānrih'tingsvərkār`	One Way
Verboden toegang vərbō'də tō'häng	Do Not Enter
Voorrang geven vôr'äng hā'və	Yield
Verboden te parkeren vərbō'də te pärkā'rə	No Parking

TAXI

I'd like to go to …	**Ik wou graag naar …** ik vou häh när …
What is the fare?	**Wat is het tarief?** vät is het tärēf?
Please stop here.	**Stopt u alstublieft hier.** stôpt ē ästēblift' hēr.
Can you wait for me?	**Kunt u op mij wachten?** kint ē ôp mī väh'tə?

GETTING AROUND ON FOOT

Excuse me, could you tell me how to get to …?	**Pardon, kunt u mij vertellen hoe ik naar … kom?** pärdôN', kint ē mī vərte'lə hōō ik när … kôm?
Is it nearby/far?	**Is het dichtbij/ver weg?** is het dihtbī'/vär veh?

276

Can I walk or should I take the bus/subway?	**Kan ik daar te voet heen of kan ik beter de bus/metro nemen?** kän ik där te vōōt hän ôf kän ik be'tər də b*ē*s'/mä'trō nä'mə?
Could you direct me to the nearest bus/subway station/stop?	**Kunt u mij de weg wijzen naar het dichtstbijzijnde busstation/metro-station/de dichtstbijzijnde bushalte?** k*i*nt *ē* mī də vä*h* vī'zə när het di*h*tst'bīzīn'də b*ē*s'täsyōn/mä'trōstäsyōn`/də di*h*tst'bīzīn'də b*ē*s'hältə?
Straight ahead.	**Rechtdoor.** re*h*'dôr.
Go right/left.	**Slaat u rechtsaf/linksaf.** slät *ē* re*h*'tsäf/lingk'säf.
At the corner/traffic light.	**Op de hoek/Bij het stoplicht.** ôp də hōōk/bī het stôp'li*h*t.
I'm lost.	**Ik ben de weg kwijt.** ik ben də vä*h* kvīt.
Could you show me where we are on this map?	**Kunt u mij op deze kaart aanwijzen waar we nu zijn?** k*i*nt *ē* mī ôp dā'zə kärt än'vīzə vär və n*ē* zīn?

EATING OUT

Could we have a table outside/inside?	**Kunnen we een tafel buiten/binnen krijgen?** k*i*'nə vä än tä'fəl be'tə/bi'nə krī'*h*ə?
Do you have a fixed-price menu?	**Heeft u een dagmenu?** häft *ē* än dä*h*'men*ē*?
Is service included?	**Is de bediening inbegrepen?** is də bədē'ning in'bə*h*äpə?
Is there a cover charge?	**Is er een toeslag voor het couvert?** is er än tōō'slä*h* vôr het kōōvär'?
Separate checks, please.	**De rekening graag apart, alstublieft.** də re'kəning *h*ä*h* äpärt', äst*ē*blift'.

277

EATING OUT

I'd like some apple/orange/grapefruit juice.

Ik had graag een appelsap/jus d'orange/grapefruitsap. ik hät *häh* än a'pəlsäp/zhē dôräNzh'/häp'frōōtsäp'.

I'd like some coffee/tea with cream/lemon.

Ik had graag een koffie/thee met creamer/citroen. ik hät *häh* än kô'fē/tā met krē'mər/sitrōōn'.

I'd like a soda/beer/mineral water.

Ik had graag een soda/pilsje/mineraalwater. ik hät *häh* än sō'dä/pils'yə/minerä'lvätər.

I'd like a glass/bottle of red/white/rose wine.

Ik had graag een glas/fles rode/witte/rosé wijn. ik hät *häh* än hläs/fles rō'də/vi'tə/rōsä' vīn.

dry/sweet

droog/zoet drōōh/zōōt

Cheers!

Proost! prōst!

What is the special of the day?

Wat is het speciale dagmenu? vät is het spesyä'lə däh'menē?

Do you have a tourist menu?

Heeft u een toeristenmenu? häft ē än tōōris'tənmenē?

What is this? (pointing to item on menu)

Wat is dit? vät is dit?

I'll have this.

Ik had dit graag. ik hät dit *häh*.

I'd like some salt/pepper/cheese/sugar/milk.

Ik had graag wat zout/peper/kaas/suiker/melk. ik hät *häh* vät zout/pā'pər/käs/se'kər/melk.

More juice/coffee/tea/cream/lemon/milk/beer/wine.

Ik had graag nog wat jus/koffie/thee/creamer/citroen/melk/bier/wijn. ik hät *häh* nôh vät zhē/kô'fē/tā/krē'mər/sitrōōn'/melk/bēr/vīn.

I cannot eat/sugar/salt/drink alcohol.

Ik mag geen suiker/zout/alcohol hebben. ik mäh *h*än se'kər/zout/äl'kôhôl he'bə.

278

I am a diabetic.	**Ik ben diabeticus.** ik ben dē·ā̆bā'tik/s.
I am a vegetarian.	**Ik ben vegetariër.** ik ben vāhetä'rē·ər.
May I have the check, please.	**Mag ik de rekening, alstublieft?** mäh ik də re'kəning, ästēblift'?
Keep the change.	**U mag het wisselgeld houden.** ē mäh het vi'səlhelt hou'də.

FOOD SHOPPING & PICNIC FOOD

Can you make me a sandwich.	**Ik had graag een broodje.** ik hät häh ān brōd'yə.
To take out.	**Om mee te nemen.** ôm mā te nā'mə.
I'd like some …	**Ik had graag …** ik hät häh …
I'll have a little more.	**Ik had graag een beetje meer.** ik hät häh ān bāt'yə mār.
That's too much.	**Dat is teveel.** dät is tevāl'.
Do you have …	**Heeft u …** häft ē …
I'd like …	**Ik had graag …** ik hät häh …

a box of …	**een doosje …** ān dōs'yə
a can of …	**een blik …** ān blik
a jar of …	**een pot …** ān pôt
a half kilo of …	**een halve kilo …** ān häl'və kë'lō
a kilo of …	**een kilo …** ān kë'lō
a half liter	**een halve liter** ān häl'və lē'tər
a liter	**een liter** ān lē'tər
a packet of …	**een pak …** ān päk
a slice of …	**een plak …** ān pläk
a bottle opener	**een flessenopener** ān fle'sənō'pənər
a can opener	**een blikopener** ān blik'ōpənər
a cork screw	**een kurkentrekker** ān kër'kəntre'kər
it sliced	**gesneden** həsnā'də

DUTCH

279

FOOD SHOPPING

Do you have any plastic forks/spoons/knives and napkins?
Heeft u plastic vorken/lepels/messen en servetten? häft ē ples'tik vôr'kə/lā'pəls/me'sə en serve'tə?

May I have a bag?
Kan ik een tas krijgen? kän ik ān täs krī'hə?

Is there a park nearby?
Is er hier in de buurt een park? is er hēr in də bērt ān pärk?

May we picnic there?
Mogen we daar picknicken? mō'hə vā där pik'nikə?

May we picnic here?
Mogen we hier picknicken? mō'hə vā hēr pik'nikə?

Fruits

apples	**appelen** ä'pələ
apricots	**abrikozen** ä'brikō'zə
bananas	**bananen** bänä'nə
blueberries	**bosbessen** bôs'besə
cantaloupe	**meloen** melōōn'
cherries	**kersen** ker'sə
dates	**dadels** dä'dəls
figs	**vijgen** vī'hə
grapefruit	**grapefruit** hāp'frōōt
grapes	**druiven** dre'və
lemons	**citroenen** sitrōō'nə
nectarines	**nectarines** nektärē'nes
oranges	**sinaasappelen** sē'näsä'pələ
peach	**perzik** per'zik
pear	**peer** pār
pineapple	**ananas** ä'nänäs
plums	**pruimen** pre'mə
raisins	**rozijnen** rōzī'nə
raspberries	**frambozen** främbō'zə
strawberries	**aardbeien** ärt'bi·ən
tangerines	**mandarijntjes** mändärīn'tyəs

| watermelon | **watermeloen** vä'təmelōōn` |

Vegetables

artichokes	**artisjokken** ärtishō'kə
asparagus	**asperges** äsper'hes
green/kidney beans	**groene bonen/kidneybonen** hōō'nə bō'nə/kid'nēbō'nə
broccoli	**broccoli** brō'kôlē
red cabbage	**rodekool** rō'dəkōl
carrots	**worteltjes** vôr'təltyəs
cauliflower	**bloemkool** blōōm'kōl
celery	**selderie** sel'dərē
corn	**maïs** mīs
cucumber	**komkommer** kômkô'mər
eggplant	**aubergine** ōberzhēn`
fennel	**venkel** veng'kəl
french fries	**frietjes** frēt'yəs
garlic	**knoflook** knôf'lōk
leeks	**prei** prī
lentils	**linzen** lin'zə
lettuce	**sla** slä
mushrooms	**champignons** shämpinyôNs`
black/green olives	**zwarte/groene olijven** zvär'tə/hōō'nə ōlī'və
onions	**uien** e'ən
peas	**erwten** är'tən
hot/sweet peppers	**Spaanse/zachte paprika's** spän'sə/zäh'tə päp'rikäs
pickles	**augurken (in het zuur)** ouhēr'kə (in het zēr)
potatoes	**aardappelen** ärt'äpələn
radishes	**radijsjes** rädīs'yəs
rice	**rijst** rīst
sauerkraut	**zuurkool** zēr'kōl
spinach	**spinazie** spinä'zē
tomatoes	**tomaten** tômä'tə
zucchini	**courgette** kōōrzhet`

DUTCH

FOOD SHOPPING

Meats/Cold Cuts

beef	**rundvlees** rĭnt'vlās
bologna	**boterhammenworst** bō'tərhämənvôrst'
chicken	**kip** kip
fish	**vis** vis
ham	**ham** häm
hamburger/ground beef	**hamburger/rundergehakt** häm'bĕrhər/rin'dərhəhäkt'
hot dogs/frankfurters	**hot dogs/frankfurter worstjes** hôdôgs'/frängk'firtər vôrst'yəs
lamb	**lam** läm
pork	**varken** vär'kə
roast beef	**rosbief** rōs'bēf
salami	**salami** sälä'mē
sausage	**worst** vôrst
turkey	**kalkoen** kälkōōn'
veal	**kalfsvlees** kälfs'vlās

Nuts

almonds	**amandelen** ämän'dələ
brazil nuts	**paranoten** pä'ränō'tə
cashews	**cashewnoten** ke'shōōnō'tə
chestnuts	**kastanjes** kästän'yəs
hazelnuts	**hazelnoten** hä'zəlnōtə
peanuts	**pinda's** pin'däs
walnuts	**walnoten** väl'nōtə

Condiments

butter	**echte boter** eh'tə bō'tər
honey	**honing** hō'ning
horseradish	**mierikswortel** mē'riksvôr'təl
jam/jelly	**jam/gelei** zhjem/zhəlī
ketchup	**ketchup** ket'shəp

margarine	**margarine** märhärē'nə
mayonnaise	**mayonaise** mīyōnä'sə
mustard	**mosterd** môs'tərt
vegetable/olive oil	**plantaardige olie/olijfolie** pläntär'dihə ō'lē/ōlif'ōlē
pepper	**peper** pā'pər
mild/hot salsa	**milde/scherpe salsa** mil'də/shär'pə säl'sä
salt	**zout** zout
sugar	**suiker** se'kər
tabasco/hot sauce	**tabascosaus/scherpe saus** täbäs'kōsous/shär'pə sous
vinegar	**azijn** äzīn'

Miscellaneous

bread	**brood** brōt
cake	**cake** kāk
candy	**snoep** snōōp
cereal	**ontbijtgranen** ôntbīt'gränə
cheese	**kaas** käs
chocolate	**chocolade** shôkôlä'də
cookies	**koekjes** kōōk'yəs
crackers	**crackers** kre'kərs
eggs	**eieren** ī'ərə
ice cream	**ijs** īs
popcorn	**popcorn** pôp'kôrn
potato chips	**chips** tships
rolls	**broodjes** brōd'yəs
spaghetti	**spaghetti** späge'tē
yogurt	**yoghurt** yō'hirt

Drinks

beer	**bier** bēr
coffee	**koffie** kô'fē

DUTCH

TELEPHONE

hot chocolate	**warme chocolademelk** vär'mə shôkôlä'dəmelk
apple juice	**appelsap** ä'pəlsäp
cranberry juice	**cranberrysap** kren'berēsäp`
grapefruit juice	**grapefruitsap** häp'frōōtsäp`
orange juice	**jus d'orange** zhē dôräNzh'
tomato juice	**tomatensap** tômä'tənsäp
milk	**melk** melk
soft drinks	**frisdrank** fris'drängk
tea	**thee** tā
sparkling/mineral water	**spuitwater/mineraalwater** spet'vätər/mineräl'vätər
red/white/rose wine	**rode/witte/rosé wijn** rō'də/vi'tə/rōzā' vīn
dry/sweet	**droog/zoet** drōh/zōōt

USING THE TELEPHONE

Can I use local currency to make a local/long-distance call or do I need to buy a phone card?	**Kan ik gewoon geld gebruiken om een lokaal/interlokaal gesprek te voeren of moet ik een telefoonkaart gebruiken?** Kän ik gəvōōn' helt həbre'kən ôm ān lôkäl'/intərlôkäl' həspräk' te vōō'rə ôf mōōt ik ān telefōn'kärt həbre'kə?
Do I need to buy tokens?	**Moet ik munten kopen?** mōōt ik min'tə kō'pə?
Where can I buy tokens?/a phone card?	**Waar kan ik munten/een telefoonkaart kopen?** vär kän ik min'tə/ān telefōn'kärt kō'pə?
… tokens, please. How much?	**… munten, alstublieft. Hoeveel is het?** … min'tən, ästēblift'. hōō'väl is het?
I'd like to buy phone card. How much does it cost?	**Ik wou een telefoonkaart kopen. Hoeveel kost dat?** ik vou ān telefōn'kärt kō'pə. hōō'väl kô'stät?

| How do you use the phone card? | **Hoe moet je een telefoonkaart gebruiken?** hōō mōōt ye ān telefōn'kärt *h*əbre'kə? |

| Excuse me, where is the nearest phone? | **Pardon, waar is de dichtstbijzijnde telefooncel?** pärdôN', vär is də di*h*tst'bīzīn`də telefōn'sel? |

| I'd like to make a collect call. | **Ik wil graag collect call bellen.** ik vil *h*äh kôlekt' kôl be'lən. |

| The number is … | **Het nummer is …** het ni'mər is … |

| Hello. This is … | **Hallo. U/Je spreekt met …** hälō'. ē/ye spräkt met … |

| May I speak to … | **Kan ik … spreken?** kän ik … sprä'kən? |

POST OFFICE

| Can you direct me to the nearest post office? | **Kunt u me de weg wijzen naar het dichtstbijzijnde postkantoor?** kint ē me də väk vī'zə när het di*h*tst'bīzīn`də pōst'käntôr`? |

| Which window is for …? | **Welk loket is voor …?** velk lô'ket is vôr … |

| stamps | **postzegels** pôst'sä*h*əls |

| sending/cashing a money order | **de verzending/ontvangst van een postwissel** də vərzen'ding/ôntvängst' vän ān pôst'visəl |

| airmail writing paper | **luchtpostpapier** li*h*t'pôstpäpēr` |

| I'd like … stamps for postcards/letters to America. | **Ik had graag … postzegels voor ansichtkaarten/brieven naar Amerika.** ik hät *h*äh … pôst'sä*h*əls vôr än'si*h*tskär`tə/brē'və när ämä'rikä. |

| I'd like to send this airmail. | **Ik wou deze luchtpostbrief versturen.** ik vou dā'zə li*h*t'pôstbrēf vərstē'rə. |

PHARMACY

How much does it
cost?

Hoeveel kost het?
hōō′vāl kô′stet?

PHARMACY & DRUGSTORE

Can you direct me to
the nearest pharmacy?

**Kunt u mijde weg wijzer naarde dichtst-
bijzijnde apotheek?** k*i*nt ē mī də vā*h* vī′zə när
də di*h*tst′bizin′də äpōtāk′?

I'd like a/an/some ...

Ik had graag een/wat ...
ik hät *h*äh än/vät ...

aspirin	**aspirine** äspirē′nə
Band-Aids	**pleisters** plī′stərs
cough medicine	**hoestmiddel** hōōst′midəl
contraceptives	**voorbehoedsmiddelen** vôr′bəhōōdsmī′dələ
eye drops	**oogdruppels** ō*h*′dripəls
insect repellant	**middel tegen insecten** mi′dəl tā′*h*ə insek′tə
sanitary napkins	**maandverband** mänt′vərbänt

Could you give me
something for ...

Kunt u mij iets geven tegen ...
k*i*nt ē mī ēts *h*ā′və tā′*h*ə ...

constipation	**verstopping** vərstô′ping
diarrhea	**diarree** dē-ärā′
a headache	**hoofdpijn** hōft′pīn
hay fever	**hooikoorts** hoi′kôrts
indigestion	**indigestie** indi*h*es′tē
itching	**jeuk** yāk
nausea/travel sick-ness	**misselijkheid/reisziekte** mi′səlikīt′/rī′sēktə
a rash	**uitslag** ət′slä*h*
sore throat	**een zere keel** än zā′rə kāl
sunburn	**zonnebrand** zô′nəbränt

May I have a/an/ some …?	**Ik had graag een/wat …** ik hät *hä*h ān/vät …
deodorant	**deodorant** dā·ōdôränt′
razor	**scheerapparaat** shār′äpärät′
razor blades	**scheermesjes** shār′mesyəs
shampoo/condi-tioner	**shampoo/conditioner** shäm′pō/kôndi′shənər
soap	**zeep** zāp
suntan oil/cream/ lotion	**zonnebrandolie/zonnebrandcrème/ zonnebrandlotion** zô′nəbränt·ōlē/ zô′nəbräntkräm`/zô′nəbräntlôsyōn`
tissues	**tissues** ti′shōōs
toilet paper	**toiletpapier** toilet′päpēr`
toothbrush	**tandenborstel** tän′dənbôr′stəl
toothpaste	**tandpasta** tänt′pästä
cleaning/soaking solution for con-tact lenses	**contactlensvloeistof** kôntäkt′lensvlō·ēstôf
How much does it cost?	**Hoeveel kost het?** hōō′vāl kô′stet?

DUTCH

TOBACCO SHOP

I'd like to buy …	**Ik had graag …** ik hät *hä*h …
a pack/carton of cigarettes.	**een pakje/slof sigaretten.** ān päk′yə/slôf si*hä*re′tə.
a cigarette lighter.	**een aansteker.** ān än′stekər.
a cigar.	**een sigaar.** ān si*hä*r′.
May I have some matches?	**Heeft u lucifers voor mij?** häft *ē* lē′sifərs vôr mī?

HEALTH

PHOTOGRAPHY

I'd like to buy a roll of film.	**Ik had graag een filmrolletje.** ik hät *häh* ān film'rôlətyə.
Black and white/Color.	**Zwart-wit/In kleuren.** zvärt-vit'/in klǟrə.
How much are they?	**Hoe duur zijn ze?** hōō dēr zīn ze?
I'd like to buy batteries for this camera.	**Ik had graag batterijtjes voor deze camera.** ik hät *häh* bätəri'tyəs vôr dā'zə kǟ'merä.

HEALTH

The Doctor

I don't feel well.	**Ik voel me niet goed.** ik vōōl mə nit hôōt.
Could you direct me to a doctor that speaks English.	**Kunt u me vertellen waar er een dokter is die Engels spreekt?** kint ē me vərte'lə vär er ān dôk'tər is dē eng'əls spräkt?
I have (a) …	**Ik heb (een) …** ik hep (ān) …
burn	**brandwond** bränt'vônt
chest pains	**pijn op de borst** pīn ôp də bôrst
cold	**verkoudheid** vərkout'hīt
cough	**hoest** hōōst
cramps	**krampen** kräm'pə
cut	**snijwond** snī'vônt
diarrhea	**diarree** dē·ärā'
fever	**koorts** kôrts
flu	**griep** hēp
infection	**infectie** infek'sē
nausea	**last van misselijkheid** läst vän mi'səlikīt'
rash	**uitslag** et'släh
sore throat	**zere keel** zä'rə kāl
sprained ankle	**verstuikte enkel** vərstek'tə eng'kəl
stomach ache	**maagpijn** mäh'pīn

It hurts here. **Het doet hier pijn.** het dōōt hēr pīn.

I've been vomiting. **Ik heb overgegeven.** ik hep ō'vərhəhā'və.

I'm having difficulty breathing. **Ik krijg moeilijk adem.**
ik krīh mōō'lik ä'dəm.

I'm allergic to penicillin. **Ik ben allergisch voor penicilline.**
ik ben älär'his vôr penisilē'nə.

I'm diabetic. **Ik ben diabeticus.** ik ben dē-äbā'tik/s.

I don't smoke/drink. **Ik rook/drink niet.** ik rōōk/dringk nit.

The Dentist

Could you direct me to a dentist that speaks English? **Kunt u me vertellen waar er een tandarts is die Engels spreekt?** k/nt ē me vərte'lə vär er ən tän'därts is dē eng'əls spräkt?

I have a toothache. This tooth. **Ik heb tandpijn. Aan deze tand.**
ik hep tänt'pīn. än dä'zə tänt.

My tooth is loose. **Mijn tand zit los.** mīn tänt zit lōs.

My tooth is broken. **Mijn tand is gebroken** mīn tänt is həbrō'kən.

I've broken/lost a filling. **Ik heb een vulling gebroken/verloren.**
ik hep ən v/'ling həbrō'kə/vərlō'rə.

Paying

How much does this cost? **Hoeveel kost het?** hōō'väl kô'stet?

I have health insurance. **Ik heb een ziektekostenverzekering.**
ik hep ən zēk'təkôstəvərzā'kəring.

I'm supposed to call this number. **Ik moet dit nummer bellen.**
ik mōōt dit n/'mər be'lə.

How much do I owe you?	**Hoeveel ben ik u verschuldigd?**
	hōō'vāl ben ik ē vərshōōl'diht?

SIGHTSEEING

Can you recommend ...?	**Kunt u mij ... aanbevelen?**
	kint ē mī ... änbəvālə?

a good, inexpensive restaurant	**een goed, niet te duur restaurant**
	ān hōōt, nit te dēr restôräNt'
a fun nightclub	**een leuke nachtclub** ān lä'kə näht'klip
a good place to dance	**een leuke danstent**
	ān lä'kə däns'tent

Can you tell me where the tourist office is?	**Kunt u mij zeggen waar het VVV-kantoor is?**
	kint ē mī ze'hə vär het vā-vā-vā'-käntōr' is?

What are the main points of interest here?	**Wat zijn de interessantste dingen hier?**
	vät zīn də intəresänt'stə ding'ə hēr?

What time does it open/close?	**Wanneer gaat het open/dicht?**
	vänār hät het ō'pə/diht?

What time is the last entry?	**Tot wanneer mag je nog naar binnen?**
	tôt vänār mäh yə nôh när bi'nə?

How much is the admission? Free.	**Hoeveel is de toegangsprijs? Gratis.**
	hōō'väl is də tōō'hängsprīs'? hä'tis.

Is there a discount for students/children/teachers/senior citizens?	**Is er korting voor studenten/kinderen/leerkrachten/ouderen?** is er kôr'ting vôr stēden'tə/kin'dərə/lär'krähtə/ou'dərə?

Is the ticket good all day?	**Geldt het ticket voor de hele dag?**
	helt het ti'ket vôr də hä'lə däh?

Is there a sightseeing tour?	**Kan ik/Kunnen we een sightseeingtoer maken?** kän ik/ki'nə vä ān sīt'sē·ingtōōr' mä'kə?

What time does it start?	**Hoe laat begint die?** hōō lät bə*h*int′ dē?	
How much does it cost?	**Hoeveel kost het?** hōō′väl kô′stet?	
How long is it?	**Hoe lang duurt hij?** hōō läng dērt hī?	
Does the guide speak English?	**Spreekt de gids Engels?** spräkt də *h*ids eng′əls?	
Am I allowed to take pictures/a video?	**Mag ik foto's/videoopnamen maken?** mä*h* ik fō′tōs/vē′dä·ō·ôprä′mə mä′kə?	
Can you direct me to the …?	**Kunt u mij de weg wijzen naar …?** k*i*nt ē mī də vä*h* vī′zə när …?	
art gallery	**de kunstgalerij** də k*i*nst′hälərī	
beach	**het strand** het stränt	
castle	**het slot** het slôt	
cathedral	**de kathedraal** də kätädräl′	
cemetery	**het kerkhof** het kerk′hôf	
church	**de kerk** də kerk	
fountain	**de fontein** də fôntīn′	
gardens	**de tuinen** də te′nə	
harbor	**de haven** də hä′və	
lake	**het meer** het mār	
monastery	**het klooster** het klō′stər	
mountains	**de bergen** də bär′*h*ə	
movies	**de bioscoop** də bē·ôskōp′	
museum	**het museum** het m*i*zē′əm	
old city	**het historische centrum** het histô′risə sen′trōōm	
palace	**het paleis** het pälīs′	
ruins	**de ruïnes** də rē·ē′nəs	
shops/bazaar	**de winkels/het warenhuis** də ving′kəls/het vä′rənhes	
statue	**het standbeeld** het stänt′bält	
tomb	**de tombe** də tôm′bə	

DUTCH

291

trails (for hiking)	**wandelroutes** vän′dəlrōō′təs
university	**de universiteit** də ēnivərsitīt′
zoo	**de dierentuin** də dē′rəntən

Is it far from here?	**Is het ver van hier?** is het vär vän hēr?
Can we walk there?	**Kunnen we er te voet heen?** kĭ′nə vä er te vōōt hān?
Straight ahead.	**Rechtdoor.** reh′dôr.
Go right/left.	**Slaat u rechtsaf/linksaf.** slät ē reh′tsäf/lĭngk′säf.
At the corner/traffic light.	**Op de hoek/Bij het stoplicht.** ôp də hōōk/bī het stôp′lĭht.

DISCOUNT INFORMATION

Do I get a discount with my student/teacher's/senior citizens card?	**Kan ik korting krijgen met mijn studentenpas/docentenpas/seniorenpas?** kän ik kôr′ting krī′hə met mīn stēden′tənpäs/dōsen′tənpäs/senyô′rənpäs?
Do I get a discount with my Eurailpass/Europass/Flexipass?	**Kan ik korting krijgen met mijn Eurailpas/Europas/Flexipas?** kän ik kôr′ting krī′hə met mīn ā′rälpäs/ā′rōpäs/flek′sēpäs?
How much of a discount?	**Hoeveel korting?** hōō′väl kôr′ting?
How much do I owe?	**Hoeveel moet ik betalen?** hōō′väl mōōt ik bətä′lə?

EMERGENCIES & ACCIDENTS

Please call the police.	**Waarschuwt u alstublieft de politie.** vär′shĭvt ē ästēblift′ də pôli′tsē.

Please call a doctor/an ambulance, quickly.	**Waarschuwt u alstublieft zo snel mogelijk een dokter/ziekenwagen.** vär'shivt ē ästēblift' zō snel mō'həlik än dôk'tər/zēkəwä'hə.
Hurry!	**Snel!** snel!
Danger!	**Pas op!** päs ôp!
Someone has been hurt/robbed.	**Er is iemand gewond/beroofd.** er is ē'mänt həvônt/bərôft'.
I'm hurt.	**Ik ben gewond.** ik ben həvônt.
Where is the hospital?	**Waar is het ziekenhuis?** vär is het zē'kənhes?
There's a fire.	**Er is brand.** er is bränt.
Help!/Thief!/Pick-pocket!	**Help!/Een dief!/Een zakkenroller!** help!/än dēf!/än zä'kərōlər!
Police!	**Politie!** pôli'tsē!
Stop that man/woman!	**Hou die man/vrouw tegen!** hou dē män/vrou tā'hə!

DUTCH

LOSS & THEFT

Can you help me, please?	**Kunt u mij helpen, alstublieft?** kint ē mī hel'pə, ästēblift'?
Where is the police station?	**Waar is het politiebureau?** vär is het pôli'tsēbirō'?
Where is the American consulate/embassy?	**Waar is het Amerikaanse consulaat/ de Amerikaanse ambassade?** vär is het ämōrikän'sə kônsēlät'/də ämārikän'sə ämbäsä'də?
Can you tell me where the lost and found is?	**Kunt u mij zeggen waar het bureau gevonden voorwerpen is?** kint ē mī ze'hə vär het birō' həvôn'də vôr'verpə.is?

293

PROBLEM PEOPLE

Someone has stolen my …	**Iemand heeft mijn … gestolen.** ē'mänt häft mīn … həstō'lə.
I have lost my …	**Ik heb mijn … verloren.** ik hep mīn … vərlô'rə.
I left my … on the bus/ train.	**Ik heb mijn … in de bus/trein laten liggen.** ik hep mīn … in də bēs/trīn lä'tə li'hə.

backpack	**rugzak** rih'säk
camera	**camera** kä'merä
credit cards	**creditcards** kre'ditkärds
glasses	**bril** bril
luggage	**bagage** bähä'zhə
money	**geld** helt
passport	**paspoort** päs'pôrt
railpass	**railpas** räl'päs
traveler's checks	**travellercheques** tre'vələrsheks`
wallet	**portefeuille** pôrtəfä'yə

DEALING WITH PROBLEM PEOPLE

Leave me alone or I'll call the police.	**Laat me met rust, of ik roep de politie.** lät me met ri̇st, ôf ik rōōp də pôli'tsē.
Stop following me.	**Blijft u mij niet achtervolgen.** blīft ē mī nit ähtərvōl'hə.
I'm not interested.	**Ik ben niet geïnteresseerd.** ik ben nit hə·in'tərəsärt`.
I'm married.	**Ik ben getrouwd.** ik ben hətrouvt.
I'm waiting for my boyfriend/husband.	**Ik wacht op mijn vriend/man.** ik väht ôp mīn vrēnt/män.
Enough!	**Hou op!** hou ôp!
Go away!	**Ga weg!** hä veh!

NUMBERS

zero	**nul** n*i*l
one	**één** ān
two	**twee** tvā
three	**drie** drē
four	**vier** fēr
five	**vijf** vīf
six	**zes** zes
seven	**zeven** zā'və
eight	**acht** *ä*ht
nine	**negen** nā'h*ə*
ten	**tien** tēn
eleven	**elf** elf
twelve	**twaalf** tvälf
thirteen	**dertien** der'tēn
fourteen	**veertien** vār'tēn
fifteen	**vijftien** vīf'tēn
sixteen	**zestien** ze'stēn
seventeen	**zeventien** zā'vəntēn
eighteen	**achttien** *ä*h'tēn
nineteen	**negentien** nā'h*ə*ntēn
twenty	**twintig** tvin'ti*h*
twenty-one	**eenentwintig** ān'entvinti*h*
twenty-two	**tweeëntwintig** tvā'entvinti*h*
twenty-three	**drieëntwintig** drē'entvinti*h*
twenty-four	**vierentwintig** vēr'entvinti*h*
thirty	**dertig** der'ti*h*
forty	**veertig** vēr'ti*h*
fifty	**vijftig** vīf'ti*h*
sixty	**zestig** ze'sti*h*
seventy	**zeventig** zā'vənti*h*
eighty	**tachtig** tä*h*'ti*h*
ninety	**negentig** nā'h*ə*nti*h*
one hundred	**honderd** hôn'dərt

DUTCH

TIME

| one thousand | **duizend** de'zənt |
| one million | **een miljoen** ān milyōōn' |

DAYS

| What day is today? | **Welke dag is het vandaag?** |
| | vel'kə dä*h* is het vändä*h*? |

| It's Monday. | **Het is vandaag maandag.** |
| | het is vändä*h*' män'dä*h*. |

… Tuesday.	**… dinsdag.** … dins'dä*h*.
… Wednesday.	**… woensdag.** … vōōns'dä*h*.
… Thursday.	**… donderdag.** … dôn'dərdä*h*.
… Friday.	**… vrijdag.** … vrī'dä*h*.
… Saturday.	**… zaterdag.** … zä'tərdä*h*.
… Sunday.	**… zondag.** … zôn'dä*h*.

TIME

Time is told by the 24 hour clock. You can also reference the numbers section.

| Excuse me. Can you tell me the time? | **Pardon, kunt u mij vertellen hoe laat het is?** pärdôN', k*i*nt ē mī vərte'lə hōō lät het is? |
| I'll meet you in … | **Ik zie u/je over …** ik zē ē/ye ō'vər … |

ten minutes	**tien minuten** tēn minē'tə
a quarter of an hour	**een kwartier** ān kvärtēr'
a half hour	**een half uur** ān hälf ēr
three quarters of an hour	**drie kwartier** drē kvärtēr'

| It is … | **Het is …** het is … |

| five past one. | **vijf over één.** vīf ō'vər ān. |
| ten past two. | **tien over twee.** tēn ō'vər tvā. |

296

a quarter past three.	**kwart over drie.** kvärt ō'vər drē.
twenty past four.	**twintig over vier.** tvin'ti*h* ō'vər vēr.
twenty-five past five.	**vijf voor halfzes.** vīf vôr hälf·zes'
half past six.	**halfzeven.** hälf·zā'və.
twenty-five to seven.	**vijf over halfzeven.** vīf ō'vər hälf·zā'və.
twenty to eight.	**twintig voor acht.** tvin'ti*h* vôr ä*h*t.
a quarter to nine.	**kwart voor negen.** kvärt vôr nā'*h*ə.
ten to ten.	**tien voor tien.** tēn vôr tēn.
five to eleven.	**vijf voor elf.** vīf vôr elf.
noon.	**middag.** mi'dä*h*.
midnight.	**middernacht.** mi'dənä*h*t.

yesterday	**gisteren** *h*i'stərə
last night	**gisteravond** *h*istərä'vônt
today	**vandaag** vändä*h*'
tonight	**vanavond** vänä'vônt
tomorrow	**morgen** môr'*h*ə
morning	**morgen** môr'*h*ə
afternoon	**namiddag** nä'midä*h*
evening	**avond** ä'vônt
night	**nacht** nä*h*t
day before yesterday	**eergisteren** ār'*h*istərə
in two/three days	**over twee/drie dagen** ō'vər tvā/drē dä'*h*ə

MONTHS

January	**januari** yä'ni·ä'rē
February	**februari** fe'bri·ä'rē
March	**maart** märt
April	**april** äpril'
May	**mei** mī
June	**juni** yē'nē
July	**juli** yē'lē

COLORS

August	**augustus** ou*his*'t*is*
September	**september** septem'bər
October	**oktober** ôktō'bər
November	**november** nōvem'bər
December	**december** dāsem'bər

Merry Christmas!	**Vrolijk kerstfeest!** vrō'lik kārst'fāst!
Happy New Year!	**Gelukkig Nieuwjaar!** həli'kih nyōō'yär!
Happy Easter!	**Vrolijk Pasen!** vrō'lik pä'sə!
Happy Birthday!	**Gelukkige verjaardag!** həli'kihə vəryär'dä*h*!

COLORS

beige	**beige** bā'zhə
black	**zwart** zvärt
blue	**blauw** blou
brown	**bruin** brən
gold	**goudkleurig** *h*out'klārih
green	**groen** *h*ōōn
gray	**grijs** *h*īs
yellow	**geel** *h*āl
orange	**oranje** ôrän'yə
pink	**roze** rō'zə
purple	**paars** pärs
red	**rood** rōt
silver	**zilverkleurig** zil'vərklā'rih
white	**wit** vit

APPENDIX

Measurements

1. Units of Length

Inches to Centimeters
1 in = 2.54 cm

Centimeters to Inches
1 cm = 0.39 in

cm	1	2	3	4	5	6	7	8	9	10
in	0.4	0.8	1.2	1.6	2	2.4	2.8	3.2	3.5	4

Feet to Meters
1 ft = 0.30 m

Meters to Feet
1 m = 3.28 ft

m	1 m	2 m	3 m	4 m	5 m	6 m	7 m	8 m	9 m	10 m
ft	3.3	6.5	9.8	13	16.4	19.7	23	26.3	29.5	33

Miles to Kilometers
1 mi = 1.61 km

Kilometers to Miles
1 km = 0.62 mi

km	10	20	30	40	50	60	70	80	90	100
mi	6	12	19	25	31	37	44	50	56	62

2. Units of Volume

Quarts to Liters
1 qt = 0.95 l

Liters to Quarts
1 l = 1.06 qt

Gallons to Liters
1 gal = 3.79 l

Liters to Gallons
1 l = 0.26 gal

l	1	5	10	15	20	25	30	35	40	45	50
gal	0.26	1.3	2.6	3.9	5.2	6.5	7.8	9.1	10.4	11.7	13

APPENDIX

3. Units of Weight

Ounces to Grams
1 oz = 28.3 g

Grams to Ounces
1 g = 0.04 oz

g	1	10	50	100	125	200	250	500
oz	0.04	0.4	1.8	3.5	4.4	7	8.8	17.6

Pounds to kilograms
1 lb = 0.45 kg

kilograms to pounds
1 kg = 2.20 lb

kg	1	2	3	4	5	10	15	20	25
lb	2.2	4.4	6.6	8.8	11	22	33	44	55

4. Sizes

Women's Dresses

American American	XS 4	S 6	8	10	M 12	L 14
German, Dutch	34	36	38	40	42	44
French	36	38	40	42	44	46
Italian, Span, Port	38	40	42	44	46	48

Women's Shoes

American	6	7	8	9	10
German	36	37	38	40	41
French	37	38	40	41	42
Italian	37	38–39	40	41	42

Men's Wear

American	S	M	L	XL	XXL
European	44/46	48/50	52/54	56/58	60/62

Men's Shoes

American	6	7	8	9	10	11	12	13	14
European	37	38	39	40	41	42.5	44	45	46

5. Temperature

Fahrenheit to Celsius
Subtract 32 from Fahrenheit
degrees and divide by 1.8.

Celsius to Fahrenheit
multiply Celsius by 1.8 and add
32.

C°	−10	−5	0	5	10	15	20	25	30	35	40
F°	14	23	32	41	50	59	68	77	86	95	100

APPENDIX

Pictograms

Bus

Parking

Airport

Information

Post office

Hotel

Restaurant

Camping

Telephone

Refreshments

Rent-a-Car

First-Aid station

No dogs allowed